Microsoft®

Expression® Web 3

Complete

Gary B. Shelly

Jennifer T. Campbell

Ollie Rivers

Microsoft®

Expression® Web 3

Complete

Gary B. Shelly

Jennifer T. Campbell

Ollie Rivers

Shelly Cashman Series®

An imprint of Course Technology, Cengage Learning

COURSE TECHNOLOGY
CENGAGE Learning™

Australia • Brazil • Japan • Korea • Mexico • Singapore • Spain • United Kingdom • United States

COURSE TECHNOLOGY
CENGAGE Learning

**Microsoft® Expression® Web 3
Complete**
Gary B. Shelly, Jennifer T. Campbell,
Ollie Rivers

Vice President, Publisher: Nicole Pinard

Executive Editor: Kathleen McMahon

Product Manager: Jon Farnham

Associate Product Manager: Aimee Poirier

Editorial Assistant: Lauren Brody

Director of Marketing: Cheryl Costantini

Marketing Manager: Tristen Kendall

Marketing Coordinator: Stacey Leasca

Senior Print Buyer: Julio Esperas

Director of Production: Patty Stephan

Content Project Manager: Jennifer Feltri

Development Editor: Susan Whalen

Copyeditor/Proofreader: Suzanne Huizenga

Indexer: Sharon Hilgenberg

QA Manuscript Reviewers: John Freitas,
  Danielle Shaw

Art Director: Marissa Falco

Cover Designer: Lisa Kuhn, Curio Press, LLC

Cover Photo: Tom Kates Photography

Compositor: PrePress, PMG

For product information and technology assistance, contact us at
Cengage Learning Customer & Sales Support, 1-800-354-9706

For permission to use material from this text or product, submit all requests online at **www.cengage.com/permissions**
Further permissions questions can be emailed to
permissionrequest@cengage.com

Library of Congress Control Number: 2010925123

ISBN-13: 978-0-538-47448-1

ISBN-10: 0-538-47448-3

Course Technology
20 Channel Center Street
Boston, Massachusetts 02210
USA

All photos are property of the author.
The art in Chapter 4 is included with the permission of Mimei Thompson.

Cengage Learning is a leading provider of customized learning solutions with office locations around the globe, including Singapore, the United Kingdom, Australia, Mexico, Brazil and Japan. Locate your local office at:
international.cengage.com/region

Cengage Learning products are represented in Canada by Nelson Education, Ltd.

Visit our Web site **www.cengage.com/ct/shellycashman** to share and gain ideas on our textbooks!

To learn more about Course Technology, visit **www.cengage.com/coursetechnology**

Purchase any of our products at your local college store or at our preferred online store: **www.CengageBrain.com**

Printed in the United States of America
1 2 3 4 5 6 7 15 14 13 12 11 10

Contents

Preface

Shelly Cashman Series® offers the finest textbooks in computer education. We are proud of the fact that our textbooks have been the most widely used books in education. *Microsoft® Expression® Web 3: Complete* continues with the innovation, quality, and reliability that you have come to expect from the Shelly Cashman Series.

Microsoft Expression Web is known as the standard in Web authoring and enhances the work experience for users by providing a WYSIWYG design environment that can be used to create complex, standards-compliant, multi-page Web sites using tools such as dialog boxes, task panes, and dynamic Web templates without needing to enter HTML or CSS code.

In this Microsoft Expression Web 3 book, you will find an educationally sound and easy-to-follow pedagogy that combines a step-by-step approach with corresponding screens. All projects and exercises in this book are designed to take full advantage of the Expression Web 3 enhancements. The Other Ways feature offers in-depth knowledge of Expression Web. The popular Q&A feature provides answers to common questions students have about the Web design processes. The Learn It Online page presents a wealth of additional exercises to ensure your students have all the reinforcement they need. The project material is developed carefully to ensure that students will see the importance of learning Expression Web for future coursework.

Objectives of This Textbook

Microsoft® Expression® Web 3: Complete is intended for a course that includes an introduction to Expression Web 3. A basic understanding of the Internet, computers, data entry, and program tools such as dialog boxes and menu bars is assumed. The objectives of this book are:

- To teach the fundamentals of Microsoft Expression Web 3

- To expose students to the planning and decision-making process involved in creating Web pages, Web sites, and style sheets

- To acquaint students with the proper procedures to create Web pages and Web sites that include text, images, and hyperlinks, and are suitable for coursework, professional purposes, and personal use

- To help students use the Expression Web tools and user interface to create Web pages, Web sites, and style sheets that are easy to create, maintain, and use

- To develop an exercise-oriented approach that allows learning by doing

Distinguishing Features

A Proven Pedagogy with an Emphasis on Project Planning Each chapter presents a practical problem to be solved, within a project planning framework. The project orientation is strengthened by the use of Plan Ahead boxes that encourage critical thinking about how to proceed at various points in the project. Step-by-step instructions with supporting screens guide students through the steps. Instructional steps are supported by the Q&A, Experimental Step, and BTW features.

A Visually Engaging Book that Maintains Student Interest The step-by-step tasks, with supporting figures, provide a rich visual experience for the student. Callouts on the screens that present both explanatory and navigational information provide students with information they need when they need to know it.

Supporting Reference Materials (Quick Reference, Appendices) The appendices provide additional information about Expression Web 3, such as the Help Feature and customizing the application. With the Quick Reference, students can quickly look up information about a single task, such as keyboard shortcuts, and find page references of where in the book the task is illustrated.

Integration of the Web The World Wide Web is integrated into the Expression Web 3 learning experience by (1) BTW annotations; and (2) the Learn It Online section for each chapter.

End-of-Chapter Student Activities Extensive end-of-chapter activities provide a variety of reinforcement opportunities for students where they can apply and expand their skills through individual and group work.

Instructor Resources CD-ROM

The Instructor Resources include both teaching and testing aids.

INSTRUCTOR'S MANUAL Includes lecture notes summarizing the chapter sections, figures and boxed elements found in every chapter, teacher tips, classroom activities, lab activities, and quick quizzes in Microsoft Word files.

SYLLABUS Easily customizable sample syllabi that cover policies, assignments, exams, and other course information.

FIGURE FILES Illustrations for every figure in the textbook in electronic form.

POWERPOINT PRESENTATIONS A multimedia lecture presentation system that provides slides for each chapter. Presentations are based on chapter objectives.

SOLUTIONS TO EXERCISES Includes solutions for all end-of-chapter and chapter reinforcement exercises.

TEST BANK & TEST ENGINE Test Banks include 112 questions for every chapter, featuring objective-based and critical thinking question types, and including page number references and figure references, when appropriate. Also included is the test engine, ExamView, the ultimate tool for your objective-based testing needs.

DATA FILES FOR STUDENTS Includes all the files that are required by students to complete the exercises.

ADDITIONAL ACTIVITIES FOR STUDENTS Consists of Chapter Reinforcement Exercises, which are true/false, multiple-choice, and short answer questions that help students gain confidence in the material learned.

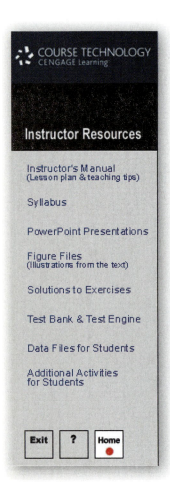

Content for Online Learning

Course Technology has partnered with the leading distance learning solution providers and class-management platforms today. To access this material, instructors will visit our password-protected instructor resources available at www.cengage.com/coursetechnology. Instructor resources include the following: additional case projects, sample syllabi, PowerPoint presentations per chapter, and more. For additional information or for an instructor username and password, please contact your sales representative. For students to access this material, they must have purchased a WebTutor PIN-code specific to this title and your campus platform. The resources for students may include (based on instructor preferences), but are not limited to: topic review, review questions, and practice tests.

CourseNotes

Course Technology's CourseNotes are six-panel quick reference cards that reinforce the most important concepts and features of a software application in a visual and user-friendly format. CourseNotes serve as a great reference tool during and after the student completes the course. CourseNotes are available for software applications, such as Microsoft Office 2007, Word 2007, PowerPoint 2007, Excel 2007, Access 2007, and Windows 7. There are also topic-based CourseNotes available for Best Practices in Social Networking, Hot Topics in Technology, and Web 2.0. Visit www.cengage.com/ct/coursenotes to learn more!

Guided Tours

Add excitement and interactivity to your classroom with the "*A Guided Tour*" product line. Play one of the brief mini-movies to spice up your lecture and spark classroom discussion. Or, assign a movie for homework and ask students to complete the correlated assignment that accompanies each topic. The "*A Guided Tour*" product line takes the prep work out of providing your students with information on new technologies and software applications and helps keep students engaged with content relevant to their lives — all in under an hour!

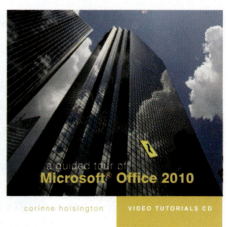

Textbook Walk-Through

The Shelly Cashman Series Pedagogy:
Project-based — Step-by-step — Variety of assessments

Plan Ahead boxes prepare students to create successful projects by encouraging them to think strategically about what they are trying to accomplish before they begin working.

Step-by-step instructions now provide a context beyond the point-and-click. Each step provides information on why students are performing each task, or what will occur as a result.

- Format text on the page.
- Use visual aids and tags.
- Save the page.
- Preview the page.
- Print the page.

General Project Guidelines   **Plan Ahead**

When creating an Expression Web site, the actions you perform and decisions you make will affect the pages and links included in the site. As you create a Web site, such as the project shown in Figure 1–1, you should follow these general guidelines:

1. **Choose a Web site structure to use as the starting point for the site.** A Web site consists of one or more Web pages. Determine the purpose of the site, such as commercial or personal, then determine the number of pages and how site users will navigate to the pages.

2. **Determine folder structure and location and file naming conventions for the Web site files.** You must save all of the related files and folders for the Web site in one location.

3. **Determine the page properties or settings that will apply to the pages.** You can choose page settings, such as page title and keywords, using the Page Properties dialog box.

4. **Decide what the page layout will look like.** Page layout, which is the placement of text and objects, contributes to the look and consistency of a site. Well-arranged elements, such as a company logo or a navigation bar with links to the main pages of a site, keep the visitor interacting with the site longer and give the site a professional look.

5. **Determine the text content for the page.** Use text to convey the message with as few words as possible. Easy-to-read content encourages visitors to consider your product or service.

6. **Design the format for the text elements on the page.** The use of headings, fonts, lists, and color helps to identify important content and assists the visitor when scanning the page for specific content.

When necessary, specific details about these guidelines are presented at appropriate points in the chapter. The chapter also will identify the tasks performed and decisions made during the creation of the Web site shown in Figure 1–1.

To Start Expression Web

The following steps, which assume Windows 7 is running, start Expression Web based on a typical installation. You may need to ask your instructor how to start Expression Web for your computer.

Note: If you are using Windows XP, see Appendix E for alternate steps. If you are using Windows Vista, see Appendix F for alternate steps.

1
- Click the Start button on the Windows 7 taskbar to display the Start menu.
- Click All Programs at the bottom of the left pane on the Start menu to display the All Programs list.
- Click the Microsoft Expression folder on the All Programs list to display the Microsoft Expression list (Figure 1–3).

Figure 1–3

2
- Click Microsoft Expression Web 3 to start Expression Web and display a new blank Web page in the Expression Web editing window (Figure 1–4).

Q&A Why does Expression Web sometimes open a Web site and other times open with a blank Web page named Untitled_1.html?

When you quit Expression Web without closing the Web site you are working on, Expression Web remembers the site and automatically opens it the next time Expression Web starts. If no previous site is in Expression Web's memory, it starts with a blank page named Untitled_1.html.

Q&A Sometimes when opening Expression Web, a server error message displays. What does that error mean?

If you quit Expression Web without closing a Web site first, Expression Web will try to open that site the next time Expression Web is started. If the site was saved on an external drive such as a USB flash drive, Expression Web looks for that drive address; if the location is not available (such as when the USB flash drive has been removed), the server error is generated. Just click OK to proceed.

Figure 1–4

Other Ways
1. Double-click the Microsoft Expression Web 3 icon on the desktop, if one is present
2. Click Microsoft Expression Web 3 on the Start menu

project in this chapter, and you want your ... uld change your screen's resolution to ... change a computer's resolution, read

BTW

File Extensions
HTML files can be saved with either the .html or .htm file extension. DOS-based operating systems restricted file extensions to three letters, necessitating the abbreviation of .html to .htm. All of today's browsers recognize both file extensions.

Navigational callouts in red show students where to click.

Explanatory callouts summarize what is happening on screen.

BTW

Screen Shots
Callouts in screen shots give students information they need, when they need to know it. The Series has always used plenty of callouts to ensure that students don't get lost. Now, we use color to distinguish the content in the callouts to make them more meaningful.

Textbook Walk-Through

Q&A boxes offer questions students may have when working through the steps and provide additional information about what they are doing right where they need it.

Experiment Steps within our step-by-step instructions encourage students to explore, experiment with, and take advantage of the features of Expression Web 3. These steps are not necessary to complete the projects, but are designed to increase students' confidence with the software and build problem-solving skills.

4

- Click Computer in the Navigation pane to display a list of available drives (Figure 1–12).
- If necessary, scroll until FLASH DRIVE or USB (G:) appears in the list of available drives.

Q&A Do I have to use a USB flash drive?

No. You can save to any device or folder. Use the same process, but select your device or network folder from the Computer list.

- Double-click FLASH DRIVE (G:) to select the USB flash drive, drive G in this case, as the new save location.

Figure 1–12

5

- If necessary, navigate to or create a folder on your drive into which you will save your Data Files.
- Click the Open button to return to

Figure 1–13

2

- Click the <li> tag on the Quick Tag Selector to select the entire bullet (Figure 1–46).

Q&A Why did a menu appear when I clicked the <li> tag?

Be sure to click the tag, not the arrow to its right.

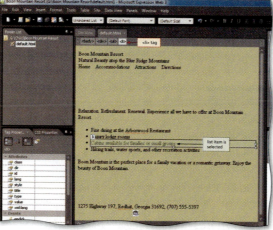

Figure 1–46

3

- Click the <ul> tag on the Quick Tag Selector to select the entire bulleted list (Figure 1–47).

⑦ Experiment

- Use the Quick Tag Selector to select other tags, such as <body>, to see how many nested elements are selected. The farther left you click on the Quick Tag Selector, the higher you are in the hierarchy of tags on the page.

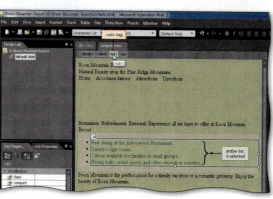

Figure 1–47

Textbook Walk-Through

Other Ways boxes that follow many of the step sequences explain the other ways to complete the task presented.

4
- Click groups in the Suggestions box.
- Click the Change button to correct the word (Figure 1–71).

Figure 1–71

5
- Click the Ignore button to skip the name of the town, Redhat (Figure 1–72).

Figure 1–72

6
- Click the OK button to close the message box indicating that spell checking is complete (Figure 1–73).
- Click the Save button on the Common toolbar to save the page.

Other Ways
1. As you are typing, right-click a flagged word to display a short-cut menu that includes a list of suggested spelling corrections
2. Press the F7 key to start the spell checker

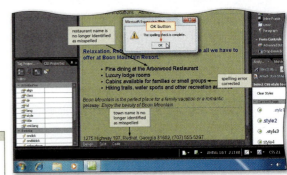

Figure 1–73

16. Press ENTER a second time after the last line to end the bulleted list.
17. Select the <ul> tag of the bulleted list and change the font color to the red co navigation text. Press the Increase Indent button eight times to indent the list
18. Add a div at the bottom of the page for the footer.
19. Press ENTER twice at the beginning of the div to add some space.
20. Type the company address and phone number in the div as follows: 14 Emer Exeter, NH 03833, (603) 555-1743.
21. Select the footer div, center and bold the div, and then change the font color previously used teal color, and then bold the div.
22. Select the body tag, then change the font family to Gill Sans, Gill Sans MT, C sans-serif.
23. Save the default.html Web page.
24. Spell check the Web page.
25. Preview the site in two different browsers or resolutions.
26. Use Print Preview to view the site.
27. Print the site.
28. Change the site properties, as specified by your instructor.
29. Close the default.html Web page and the site.
30. Rename the site using the filename, Apply 1-1 Jewelry Site using Windows Explorer.
31. Submit the revised site in the format specified by your instructor.

Extend Your Knowledge

Extend the skills you learned in this chapter and experiment with new skills. You may need to use Help to complete the assignment.

Formatting a Web Site

Instructions: Start Expression Web. Open the Web site, Extend 1-1 Music Festival, from the Data Files for Students. See the inside back cover of this book for instructions for downloading the Data Files for Students, or see your instructor for information about accessing the required files.
 Enhance the Web page to match the one shown in Figure 1–93.

Perform the following tasks:
1. Use Help to learn about changing the default font color and how to insert a horizontal line.
2. Print the default.html page.
3. Make notes on the hard copy as to how you will change the Web page to more closely match Figure 1–93.
4. Use the Page Properties dialog box to change the page background to orange (255, 204, 102) and the default font color to blue (0, 51, 153). (*Hint:* Click Custom in the More Colors dialog box to enter Red, Green, and Blue values.)
5. Change the font family of the masthead div using a font family containing Gill Sans (or another font family of your choice) and the font color to red. Bold and center the masthead text and change the font size to x-large.

Continued >

Extend Your Knowledge projects at the end of each chapter allow students to extend and expand on the skills learned within the chapter. Students use critical thinking to experiment with new skills to complete each project.

Textbook Walk-Through

Extend Your Knowledge *continued*

6. Click at the end of the masthead text and press ENTER. Double-click the Horizontal Line tag in the Toolbox to insert a horizontal line under the masthead.

7. Change the font family of both the bulleted list and the paragraph to one containing Arial.

8. Increase the font size of the bulleted list text to large and apply the bold attribute.

9. Select the text, Incoming Flight, then click the Italic button on the Common toolbar.

10. On a separate piece of paper, draw a mock-up of the final page, identifying each part of the page. Make two suggestions for changes based on your own design preferences.

11. Change the site properties, as specified by your instructor.

12. Save and close the default.html page and the Web site. Using Windows Explorer, rename the Extend 1-1 Music Festival site folder as Extend 1-1 Music Site.

13. Submit the revised site in the format specified by your instructor.

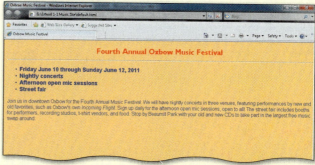

Figure 1–93

Make It Right projects call on students to analyze a file, discover errors in it, and fix them using the skills they learned in the chapter.

Make It Right

Analyze a site and correct all errors and/or improve the design.

Increasing Readability and Correcting Spelling Errors

Instructions: Start Expression Web. Open the Web site, Make It Right 1-1 Swim Club, from the Data Files for Students. See the inside back cover of this book for instructions for downloading the Data Files for Students, or see your instructor for information about accessing the required files.

The site's font colors and sizes do not provide enough contrast to be easily readable from the screen, and the Expression Web dictionary has flagged several words as being erroneous. Using Figure 1–94 to guide you, change the background color of the page, bullet and indent the list, change the text alignment, and then change the font sizes and colors to make the text more readable and to show a hierarchy of information. Apply a font family with Franklin Gothic Medium in it to the entire page. Correct each spelling error by right-clicking the flagged text and clicking the appropriate correction or option on the shortcut menu, then run the spelling checker to make sure there are no other errors. Change the page title in the Page Properties dialog box to Macon Waves Swim Club.

Cases and Places

Apply your creative thinking and problem-solving skills to

• EASIER •• MORE DIFFICULT

• 1: Work with the Expression Web Window

You want to practice working with the Expression Web window. Chapter 1, then open that site's default.html page. Use the Page word. Switch to Code view, then split the view. Select text in Co to the HTML code. Switch to Design view. Insert a new paragra graph, create a numbered list with three items, and include one Expression Web identifies as a misspelling. Check the spelling o and ignore the name. Select one item using the Quick Tag Selec select the entire list. Close the default.html page without saving quit Expression Web.

• 2: Design and Plan a School Web Site

You have just finished a class on Web design. The school administration of Pinkham Academy, a private high school, would like to plan a Web site that will include a home page, and eventually it will add other pages. Sketch a plan on a piece of paper for the home page of the Web site that you can present to the administration and use to gather its feedback. Include a masthead that lists the school name and a navigation bar with links to the library, administration, and calendar. The administration wants to include the school logo on the home page. Include an area for a letter from the principal and a footer for the address. The school's colors are blue and white; indicate on the Web site sketch how you will incorporate the school's colors.

•• 3: Format a One-Page Alumni Web Site

You have recently joined the Connecticut branch of your college alumni association. You have been working on a home page that can tell other local graduates of Gulliver College about upcoming alumni events. You have already entered the text for the home page. Open the site Cases and Places 3 Alumni, then open the page default.html. Use the page properties to add a title, a description, and four appropriate keywords. Use the heading style and other formatting techniques to apply italics, bold, center alignment, and indentations to make the home page easy to read.

•• 4: Create a Job Search Home Page

Make It Personal

When you are looking for a job, it is helpful to have a résumé or list of your skills that you can share with potential employers. What is your dream job? Imagine yourself a decade from now—what amazing skills and job experiences will you have collected? Will you have won any awards, made a scientific discovery, learned a foreign language, or gone to art school? Create a one-page Web site that you can use to show potential employers all of the things that you might have learned and done over the next 10 years that would qualify you for your dream job. Include a masthead, bulleted list, footer, and any other information you think is relevant. Format the Web site attractively, including adding a background color, changing the fonts, and applying effects such as bold and italics. Add a page title, a description, and keywords.

Found within the Cases and Places exercises, the **Make It Personal** exercises call on students to create an open-ended project that relates to their personal lives.

1 | Creating an Expression Web Site

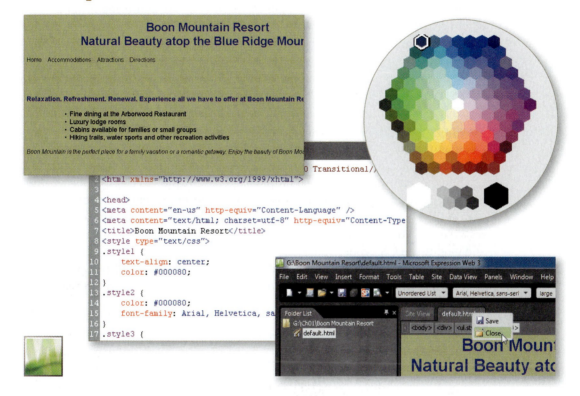

Objectives

You will have mastered the material in this chapter when you can:

- Start and quit Expression Web
- Describe the features of Expression Web's main window
- Create a new Expression Web site
- Set page properties
- Enter and format text
- Create headings and lists

- Switch views
- Spell check a page
- Save a page
- Show and hide visual aids
- Use Quick Tag Selectors
- Display a page in a browser
- Close an Expression Web site

1 | Creating an Expression Web Site

What Is Microsoft Expression Web?

Microsoft Expression Web 3 is a full-featured Web site authoring program that allows you to create professional looking Web sites. A **Web site** is a collection of connected Web pages that contain text, images, or video. With Expression Web, you can create any type of Web site, from a one-page personal site to a sophisticated professional site consisting of hundreds of pages. Expression Web provides a **What You See Is What You Get (WYSIWYG)** design interface; in Design view, you can see exactly how the layout and formatting will appear in a browser and make necessary changes while editing. Expression Web provides automated tools for creating Web pages and Web sites.

You can use Expression Web to create and edit HTML files that contain the content of a page, and Cascading Style Sheets (CSS) files that control the formatting and layout of text and objects on a page or on multiple pages. Expression Web tools such as the design interface, panel, and dialog boxes assist you in entering content and defining the style rules, without you having to know CSS and HTML codes. Expression Web also provides a full-featured HTML/XHTML editor for viewing and entering code, and allows you to view and modify the CSS code.

Expression Web is part of the **Microsoft Expression Studio 3** program suite. Appendix D provides more information on the various products in Expression Studio and describes how they work together.

Project Planning Guidelines

> Before you can begin to create a Web site, you must do some initial planning and get approval on the plan from your client or colleagues. You will need to establish the goal or purpose of the Web site and the type of site (such as informational or e-commerce), and identify the target users you want to attract to your site. Next, you should conduct research to learn how comparable sites are designed. With these elements defined, you should create a plan that specifies the content and layout of your site. After establishing the basic structure and content of your site, you will be ready to develop the site and test it with multiple browsers. Finally, after the site is complete, you can publish it to a Web server and begin marketing your site to attract visitors. Each project in this book provides practical applications of these guidelines.

Project — Home Page

Boon Mountain Resort is located in Redhat, Georgia. The resort has been in business for one year and now would like to have a Web site to promote its many features. The resort has an excellent restaurant, luxury lodge rooms, and individual cabins located throughout the property. Nearby hiking trails and water sports are available for guests. The resort intends to promote itself to potential guests through a Web site with pages for accommodations, attractions, and directions, along with a home page.

The project in this chapter follows general guidelines and uses Expression Web to create the home page shown in Figure 1–1. This home page is the entry to the Boon Mountain Resort Web site, and will need text and formatting, and, eventually, graphics and hyperlinks. You will create a navigation bar to which you will add links to other site pages in the next chapter. In Chapter 1, you will create the text for the Boon Mountain Resort home page, and in the next chapter, you will enhance your Web site by adding pages, images, and links.

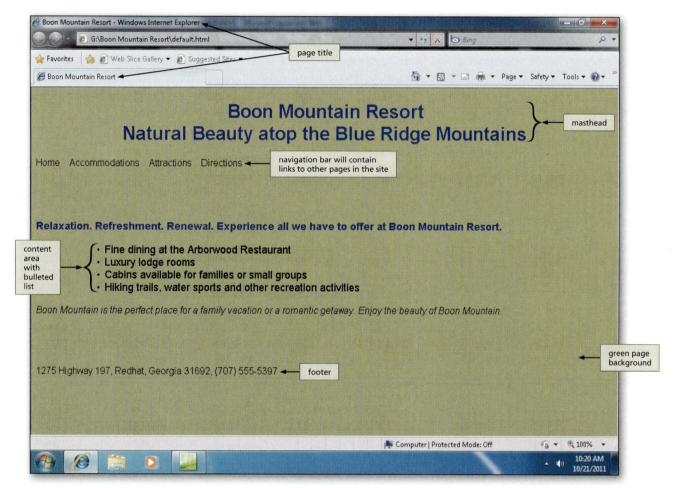

Figure 1–1

Figure 1–2 illustrates a plan for the layout and content of the default.html page of the Boon Mountain Resort Web site.

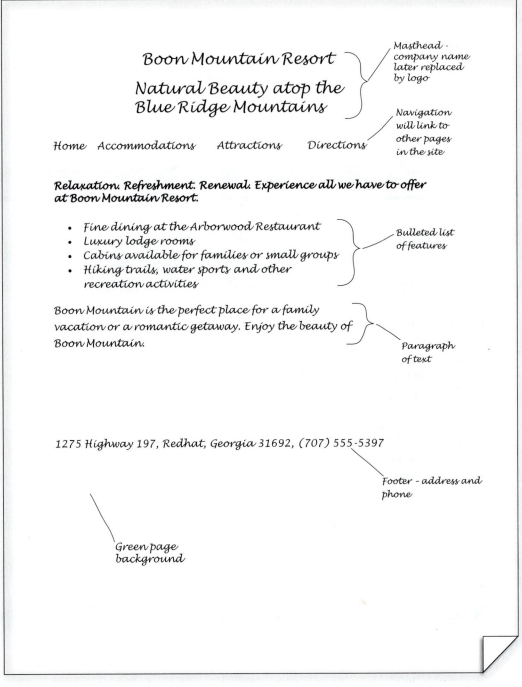

Figure 1–2

Overview

As you read this chapter, you will learn how to create the Web site shown in Figure 1–1 by performing these general tasks:

- Open the Expression Web program.
- Create an Expression Web site.
- Set page properties.
- Add page divisions.
- Enter text on the page.

- Format text on the page.
- Use visual aids and tags.
- Save the page.
- Preview the page.
- Print the page.

Plan
Ahead

General Project Guidelines

When creating an Expression Web site, the actions you perform and decisions you make will affect the pages and links included in the site. As you create a Web site, such as the project shown in Figure 1–1, you should follow these general guidelines:

1. **Choose a Web site structure to use as the starting point for the site.** A Web site consists of one or more Web pages. Determine the purpose of the site, such as commercial or personal, then determine the number of pages and how site users will navigate to the pages.

2. **Determine folder structure and location and file naming conventions for the Web site files.** You must save all of the related files and folders for the Web site in one location.

3. **Determine the page properties or settings that will apply to the pages.** You can choose page settings, such as page title and keywords, using the Page Properties dialog box.

4. **Decide what the page layout will look like.** Page **layout**, which is the placement of text and objects, contributes to the look and consistency of a site. Well-arranged elements, such as a company logo or a navigation bar with links to the main pages of a site, keep the visitor interacting with the site longer and give the site a professional look.

5. **Determine the text content for the page.** Use text to convey the message with as few words as possible. Easy-to-read content encourages visitors to consider your product or service.

6. **Design the format for the text elements on the page.** The use of headings, fonts, lists, and color helps to identify important content and assists the visitor when scanning the page for specific content.

When necessary, specific details about these guidelines are presented at appropriate points in the chapter. The chapter also will identify the tasks performed and decisions made during the creation of the Web site shown in Figure 1–1.

Starting Expression Web

If you are using a computer to step through the project in this chapter, and you want your screen to match the figures in this book, you should change your screen's resolution to 1024×768. For more information about how to change a computer's resolution, read Appendix G.

BTW

File Extensions
HTML files can be saved with either the .html or .htm file extension. DOS-based operating systems restricted file extensions to three letters, necessitating the abbreviation of .html to .htm. All of today's browsers recognize both file extensions.

To Start Expression Web

The following steps, which assume Windows 7 is running, start Expression Web based on a typical installation. You may need to ask your instructor how to start Expression Web for your computer.

Note: If you are using Windows XP, see Appendix E for alternate steps. If you are using Windows Vista, see Appendix F for alternate steps.

- Click the Start button on the Windows 7 taskbar to display the Start menu.

- Click All Programs at the bottom of the left pane on the Start menu to display the All Programs list.

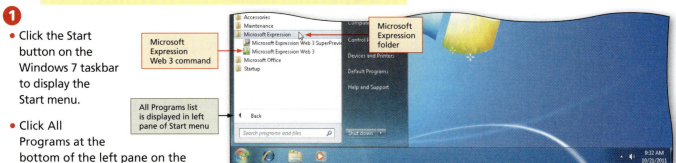

Figure 1–3

- Click the Microsoft Expression folder on the All Programs list to display the Microsoft Expression list (Figure 1–3).

- Click Microsoft Expression Web 3 to start Expression Web and display a new blank Web page in the Expression Web editing window (Figure 1–4).

Q&A Why does Expression Web sometimes open a Web site and other times open with a blank Web page named Untitled_1.html?

When you quit Expression Web without closing the Web site you are working on, Expression Web remembers the site and automatically opens it the next time Expression Web starts. If no previous site is in Expression Web's memory, it starts with a blank page named Untitled_1.html.

Q&A Sometimes when opening Expression Web, a server error message displays. What does that error mean?

If you quit Expression Web without closing a Web site first, Expression Web will try to open that site the next time Expression Web is started. If the site was saved on an external drive such as a USB flash drive, Expression Web looks for that drive address; if the location is not available (such as when the USB flash drive has been removed), the server error is generated. Just click OK to proceed.

Figure 1–4

Other Ways

1. Double-click the Microsoft Expression Web 3 icon on the desktop, if one is present
2. Click Microsoft Expression Web 3 on the Start menu

Expression Web Workspace

Expression Web opens with a menu, a toolbar, a status bar, an editing window, and four panels for adding components and managing site content. When you first open Expression Web, a new blank HTML page displays with the name, Untitled_1.html.

The Workspace Window

The workspace window shown in Figure 1–5 is where you build your Web site. The **workspace** contains the tools necessary to edit and manage Web pages. You can customize the workspace to contain the tools you use most often.

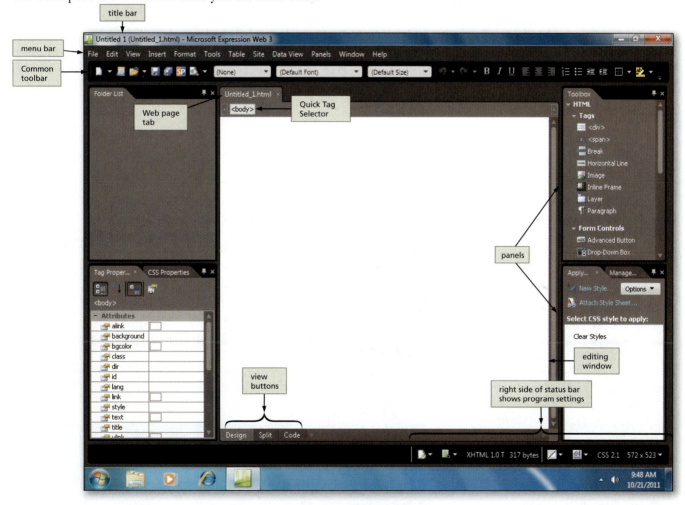

Figure 1–5

Title Bar The **title bar** at the top of the screen shows the application name and filename of the current Web page.

Menu Bar The **menu bar** at the top of the workspace contains all of the Expression Web commands.

Common Toolbar The **Common toolbar** is located below the menu bar and contains buttons for the most commonly used commands.

BTW

Other Views
When the Site View tab is active, the view buttons change to Folders, Publishing, Reports, and Hyperlinks. Folders view is used to manage files and folders. Publishing view shows files located on a remote server. Reports view shows content and status of site elements, and Hyperlinks view shows links to pages within the site.

Editing Window   The **editing window** is where you create your Web page using the various Expression Web tools.

Web Page Tab   The **Web page tab** shows the filename of the page being edited as well as any other open pages.

Quick Tag Selector   The **Quick Tag Selector**, located just below the Web page tab, shows the underlying HTML tags generated as you add content to the page.

Panels   There are four default **panels:** two on the left (Folder List and Tag Properties) and two on the right (Toolbox and Apply Styles). Panels are moved or replaced to reflect the current task.

View Buttons   The **view buttons** are located at the lower left of the editing window and change depending on which tab is active (Web Site tab or Web page tab). When a Web page is open, the available view buttons are Design, Split, and Code. Design view is the WYSIWYG view. Split view shows the HTML tags at the top of the screen and the WYSIWYG page on the bottom. Code view shows only the HTML code.

Status Bar   The right side of the **status bar** shows HTML incompatibilities and code errors, XHTML version, the status of visual aids, page size dimensions, and the XHTML and CSS versions Expression Web is using to code your pages.

Toolbars

Expression Web's default toolbar is the Common toolbar. To display the menu of toolbar options, right-click a toolbar (Figure 1–6). In addition to the Common toolbar, Expression Web has 10 other task-specific toolbars that you can display when needed to perform a specific task, such as working with a table. When Expression Web opens for the first time, the Common toolbar is the only one visible. When you open a toolbar, it remains open each time the program is started, until you close it manually. Depending on past usage, your toolbar buttons may differ slightly. A check mark next to the toolbar name indicates it is visible. To show a toolbar, click the toolbar name to add a check mark. To hide a toolbar, click the name that contains the check mark to remove the check mark.

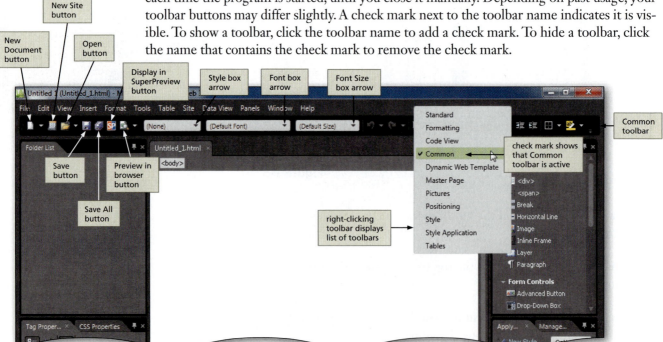

Figure 1–6

To Reset Workspace Layout

As you work with Expression Web, you may rearrange the toolbars and panels by opening, moving, maximizing, or closing them. To make your screen match the figures in this book and to ensure that you start from the same point during each work session, you should reset the workspace to the default layout, and close any open sites. The following steps restore all panels and content areas to the default sizes and locations, and close any open sites.

 1

- Click Panels on the menu bar to open the Panels menu and then point to Reset Workspace Layout (Figure 1–7).

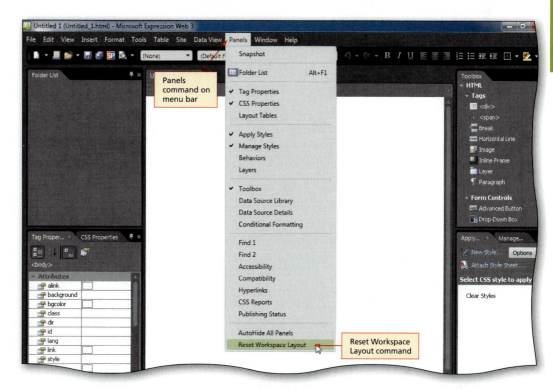

Figure 1–7

 2

- Click Reset Workspace Layout to restore the panels to their default layout.

- If a site is open, click Site on the menu bar to open the Site menu, and then click Close to close the site (Figure 1–8).

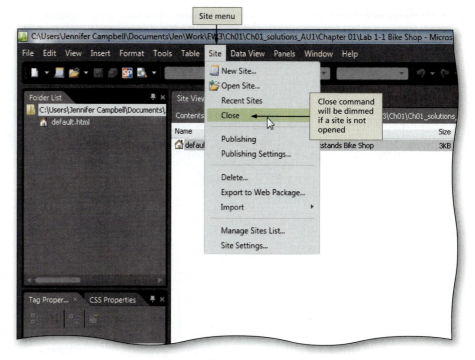

Figure 1–8

Naming Files and Folders

The site name, which is the folder that contains the site contents, can include spaces. Within the site, folders and filenames cannot contain uppercase letters, spaces, or certain characters, such as the pound sign (#) or an asterisk (*). You can separate words in a filename by using an underscore (_), such as in the folder name assets_images or the filename web_page2.html.

Creating a Web Site

A Web site consists, at minimum, of a folder and an HTML file. Once these two basic components are created, you can enhance the site with additional HTML files, embed images and style sheets, and organize the files into folders and subfolders. The first Web page in the site is the **home page**. The home page provides access to the other Web pages in the site by including hyperlinks in a navigation bar.

When creating an Expression Web site, you are actually creating a root folder to store all the files and subfolders for your site. When you create a new one-page Web site, Expression Web creates a root folder and a file named default.html, which serves as the home page for the site. Expression Web uses the default.html name because the Web servers on which Web pages are stored look for a home page named default.html or index.html.

Plan Ahead

> **Choose the Web site structure to use as the starting point for the site.**
> You must first decide whether to begin your Web site by using a blank Web site, modifying an existing Web site, using a template, or importing an existing site from the Internet or other location into Expression Web.
>
> **Determine folder structure and location and file naming conventions for the Web site files.**
> Saving an Expression Web site is different from saving an individual file created in another program. A site consists of HTML files that store content, style sheets that indicate how formatting is applied, and elements such as graphics and media files. It is important to plan how you will name and organize the files and folder structure where you will store the site's pages, style sheets, and graphics and media files.

To Create a Web Site

If you need your site to be portable so that you can work on it on different computers, you should store the site on an external storage device such as a USB flash drive. The following steps create the Web site folder for the Boon Mountain Resort site and a one-page blank HTML file, and save them to the USB flash drive.

1

• With a USB flash drive connected to one of the computer's USB ports, click Site on the menu bar to open the Site menu, then point to New Site (Figure 1–9).

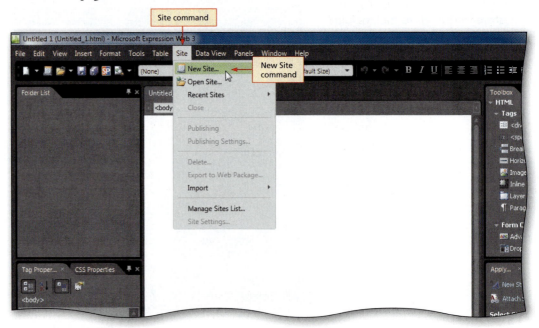

Figure 1–9

2

- Click New Site on the Site menu to display the New dialog box (Figure 1–10).

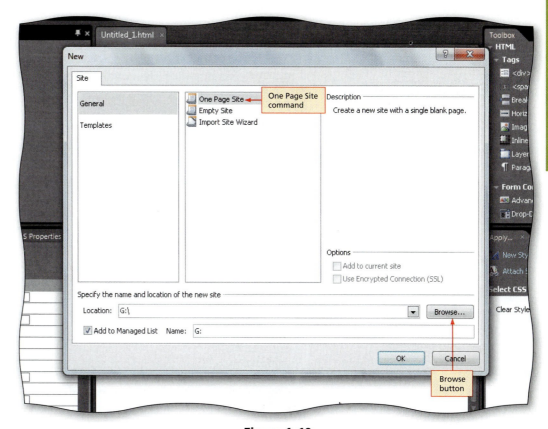

Figure 1–10

3

- In the middle pane, click One Page Site.

- Click the Browse button to open the New Site Location dialog box (Figure 1–11).

Figure 1–11

- Click Computer in the Navigation pane to display a list of available drives (Figure 1–12).

- If necessary, scroll until FLASH DRIVE or USB (G:) appears in the list of available drives.

Q&A Do I have to use a USB flash drive?

No. You can save to any device or folder. Use the same process, but select your device or network folder from the Computer list.

- Double-click FLASH DRIVE (G:) to select the USB flash drive, drive G in this case, as the new save location.

Figure 1–12

- If necessary, navigate to or create a folder on your drive into which you will save your Data Files.

- Click the Open button to return to the New dialog box (Figure 1–13).

Q&A What if my USB flash drive has a different name or letter?

It is likely that your USB flash drive will be named differently and be connected to a different lettered port. Use the device, folder, or drive where you save your files.

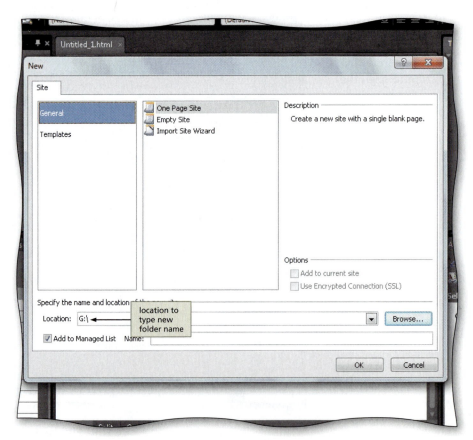

Figure 1–13

- Click in the Location text box, then click after the text to position the insertion point to create a new Web site folder.
- Type `Boon Mountain Resort` to specify the site folder name (Figure 1–14).

Figure 1–14

- Click the OK button to close the New dialog box, open the Web site folder for the site, and create the default.html page (Figure 1–15).

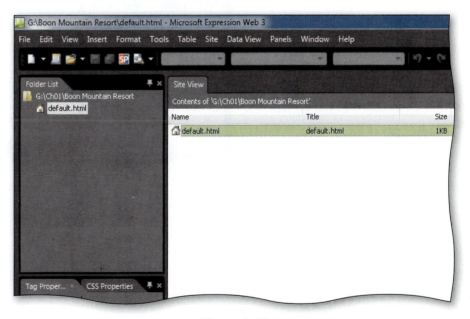

Figure 1–15

To Open a Web Page

Now that you have created the Web site, you are ready to add content to the home page. The home page will contain links to the other pages in the site and information about the Boon Mountain Resort. The following step opens the HTML file that will contain the home page content.

- Double-click default.html in the Folder List panel to open the page (Figure 1–16).

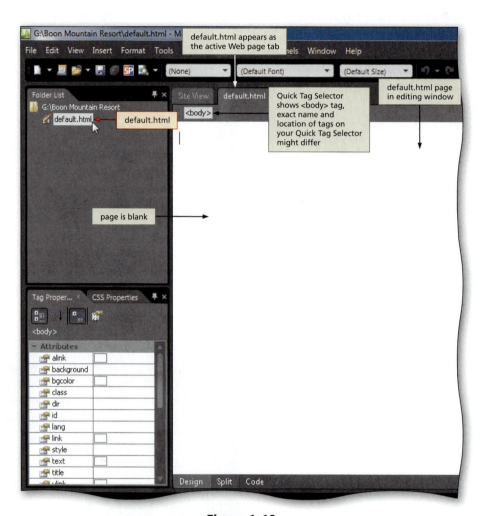

Figure 1–16

Other Ways		
1. Double-click the filename in the Site View tab	2. Click File on the menu bar, then click Open to open the Open File dialog box. Click the filename, then click the Open button	3. Press CTRL +O to open the Open File dialog box. Click the filename, then click the Open button

Setting Page Properties

Each page in the site can have unique page properties. These properties include file location, page title, page description, keywords, background sound, background image, hyperlink colors, and margins. Such properties can add visual interest, increase readability, and reflect a company's identity, in addition to making your site easier for search engines to find. You can use a predefined color for the page background, or define characteristics to create a custom color.

The **page title** displays on the title bar of a browser and should be meaningful to a visitor. If the visitor adds the page to his or her browser Favorites or Bookmarks list, the page title is often what appears in the Favorites list, depending on the browser. Search engines display the **page description** in search results, and use **keywords** to place your page in search results by matching the keywords listed in the site with the user's search criteria.

> **Determine the page properties or settings that will apply to the page.**
> You can set page properties at any time, but it is a good design strategy to set them before you enter text onto the page. These page specifications should be determined during the planning and design stage while you are making decisions about the site color scheme and layout.
>
> When deciding on a background color or graphic, keep in mind that the text on the page should be easy to read. A dark background or busy graphic might distract from the content and could cause your site visitors to miss important information.

Plan Ahead

BTW

Misspellings
If some of your keywords include common mis-spellings, or British and American English spelling variations (such as *colour* and *color*), be sure to include them in the Page Properties dialog box.

To Set Page Properties

To enter or change the page description and keywords, you use the General, Formatting, and other tabs in the Page Properties dialog box. The following steps change the page properties and add a custom color background to the page.

- Click File on the menu bar to display the File menu, then click Properties to display the Page Properties dialog box (Figure 1–17).

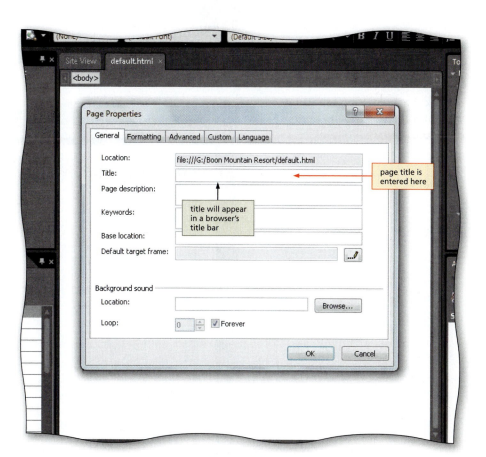

Figure 1–17

2

- On the General tab, type `Boon Mountain Resort` in the Title text box to specify the page title.

- Press the TAB key to move to the Page description text box.

- Type `Magnificent resort atop the majestic Blue Ridge Mountains.`

- Press the TAB key to move to the Keywords text box.

- Type `resort, cabins, mountains, romantic getaway, family vacation, Blue Ridge Mountains, Redhat, Georgia` (Figure 1–18).

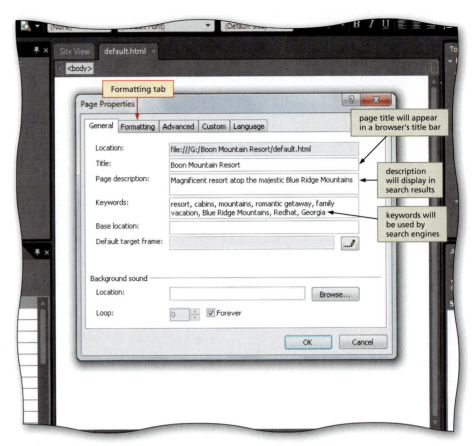

Figure 1–18

3

- Click the Formatting tab to display the background options (Figure 1–19).

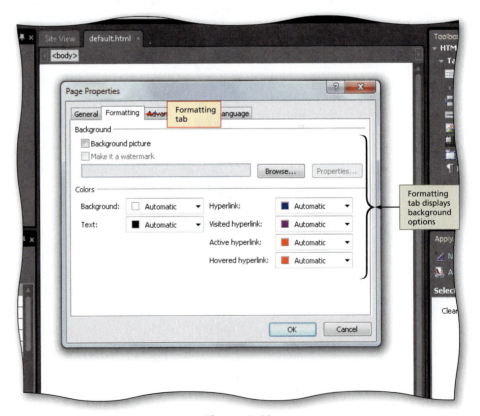

Figure 1–19

4
- In the Colors area, click the Background color button arrow to display the color palette (Figure 1–20).

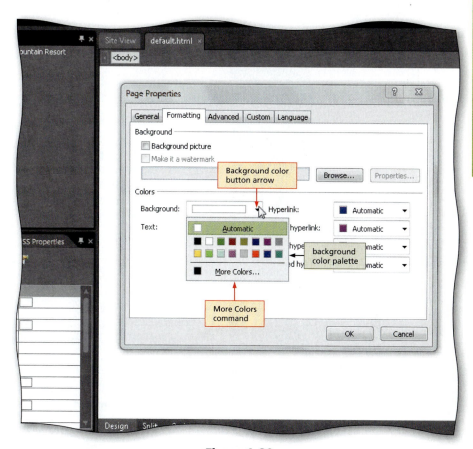

Figure 1–20

5
- Click More Colors to display the More Colors dialog box (Figure 1–21).

Q&A What is a custom color?

A custom color is created by using numbers to define characteristics such as hue, saturation, and luminosity or red, green, and blue.

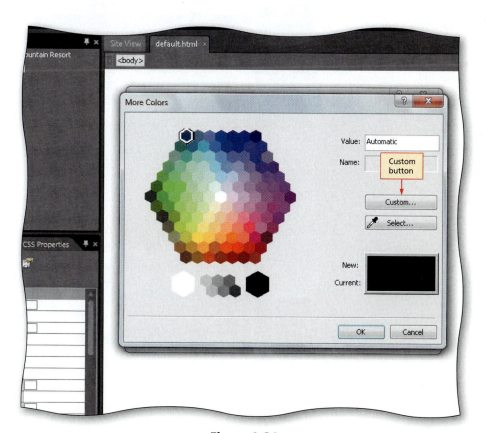

Figure 1–21

6
- Click the Custom button to open the Color dialog box.

- Double-click in the Hue box, then type 40.

- Press TAB and then type 80 in the Sat box.

- Press TAB, and then type 137 in the Lum box to define a green custom color (Figure 1–22).

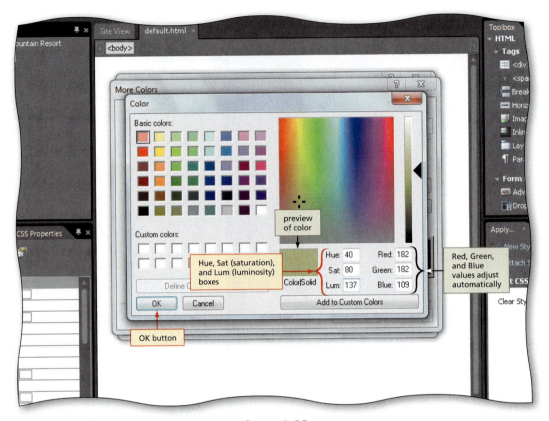

Figure 1–22

7
- Click the OK button to close the Color dialog box (Figure 1–23).

 Q&A What is a hex color value?

A hex color value is a number that represents color in the format that is used in HTML code.

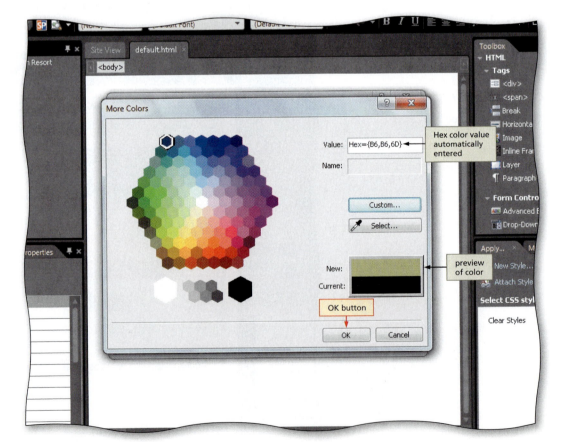

Figure 1–23

- Click the OK button to close the More Colors dialog box.

- Click the OK button to close the Page Properties dialog box and view the green page background (Figure 1–24).

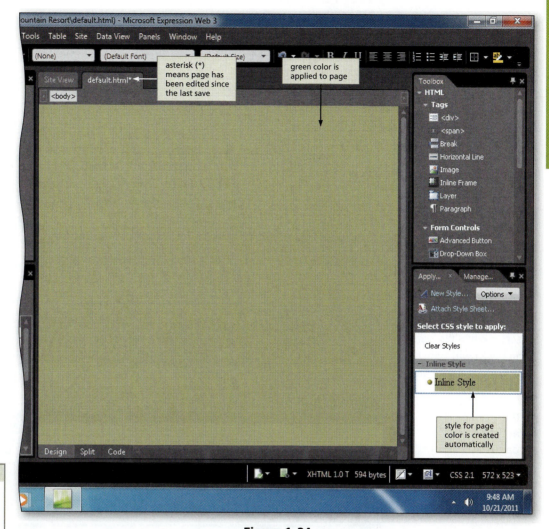

Figure 1–24

Other Ways

1. Right-click anywhere in the page to display the shortcut menu, then click Page Properties to open the Page Properties dialog box

---

Decide what the page layout will look like.
Most pages on the Internet follow similar layout rules because of the restrictions of HTML. Using a layout with which users feel comfortable allows them to focus on the content and message of your site.

- Some common elements found on each page of most professionally developed Web sites include a masthead or page banner, one or more navigational systems, a content section divided into one or more columns, and a footer area. Minor variations of page layouts throughout the site can add interest and variety to the site to enhance the visitor experience, but the overall structure should be consistent.

- A page mockup for each page, either hand drawn or computer generated, indicates what a finished page will look like.

- Select font families, color schemes, or palettes to provide contrast, set the mood, and maintain consistency throughout the site.

Determine the text content for the page.
Avoid long paragraphs of text. Use short sentences, bulleted lists, and boldface key terms to show the main points of a page without bogging down the reader. Divide content among site pages to avoid having visitors scroll to read all information on a page.

Plan Ahead

BTW

Web Standards
Web standards are guidelines for Web development, defined by the World Wide Web Consortium (W3C), an international organization of Web developers (www.w3c.org). Web standards ensure that viewers of a Web site who are using different browsers have a common experience.

Entering Text

Faster Downloading
Another advantage of using a division-based layout is that it reduces the number of lines of code needed to create a page, resulting in faster downloading from the Internet.

A basic Web page layout typically contains four sections: masthead, navigation, content, and footer. These sections are usually enclosed within division containers made up of <div>…</div> tag elements. This method of layout is called **division-based layout**. The purpose of using <div> </div> tags, or **divs**, is to define an area of the page that you can format using **styles**, which are collections of formatting attributes.

Using the page layout mockup shown in Figure 1–2, the home page shows the company name and tagline at the top of the page, called the **masthead**. The **navigation bar** includes the names of the other site pages, each of which will contain information relating to a specific topic, and to which you will later add links. The body of the home page, called the content area, contains a bulleted list that highlights important features of the resort. The page is visually appealing and easy to read because of the varying font colors used for emphasis and the green page background.

Once the layout is defined, you can start entering text by clicking in a div and typing.

To Add a <Div> Tag

As shown in Figure 1–1, the final page will include four text areas: a masthead, a navigation bar, a page content area, and a footer. To define the masthead section of the page where the company name and tagline will appear, you will insert a <div> tag before typing text. You will also need to add a <div> tag, to define the navigation bar of the page, into which you will type the names of the other site pages. In a later chapter, you will add links to those pages. The following steps create the first two tags and their content.

1
- If necessary, click at the top of the page to position the insertion point where you want the <div> tag to appear (Figure 1–25).

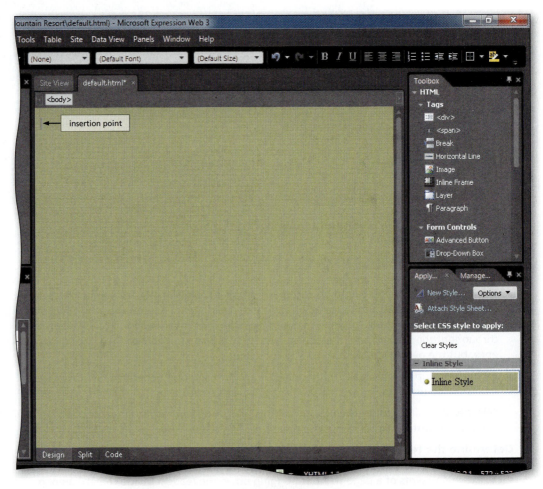

Figure 1–25

2

- Double-click the <div> tag in the Toolbox to place a <div> division container on your page at the insertion point's location (Figure 1–26).

Q&A What if I double-click too many times and get more than one tag on my page?

Click the Undo button on the Common toolbar.

Q&A What should I do if I cannot see the new div?

Point to Visual Aids on the View menu, and then click Show.

Other Ways

1. Click the <div> tag in the Toolbox, then drag the <div> tag to where you want it on the page
2. Click the <div> button on the Common toolbar

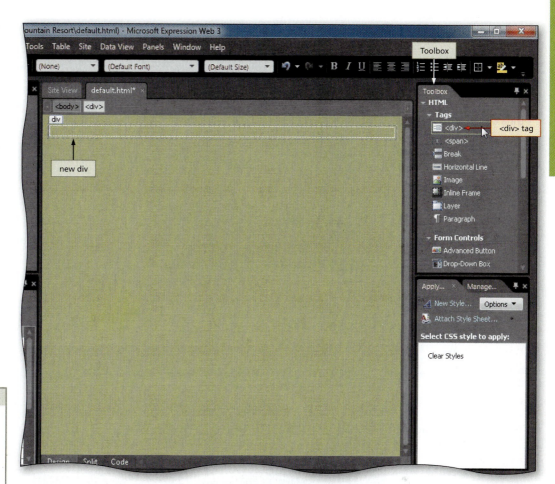

Figure 1–26

3

- Type Boon Mountain Resort, then press the ENTER key to move the insertion point to the next line (Figure 1–27).

Q&A What if my insertion point is not inside the <div> container?

Click inside the <div> container.

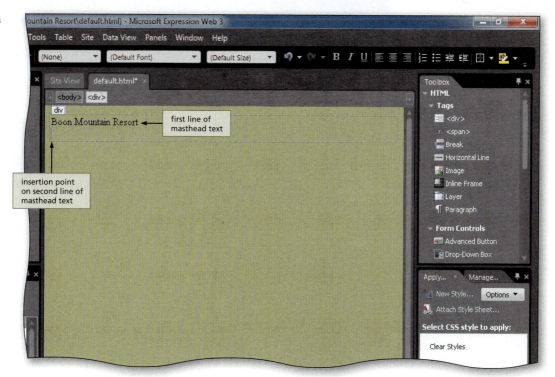

Figure 1–27

4

- Type Natural Beauty atop the Blue Ridge Mountains, then click a blank spot on the page outside of the <div> tag to indicate you are finished entering data into it (Figure 1–28).

Figure 1–28

5

- Double-click the <div> tag in the Toolbox to place a division container at the insertion point's location (Figure 1–29).

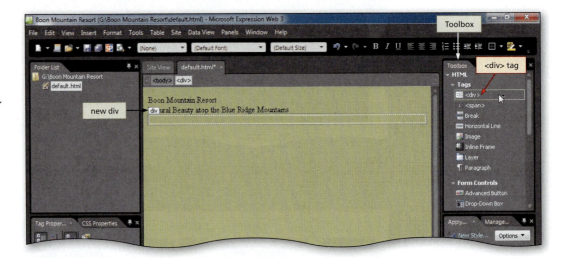

Figure 1–29

6

- Be sure the insertion point is inside the <div> tag. Type Home, then press TAB to enter the text for the first navigational link (Figure 1–30).

Q&A

Why do I press TAB instead of the SPACEBAR?

Pressing TAB inserts more space than pressing the SPACEBAR. TAB is used to insert a consistent amount of space between words.

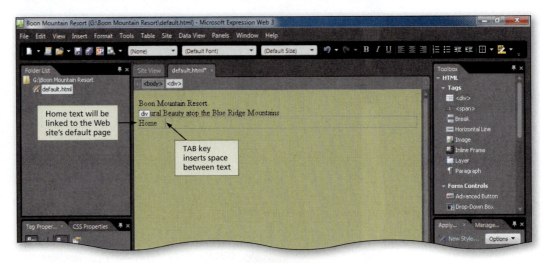

Figure 1–30

7

- Type
Accommodations
as the text for the
second link, then
press TAB.

- Type Attractions
as the text for the
third link, then
press TAB.

- Type Directions as
the text for the final
navigational link,
then click a blank
spot on the page
outside of the <div>
to indicate you are
finished entering
data into it
(Figure 1–31).

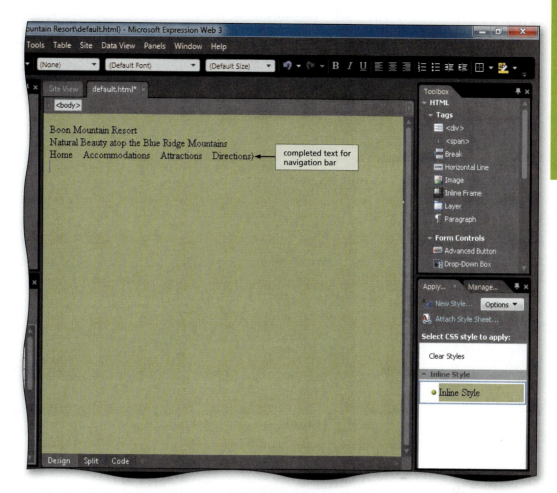

Figure 1–31

To Add Paragraph Text

A paragraph is specified by using the <p> tag, and is used to contain text. When you press ENTER in a <p> tag, a new paragraph is inserted, with line space between the two paragraphs. The following steps add another <div> . . . </div> container to hold the rest of the page content, then add space between divs on the page. Within the new <div> tag you will embed a paragraph <p> tag and enter content. When Expression Web 3 inserts <p></p> tags they are represented in Design view by a <p> on the Quick Tag Selector and a p tab and container in the editing window.

1

- Double-click the <div>
tag in the Toolbox
to place a division
container at the inser-
tion point's location
(Figure 1–32).

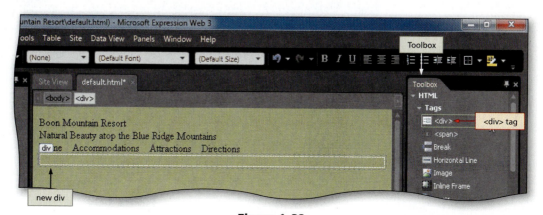

Figure 1–32

2

- With the insertion point still inside the <div> tag, press the ENTER key four times to add line spacing inside the <div> tag container (Figure 1–33).

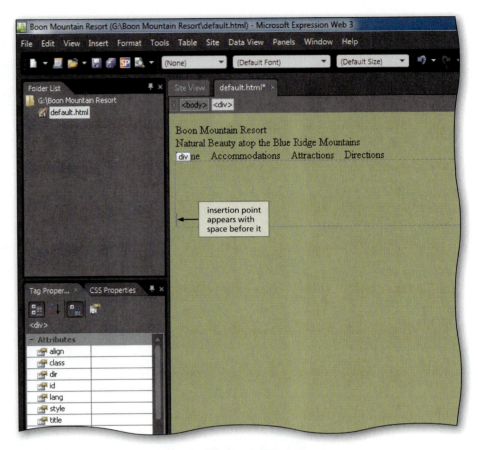

Figure 1–33

3

- Double-click the Paragraph tag in the Toolbox to place a paragraph <p> tag on the page inside of the <div> tag container (Figure 1–34).

Q&A Why should I add extra lines on the page?

Using generous blank areas, or white space, helps to avoid a cluttered page.

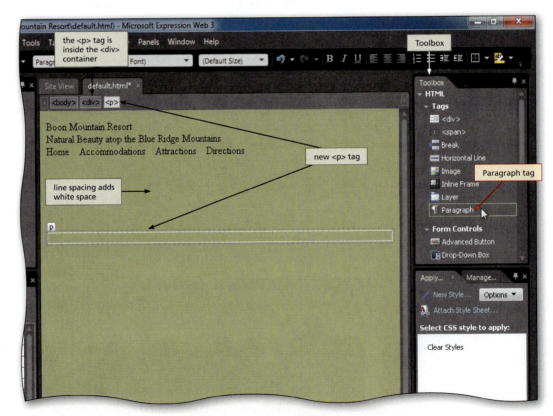

Figure 1–34

4

- With the insertion point inside the Paragraph tag, type Relaxation. Refreshment. Renewal. Experience all we have to offer at Boon Mountain Resort., then press ENTER to insert a new <p> tag (Figure 1–35).

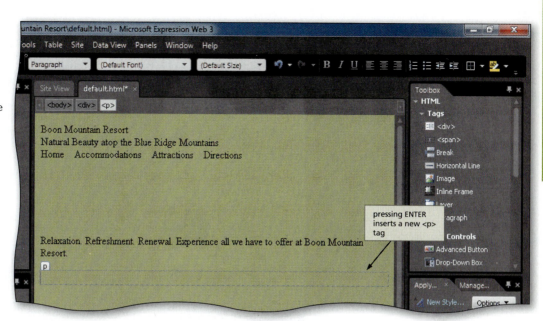

Figure 1–35

To Add a Bulleted List

A **bulleted list** is used to portray several points that do not need to appear in any specific order. The following steps add features to extol the benefits of the Boon Mountain Resort by creating a bulleted list.

1

- Be sure the insertion point is inside the new <p> tag and then click the Bullets button on the Common toolbar to create the first bullet (Figure 1–36).

Q&A

What happened to the <p> tag?

The <p> tag was replaced with the <ul> tag when the Bullets button was clicked.

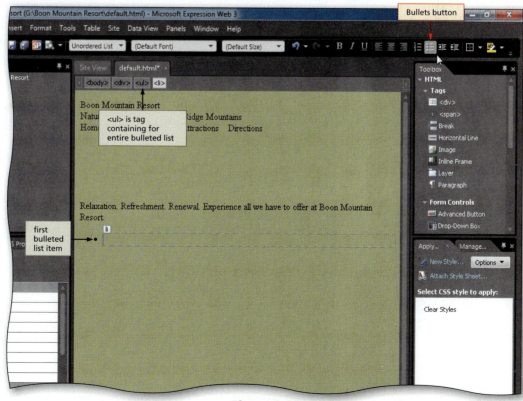

Figure 1–36

2

- Type Fine dining at the Arborwood Restaurant, then press ENTER to start a new bullet (Figure 1–37).

Q&A What is the red, wavy line under Arborwood?

Words with a red, wavy line are not in the Expression Web dictionary. If you don't see the line, click Tools on the menu bar, point to Spelling, click Spelling Options to open the Spelling Options dialog box, click the 'Check spelling as you type' check box to select it, then click the OK button to close the dialog box. You will check spelling later in Chapter 1.

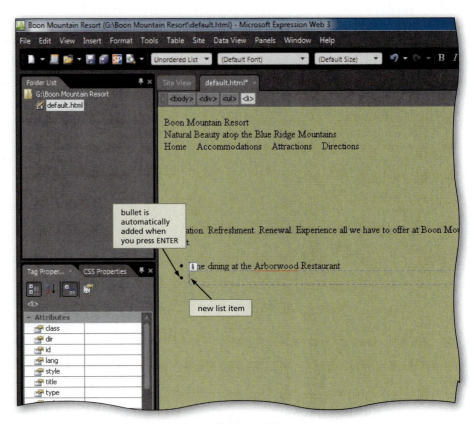

Figure 1–37

3

- Type Luxury lodge rooms as the text for the second bullet, then press ENTER.

- Type Cabins available for families or small groups as the third list item, then press ENTER.

- Type Hiking trails, water sports and other recreation activities, then press ENTER to start a new line (Figure 1–38).

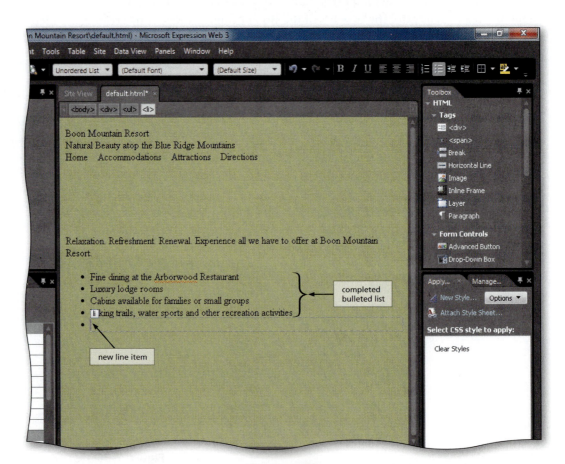

Figure 1–38

- Click the Bullets button on the Common toolbar to end the bulleted list. Expression Web starts a new paragraph by inserting a <p> tag (Figure 1–39).

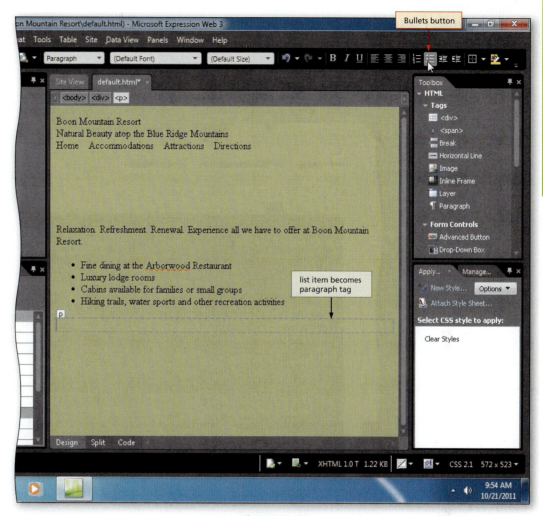

Figure 1–39

To Complete Page Content

The last <p> tag in the content area on the default page will contain the resort's advertising slogan. The final <div> tag, which you add in the following steps, will be used as the footer area on the page. The following steps enter the content for the slogan and add the footer.

- With the insertion point inside the new <p> tag, type Boon Mountain is the perfect place for a family vacation or a romantic getaway. Enjoy the beauty of Boon Mountain., but do not press ENTER (Figure 1–40).

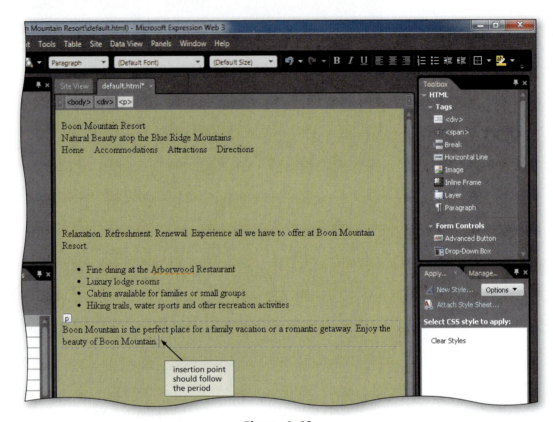

Figure 1–40

- Click a blank area under the <p> tag, then press ENTER twice to add white space to the page (Figure 1–41).

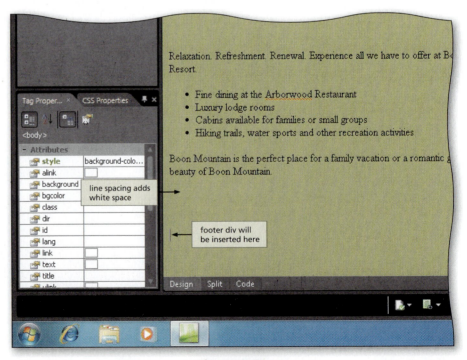

Figure 1–41

3

- Double-click the
<div> tag in the
Toolbox to place
a division container
at the insertion
point's location
(Figure 1–42).

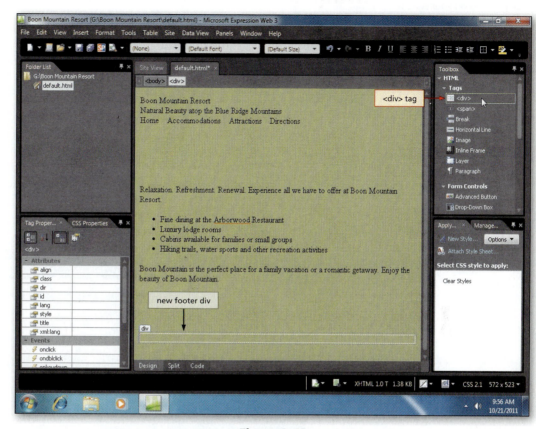

Figure 1–42

4

- Type 1275 Highway 197,
Redhat, Georgia 31692,
(707) 555-5397 (Figure 1–43).

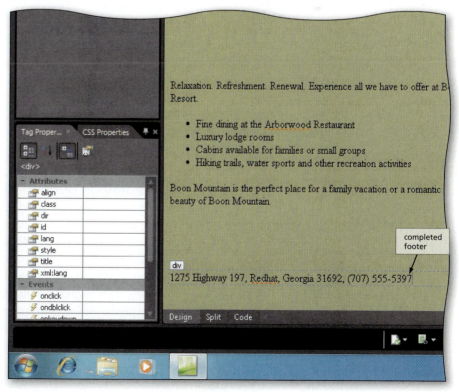

Figure 1–43

AutoSave
Depending on your system settings, Expression Web may save pages automatically as you work. If you get an error message indicating that a more recent version of the file was saved to the server, click Yes to overwrite the file.

Saving Individual Web Pages

As you make changes to a page, an asterisk (*) appears next to the page name on the tab at the top of the editing window, indicating that it needs to be saved before your changes will be reflected in a browser. You should save your pages frequently while editing so that you do not lose any content, layout, or other work you have done on your site.

To Save a Web Page

It is a good habit to save your page often as you are creating it. The following step saves the page you are working on.

1
- Click the Save button on the Common toolbar (Figure 1–44).

Figure 1–44

Other Ways
1. Right-click the page tab at the top of the Editing window, then click Save   2. Click File on the menu bar, then click Save   3. Press CTRL+S

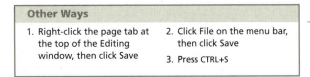

Web Accessibility
See Appendix B for more information about accessibility and assistive technology.

Applying Formatting and Styles

Formatting is the combination of design characteristics that are applied to text, specifying a hierarchy of headings and text levels. Consistently applied formatting can guide the reader through the content on your site. Formatting techniques include changing fonts and font sizes, applying font attributes such as bold and italics, and changing the alignment and indentation of lines and paragraphs of text. To emphasize just one word or a series of words in a paragraph, you can apply the bold or italic font attribute by using formatting buttons or keyboard shortcuts.

You can apply formatting such as bold as you enter text (just as you would in a word processing program) or apply predefined or custom styles that combine a variety of attributes.

Heading and subheading styles indicate the relative importance of each line of text. HTML supports six levels of heading style tags: <h1>, the largest, through <h6>, the smallest. All heading styles apply the bold attribute automatically but use different font sizes to show the level. Using styles, as opposed to applying formatting directly, ensures consistency in a large site so that if you change an attribute of a style, it applies automatically to other elements that share that style.

As you apply various formatting to text on the page, Expression Web creates a style in the Apply Styles panel. The styles are given a default number as they are applied and that number becomes part of the HTML tag. You can then apply these styles to different areas of the page or site, such as for bulleted lists. You will work with the Apply Styles panel in Chapter 3.

Design the format for the text elements on the page.

When formatting fonts, you should select font families and assign formatting characteristics for headings, captions, and lists that help make your page attractive and easy to read.

- Readability is the first consideration for text formatting. Font size should be neither too small, which is difficult to read, nor too large, which looks unprofessional and wastes screen space.

- Use headings and subheadings to emphasize important words and to draw the reader's eye to that location of the screen.

- Limit the number of fonts used in your site to two or three. Choose common fonts or font families that will be recognizable to many browsers. Avoid ornate fonts, such as hand-writing or scroll fonts, because they are difficult to read and are not recognized by many browsers. If your company uses a custom or fancy font in its logo, create the logo as a graphic element rather than text to ensure that it appears the same in all browsers.

- Use font color as emphasis on important words within a paragraph or bulleted text rather than applying a color to the entire text section. Consider the background of the page and make sure that the font color you choose provides contrast.

- Avoid using underlined text, which usually represents a hyperlink.

Plan Ahead

To Use the Quick Tag Selector

Use the Quick Tag Selector to confirm that you have selected an entire element before applying formatting or making changes to the text. The following step selects a list item and a list using the Quick Tag Selector.

- Click in the text of the third bullet to display the <li> tag for the list item (Figure 1–45).

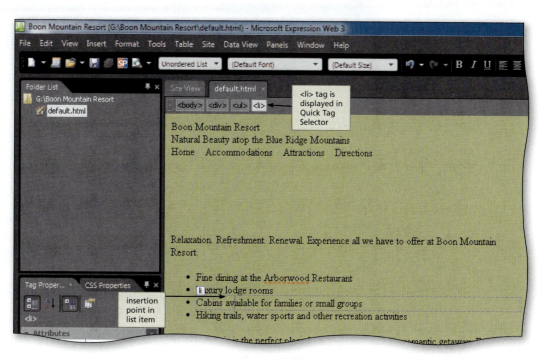

Figure 1–45

2

• Click the <li> tag on the Quick Tag Selector to select the entire bullet (Figure 1–46).

Q&A

Why did a menu appear when I clicked the <li> tag?

Be sure to click the tag, not the arrow to its right.

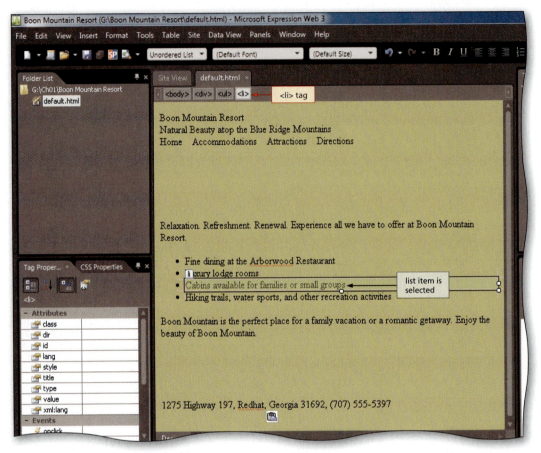

Figure 1–46

3

• Click the <ul> tag on the Quick Tag Selector to select the entire bulleted list (Figure 1–47).

Experiment

• Use the Quick Tag Selector to select other tags, such as <body>, to see how many nested elements are selected. The farther left you click on the Quick Tag Selector, the higher you are in the hierarchy of tags on the page.

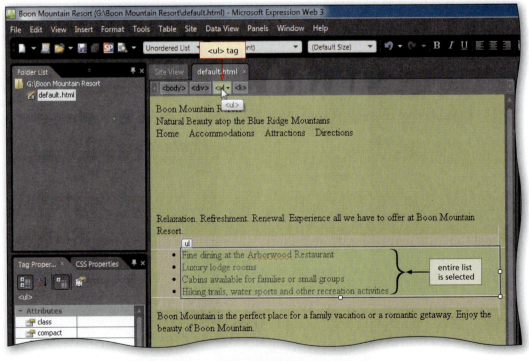

Figure 1–47

To Apply a Heading Style

In addition to providing a visual cue as to a heading's relative importance, using the heading style ensures that assistive technology can distinguish how the text has been formatted, to accurately represent it to vision-impaired site visitors. The following steps use heading styles to change the font size and apply the bold attribute.

- Click after the words, Blue Ridge Mountains, at the top of the page inside the first <div> tag (Figure 1–48).

Q&A Can I still apply the heading style if only a few words of the div are selected?

To ensure that the heading style is applied to all of the text, click the <div> tag on the Quick Tag Selector to select all of the text at once.

Figure 1–48

- With the insertion point inside the first div, click <div> on the Quick Tag Selector to select the entire two lines of text inside the <div> tag container (Figure 1–49).

Q&A Can I select the individual words rather than the entire <div> tag container?

Yes, but Expression Web will assign the code to only the selected text, which will cause problems if you later attempt to apply styles using CSS.

Figure 1–49

- Click the Style box arrow on the Common toolbar to display the Style menu (Figure 1–50).

Figure 1–50

4

• Click Heading 1 <h1> to apply it (Figure 1–51).

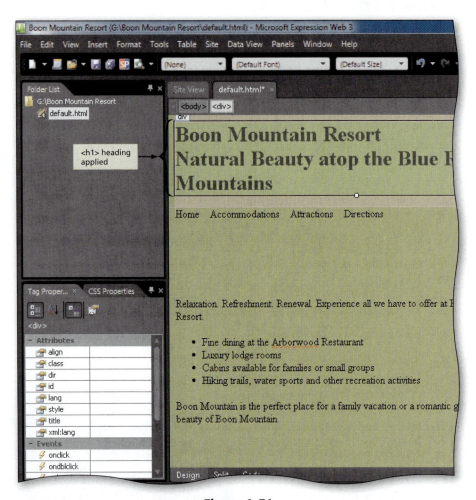

Figure 1–51

5

• Click in the word, Relaxation, to position the insertion point.

• Click the <p> tag on the Quick Tag Selector to select the paragraph tag (Figure 1–52).

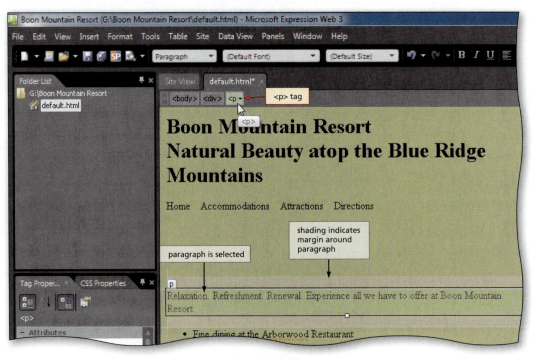

Figure 1–52

6

- Click the Style box arrow on the Common toolbar to display the menu.

- Click Heading 2 <h2> to apply it (Figure 1–53).

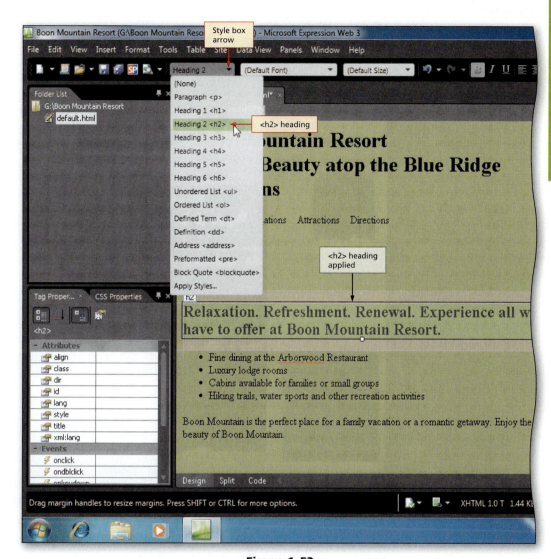

Figure 1–53

To Center Text

When all of the text is aligned to the left side of a Web page, it is difficult for the visitor to scan the page. Using centered text draws the eye to certain headings and paragraphs, and improves the overall look of the page. In the following steps, you will apply center alignment to the company name and tagline.

1

- Click in the masthead, then click the <div> tag on the Quick Tag Selector to select the div.

- Click the Center button on the Common toolbar to center the selected text (Figure 1–54).

- Click the Save button on the Common toolbar to save the page.

 Experiment

- Click the Align Text Right button to see the effect. Press CTRL+Z to undo the change.

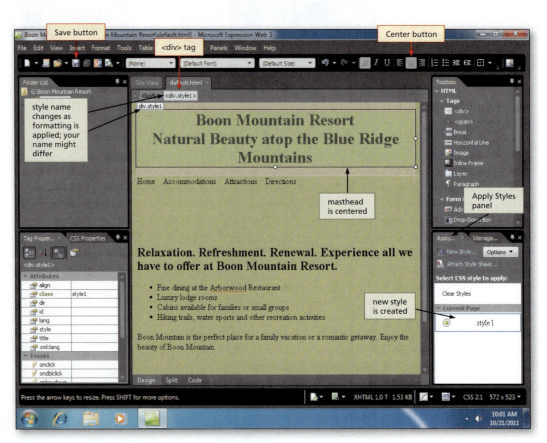

Figure 1–54

Applying Font Characteristics

Centering Usage
Centering, like all formatting techniques, should not be overdone. Apply centering to headings or elements such as footers. Paragraphs and lists are usually left-aligned.

Text attributes can include the font family (such as Arial or Times New Roman), as well as the size, color, alignment, and other attributes of individual characters or words, such as blinking or small capital letters.

Fonts help establish the mood of the site. Clean, simple fonts convey professionalism and clarity, whereas ornate fonts can provide a feeling of excitement or creativity. Fonts with serifs (strokes at the ends of lines that make up letters) are considered easier to read in paragraphs of text. Fonts without serifs, called sans serif fonts, are often used for headings. For more information on fonts, see Special Feature 1.

Font color is also an important consideration. Most sites use a dark font on a light background, or vice versa, which provides good contrast and is easy to read. Royal blue or purple underlined text often indicates a hyperlink, so avoid using this combination of characteristics unless it is for a link.

To Change Font Color

Many sites use colored fonts to distinguish headers but use black for paragraphs of text. The following steps add font colors to selected text to contrast with the green page background.

1

- With the company name and tagline div still selected, click the Font Color button arrow on the Common toolbar to display the Font Color palette (Figure 1–55).

Q&A

The Font Color button is not on my Common toolbar.

Depending on your screen resolution and toolbar setup, you may have to click the More button to the right of the Common toolbar to access additional buttons, as shown in Figure 1–55.

Figure 1–55

2

- Click the #000080 button on the Standard Colors palette, then click Apply to make the masthead text navy blue (Figure 1–56).

Experiment

- Select a lighter font color to see how difficult it is to see a color that does not contrast with the page background. Press CTRL+Z to undo the change.

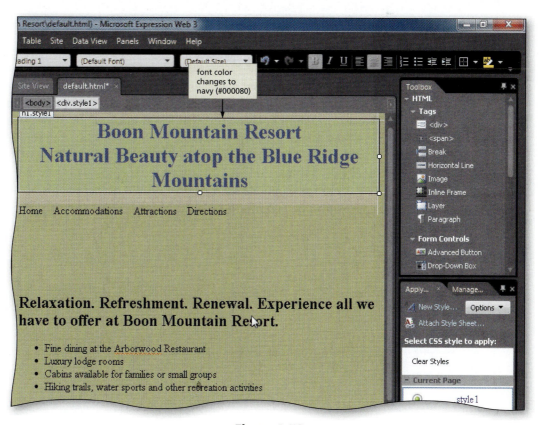

Figure 1–56

3

- Click at the end of the word, Relaxation, to place the insertion point inside the <h2> tag.

- Click the <h2> tag on the Quick Tag Selector to select the tag.

- Click the Common toolbar More button if necessary, then click the Font Color button on the Common toolbar to format the text with blue (Figure 1–57).

- Click the Save button on the Common toolbar to save the page.

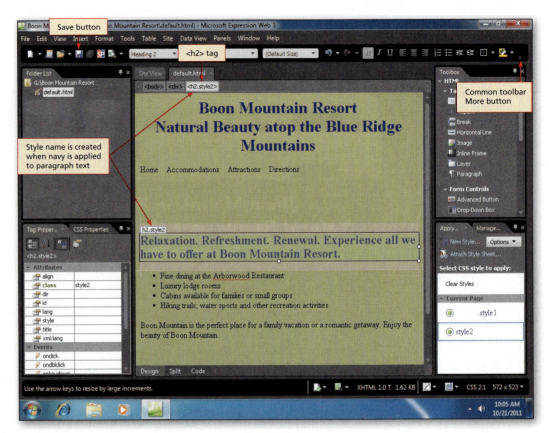

Figure 1–57

Quick Reference

For a table that lists how to complete the tasks covered in this book using the mouse, shortcut menu, and keyboard, see the Quick Reference Summary at the back of this book, or visit the Expression Web 3 Quick Reference Web page (scsite.com/ew3/qr).

Changing Font Sizes

Unlike in printed documents, the appearance of the actual point size of fonts in a Web page depends on the screen size and resolution of the viewer's computer setup and browser resolution. Using text that is too small might cause you to lose visitors with poor eyesight. Avoid text that is too large to conserve space and retain a professional look. Using all capital letters, except in a heading, is difficult to read and is the Web equivalent of SHOUTING.

Font size options use a relative system of increments, such as xx-small, which is approximately 8 points, to xx-large, which is approximately 36 points.

To Change Font Size

The default font size for the <h2> heading style is x-large. The default font size of plain text is medium. The following steps change the font size of the bulleted list and the paragraph above it.

1

- With the h2 tag still selected, click the Font Size box arrow on the Common toolbar to display the Font Size menu (Figure 1–58).

Figure 1–58

2

- Click large (18 pt) to decrease the size of the text (Figure 1–59).

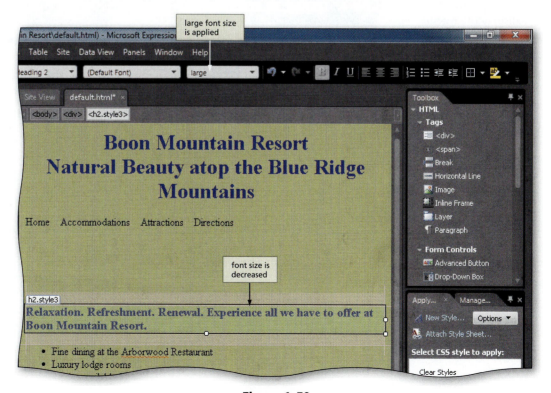

Figure 1–59

• Click at the end of the first bulleted item after the word, Restaurant.

• Click the <ul> tag on the Quick Tag Selector to select all four lines of the bulleted list (Figure 1–60).

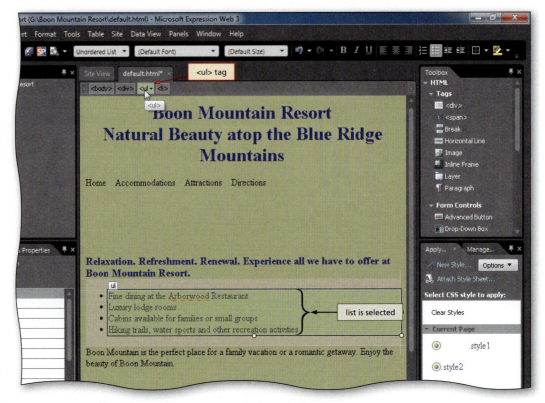

Figure 1–60

• Click the Font Size box arrow on the Common toolbar to display the menu.

• Click large (18 pt) to apply it (Figure 1–61).

Q&A

Why does my Apply Styles task pane show different styles?

Depending on the exact steps you perform, your Apply Styles task pane might show more, fewer, or differently numbered styles. Follow the figures in the text to make sure you are applying formatting to the correct tag.

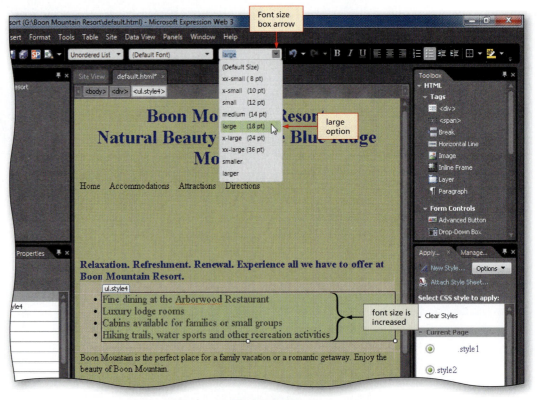

Figure 1–61

To Indent Text

Indenting text moves it away from the margin. Usually, you will see text indented from the left margin, such as at the beginning of the first line of a paragraph of text. You can also indent multiple lines at once to nest them below a heading. The following step indents the bulleted list.

1

- With the bulleted list still selected, click the Increase Indent Position button on the Common toolbar to move the list to the right (Figure 1–62).

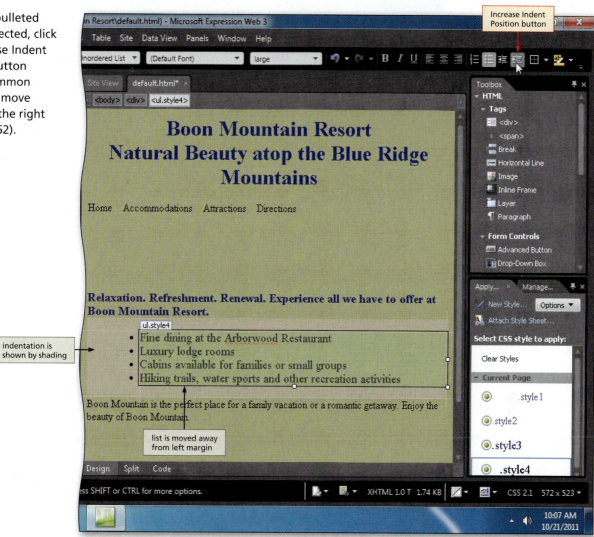

Figure 1–62

BTW

Indent Size
To indent further, click the Increase Indent Position button until you reach the desired indentation. Click the Decrease Indent Position button to move closer to the left margin. Clicking Paragraph on the Format menu opens the Paragraph dialog box, where you can specify indentation from the left and right margins, or for the first line of text only.

To Italicize Text

Italicized text appears slanted and is another type of font attribute. The following steps italicize the text below the bulleted list.

- Click anywhere in the first sentence below the bulleted list.

- Click the <p> tag on the Quick Tag Selector to select both sentences in the tag (Figure 1–63).

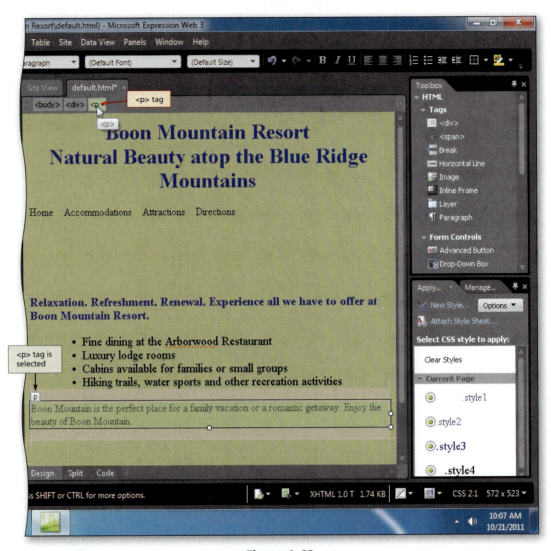

Figure 1–63

2

- Click the Italic button on the Common toolbar to apply the italic attribute to the selected text (Figure 1–64).

- Click the Save button on the Common toolbar to save the page.

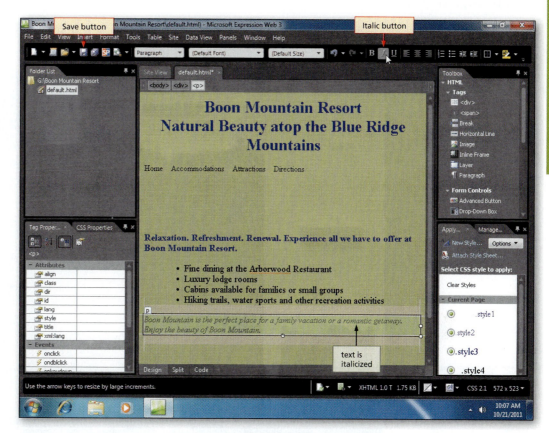

Figure 1–64

Choosing a Font

The fonts that appear on a Web page in the visitor's browser depend on the fonts installed on his or her computer. Expression Web provides font families (groups of similar fonts) to control how your pages appear. If your pages use font families, the page will default to the next available font in the family if the first font choice is not available to your visitor's browser.

BTW

Microsoft Expression Web User Guide

The best way to become familiar with the Microsoft Expression Web User Guide is to use it. Appendix A includes detailed information about the Microsoft Expression Web User Guide and exercises that will help you gain confidence in using it.

To Change a Font

The following steps change the font family from the default to a sans serif font family.

- Click the <body> tag on the Quick Tag Selector to select all of the page content (Figure 1–65).

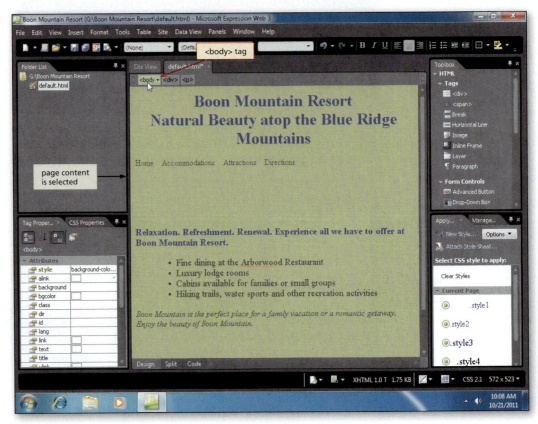

Figure 1–65

- Click the Font box arrow to display the Font gallery (Figure 1–66).

Experiment

- Scroll in the list of fonts to view the various fonts and font families available.

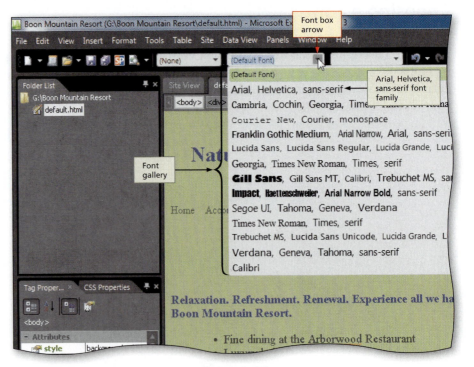

Figure 1–66

3

- Click the Arial, Helvetica, sans-serif font family to apply it (Figure 1–67).

- Click the Save button on the Common toolbar to save the page.

Q&A

What if my list of fonts differs?

Depending on your installation, you may have different fonts and font families available to you. Choose a similar font family or one that appeals to you.

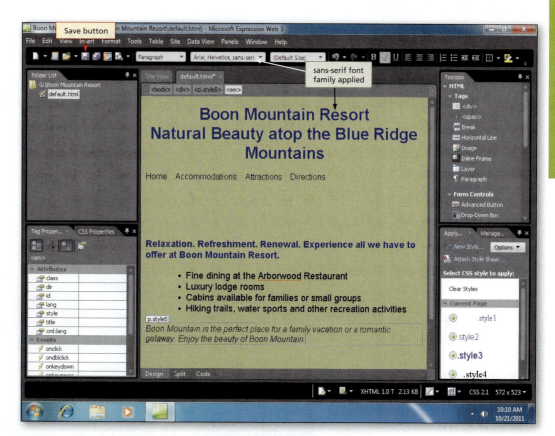

Figure 1–67

Spell Checking Pages

Spelling and grammar errors can distract a reader and make your site look unprofessional. Expression Web has a built-in **spell checker** that displays a red wavy line below words that are not included in the Expression Web dictionary. Words that Expression Web flags as being misspelled are not necessarily incorrect; for example, Expression Web's spell checker does not recognize some proper nouns. Using the spell checker, you can correct misspelled words and choose to ignore words that are proper nouns, or that are otherwise acceptable.

To Spell Check a Page

It is a good idea to check for spelling errors when you are finished entering text. The following steps introduce a spelling error, then correct that error as well as any others you might have made while entering text.

- Select the word, groups, in the third line of the bulleted list.

- Type gourps, then press the SPACEBAR to make the word appear with a red wavy line below it (Figure 1–68).

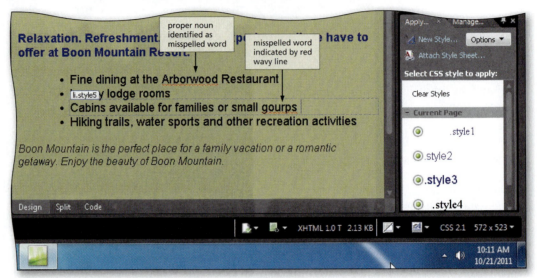

Figure 1–68

- Click a blank area of the page to deselect all text.

- Click Tools on the menu bar to open the Tools menu and then point to Spelling to display the Spelling submenu. Point to Spelling on the Spelling submenu (Figure 1–69).

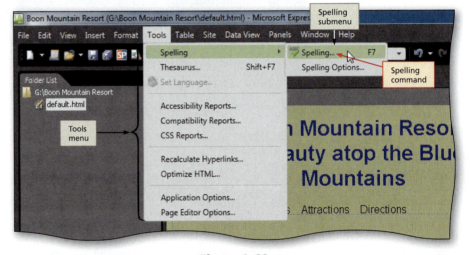

Figure 1–69

- Click the Spelling command to start the spell checker and open the Spelling dialog box.

- Click the Ignore button to skip the name of the restaurant, Arborwood, because it is correct (Figure 1–70).

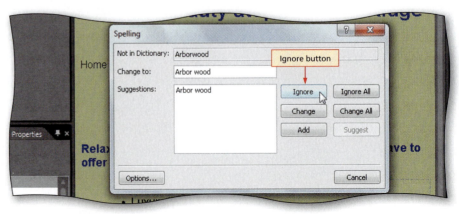

Figure 1–70

- Click groups in the Suggestions box.

- Click the Change button to correct the word (Figure 1–71).

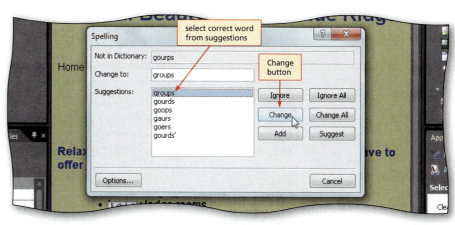

select correct word from suggestions

Change button

Figure 1–71

- Click the Ignore button to skip the name of the town, Redhat (Figure 1–72).

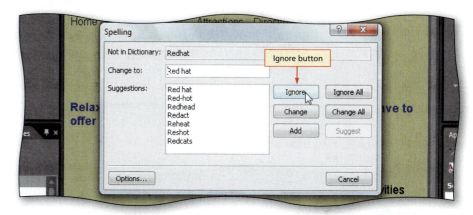

Ignore button

Figure 1–72

6

- Click the OK button to close the message box indicating that spell checking is complete (Figure 1–73).

- Click the Save button on the Common toolbar to save the page.

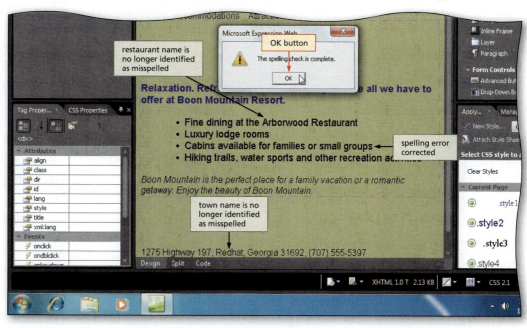

OK button

restaurant name is no longer identified as misspelled

spelling error corrected

town name is no longer identified as misspelled

Figure 1–73

Other Ways

1. As you are typing, right-click a flagged word to display a short-cut menu that includes a list of suggested spelling corrections

2. Press the F7 key to start the spell checker

Switching Views

BTW

Learning HTML
Working in Split view
is an excellent way to
learn HTML, as you can
see how the changes
you make in Design view
translate into HTML.

A Web page is created using **Hypertext Markup Language (HTML)** and **Extensible Hypertext Markup Language (XHTML)** tags. HTML and XHTML tags consist of the code within a Web page that instructs a browser where formatting is to be applied, how the layout should appear, and where images should be placed. A **browser** is software that is used to display Web pages. HTML and XHTML are the markup languages used to create Web documents. You do not need to know how to write or use HTML/XHTML codes to create Web pages in Expression Web, because as you enter and format content onto your page, Expression Web inserts the appropriate **HTML tags** to define position and formatting attributes.

Expression Web provides four views for working with Web pages. Thus far in this chapter, you have used **Design view**, which gives you a general idea of what your page will look like when viewed in a browser. **Code view** displays the underlying HTML code, which is the data that the browser will use to interpret the content, formatting, and layout when displaying your site on the Internet. In **Split view**, you can see the underlying HTML code in the top half of the Editing window and your page in the bottom half of the editing window. A fourth view, **Snapshot view**, which is available from the Panels menu, displays the page as it would appear in Internet Explorer. Snapshot view is used to do a quick check to make sure the layout of your page appears as intended; you cannot edit the page or test any hyperlinks using Snapshot view.

Looking at the code generated by Expression Web will help you become more familiar with how HTML tags are applied to your page. Figure 1–74 shows part of the code for the Boon Mountain Resort home page.

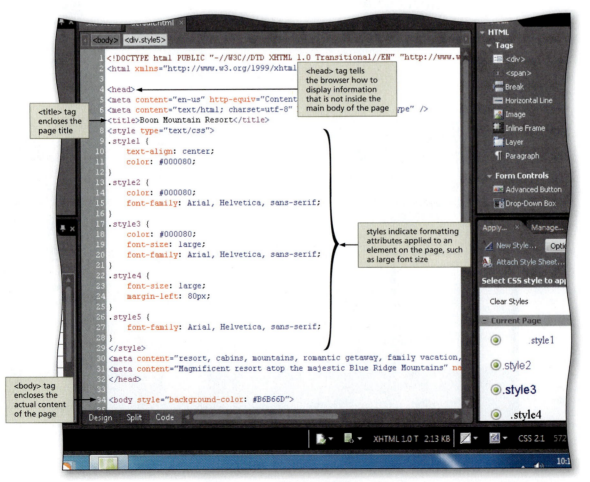

Figure 1–74

To Show Code and Split Views

Now that you have added content to the page, the following steps use the various view buttons to display the HTML code Expression Web has generated.

1

- Click the Show Code View button at the bottom of the editing window to see the HTML tags and the assigned styles (Figure 1–75).

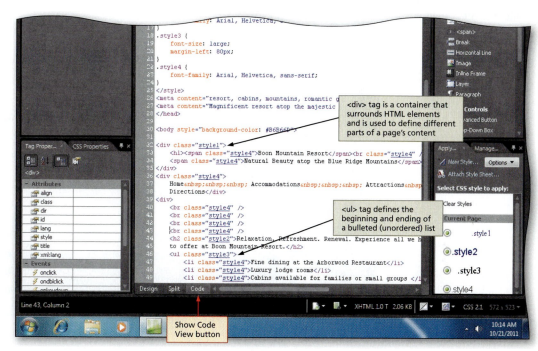

Figure 1–75

2

- Click the Show Split View button at the bottom of the Editing window to show both Code and Design views simultaneously. In Code view, drag the scroll box up to show the head area of the code as shown in the figure (Figure 1–76).

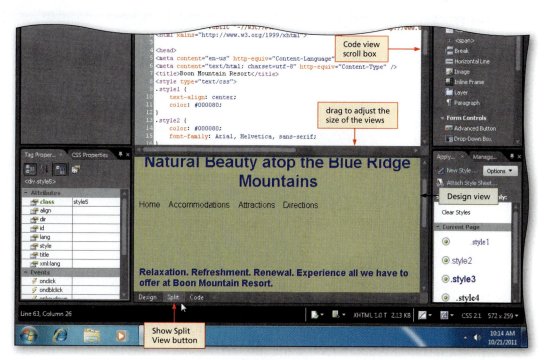

Figure 1–76

3

- Drag the separator that divides the two sections up to display more of the Design view window (Figure 1–77).

Q&A

I am having trouble moving the separator up.

Make sure you are pointing to the underside of the separator so that the pointer shown in the figure appears. Then drag the separator up.

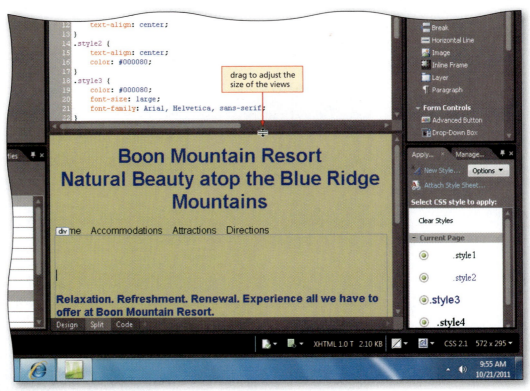

Figure 1–77

4

- Select the words, Natural Beauty, in the Design view window. Expression Web will also select them in the Code view window (Figure 1–78).

- Click anywhere in the Design view window to deselect the text.

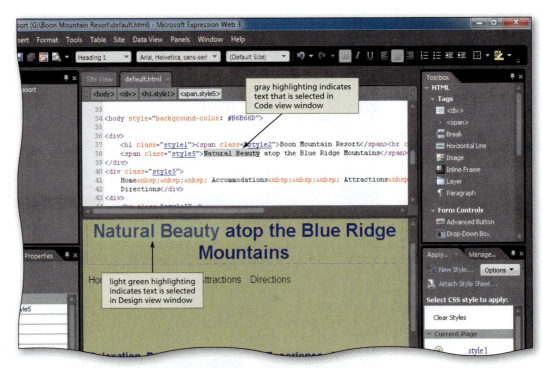

Figure 1–78

5

- Click the Show Design View button to close Code view (Figure 1–79).

Q&A Why would I want to learn HTML if Expression Web generates the code for me?

As you become a more experienced Web designer, you will find it easier to make changes and troubleshoot errors by editing the HTML code directly.

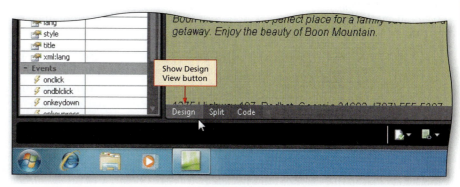

Figure 1–79

To View the Page in the Snapshot Panel

The following steps display the default.html Web page in Snapshot view, which demonstrates how it will appear in Internet Explorer 8.

1

- Click Snapshot on the Panels menu to open the Snapshot panel (Figure 1–80).

Q&A The panel opens, but I only see a clock.

You may have to wait a few moments while Expression Web generates a snapshot of the Web page and checks compatibility.

Figure 1–80

2

- Drag the Snapshot panel scroll box down to see the rest of the default.html page (Figure 1–81).

- Click the Close button to close the Snapshot panel.

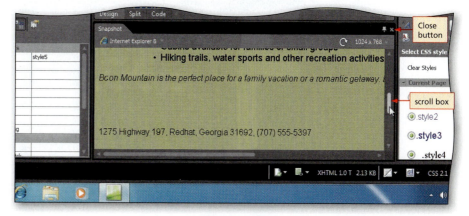

Figure 1–81

Toggle Commands
Visual aids are a toggle command, meaning that you click the same command to turn them both on and off.

Visual Aids and Quick Tags

Expression Web uses visual aids to make it easier to work with page elements, such as layers, borders, and padding, while in Design View. **Visual aids** are onscreen labels that do not appear on the actual Web page, but in Expression Web, they allow you to see the HTML tags and sizing information for elements in order to better work with them. Visual aids can also help make sure that you are selecting an entire div, or tag, before applying formatting or making other changes. By default, visual aids are turned on. You can turn them off to have a better sense of how your final page will look, then turn them back on to fine-tune elements.

Quick tags are a type of visual aid that display labels for the HTML elements on a Web page, such as paragraphs, tables, and headers. When a page element is selected, a box with a label appears around the element; this box is the selected element's visual aid. The tag for the item also appears on the Quick Tag Selector. With some page elements, such as an item in a bulleted list, you can select just one line (the tag <li> for line item), or click the tag to the left of it (the tag <ul> for unordered list) to select the entire list. Use the Quick Tag Selector to make sure that you have selected the correct item before applying formatting or making other changes.

To Hide and Display Visual Aids

You can choose to show only certain types of visual aids, such as margins or padding, or choose to show or hide all types. The visual aid settings are shown as On or Off on the status bar. The following step uses the View menu to turn off all visual aids to view the page as it would appear when finished, then turns them back on.

- Click in the first line of the bulleted list to select the first item, and notice that the <li.style5> tag name appears on a tab above the element (Figure 1–82).

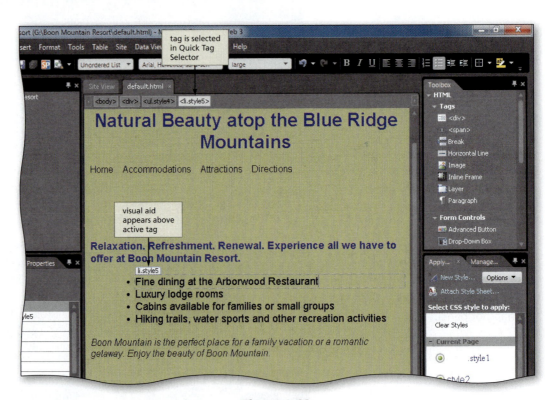

Figure 1–82

2

• Click View on the menu bar to open the View menu, point to Visual Aids to display the Visual Aids submenu, and then click Show to turn off visual aids.

• Click the second line of the bulleted list, and notice that no tag name appears above the line (Figure 1–83).

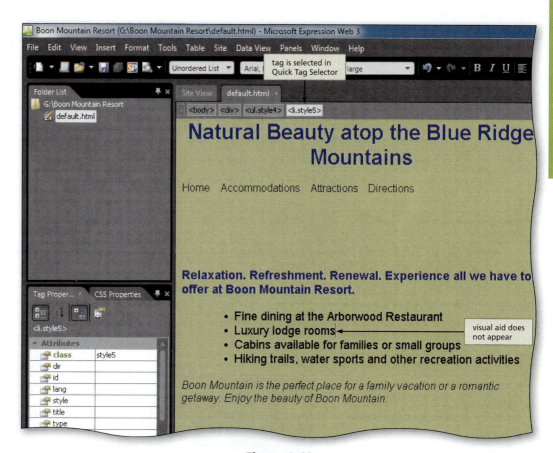

Figure 1–83

3

• Click View on the menu bar to open the View menu, point to Visual Aids to display the Visual Aids menu, then click Show to display visual aids.

• If necessary, click the second line of the bulleted list and notice that the <li> tag name appears above the line (Figure 1–84).

Other Ways

1. Click the Visual Aids button arrow on the status bar and then click Show to turn visual aids off and on

2. Press CTRL+/ to turn visual aids off and on

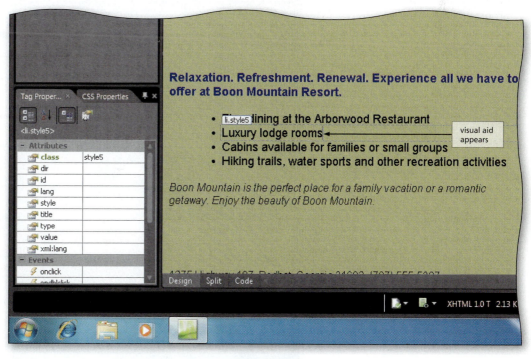

Figure 1–84

BTW

Publishing a Site
See Appendix C for more information about publishing to the Web.

Previewing in Browsers

Web surfers use a variety of browsers. The most popular are Windows Internet Explorer, Mozilla Firefox, Opera, Google Chrome, and Apple Safari. Variations among browsers can cause your pages to appear slightly differently from browser to browser, so it is important to test your pages in as many different browsers as possible before publishing your site to a Web server. Expression Web uses Windows Internet Explorer as the default browser, but you can add others to the browser list. Although you can view a page as it would appear in Internet Explorer using Snapshot view, it is always best to also view the page in a browser window. Browsers allow you to see a full view of your page as it will appear to visitors to your site, as well as allow you to test any hyperlinks, such as to other site pages.

To Preview in a Browser

Although the WYSIWYG interface of Expression Web and Snapshot view give a reasonable sense of how the page will look in a browser, it is still a good idea to preview the page from within the browser program to check for any obvious errors. You can also simulate various page sizes that represent a range of screen resolutions to get a better idea of how the visitor's browser will render your page. If your browser was maximized the last time you used it, the different resolutions will not be demonstrated when the page is previewed. The following steps preview the site in Internet Explorer.

- Click the Preview in Windows Internet Explorer 8.0 button arrow to display the browser list (Figure 1–85).

Experiment

- Choose different browser programs and/or resolutions to view any differences in how the site appears.

Q&A Why did a dialog box appear?

If a Microsoft Expression Web dialog box appears instructing you to save your changes, then you've made a change to your page since the last save. Click OK to save your changes and preview the page.

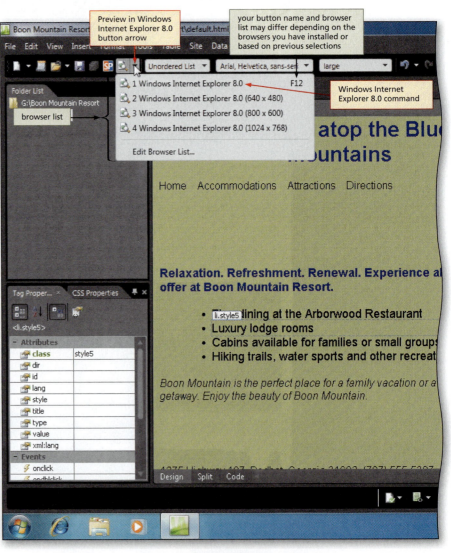

Figure 1–85

2

- Click Windows Internet Explorer 8.0 in the menu to view the page in a browser (Figure 1–86).

- If the Maximize button appears, click it to view the browser window maximized.

3

- When you are finished looking at your page in the browser, click the Close button on the browser's title bar to return to Expression Web.

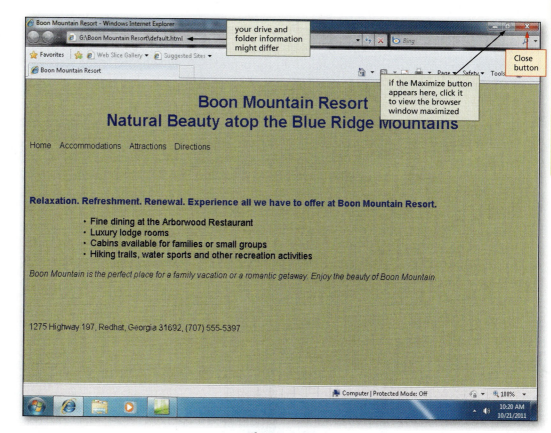

Figure 1–86

Other Ways
1. Press the F12 key to preview the site using the most recently used browser   2. Click the Preview button on the Common toolbar

Printing a Web Page

Expression Web allows you to print a page that looks just like it will appear in a browser. You might want a printout or hard copy of your site pages for proofreading or design markup. Printouts can also be used as archive copies and for distributing to clients.

BTW

Conserving Ink and Toner

You can print a Web page in black-and-white to conserve ink or toner by clicking the Properties button in the Print dialog box to open the properties dialog box. Click the tab and select any option(s) necessary to print in grayscale using black ink, then click OK to close the properties dialog box.

To Print a Web Page

To save ink and paper, use the Print Preview feature before printing a page to make sure that it fits on a reasonable number of pages. Expression Web adds the page title and a page number to the printed page. Web page background images or colors do not appear on the printed output. The following steps preview and then print the Boon Mountain Resort home page.

- Click File on the menu bar to open the File menu, and then point to Print to display the Print submenu.

- Click Print Preview on the Print sub-menu to see what the page will look like before printing it (Figure 1–87).

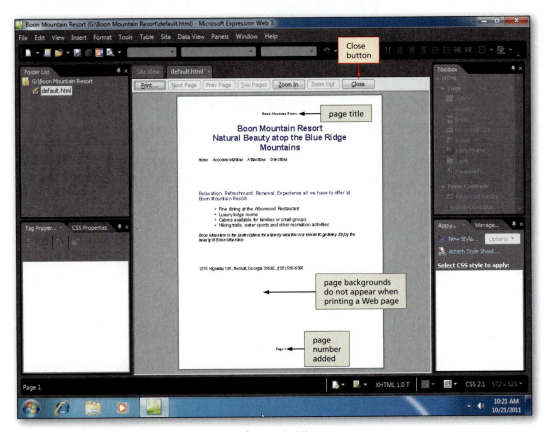

Figure 1–87

- Click the Close button at the top of the Print Preview window to close Print Preview.

- Click File on the menu bar to open the File menu, and then point to Print to display the Print submenu.

- Click Print to open the Print dialog box (Figure 1–88).

- Click the OK button in the Print dialog box to begin printing.

Q&A What if I do not want to print at this time?

Click the Cancel button to close the Print dialog box.

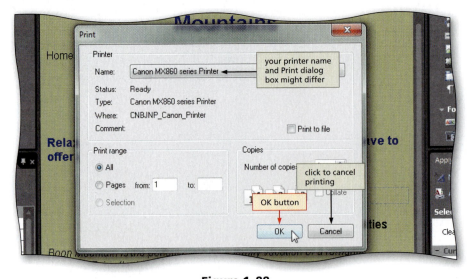

Figure 1–88

Other Ways

1. Press CTRL+P, then press the ENTER key

Closing Expression Web

If you quit Expression Web without closing the Web page, Expression Web will attempt to open the page when the program is restarted. If you are not the next user of the program, others might have access to your work. If you are storing your Web page files on a portable device such as a flash drive, Expression Web will display an error message if the portable device is not connected. To avoid these pitfalls, it is a good policy to save and close your files before you exit the Expression Web program.

BTW

Saving Before Closing
If you have made changes since the last time a page was saved, you will be prompted to save the page before closing the site.

To Close a Web Page

Now that you are finished working on the Boon Mountain home page, the following steps close the page, then close the site.

- Right-click the default.html tab at the top of the editing window and then point to Close (Figure 1–89).

Figure 1–89

- Click Close on the shortcut menu.

- Click Site on the menu bar to open the Site menu, then click the Close command (Figure 1–90).

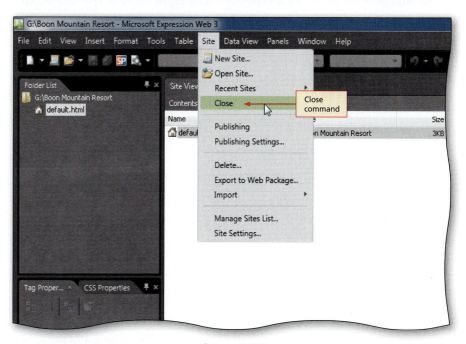

Figure 1–90

Other Ways

1. Click the Close button in the upper-right corner of the Editing window

To Quit Expression Web

You have finished the initial text design and formatting for the Boon Mountain Resort Web site. The following step closes Expression Web.

- Click File on the menu bar to open the File menu and then point to Exit (Figure 1–91).

- Click the Exit command to quit Expression Web.

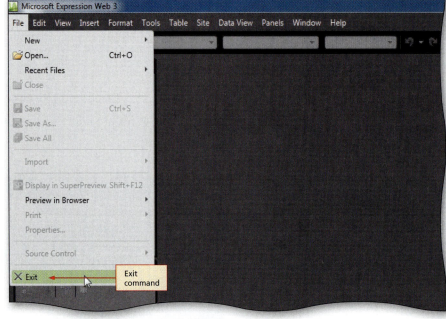

Figure 1–91

Other Ways
1. Click the Close button on the Expression Web title bar to close the program

Chapter Summary

In this chapter, you have learned how to use Expression Web to open a Web site, enter text, modify text, apply styles, and preview and print a Web page. The items listed below include all the new Expression Web skills you have learned in this chapter.

1. Start Expression Web (EW 6)
2. Reset Workspace Layout (EW 9)
3. Create a Web Site (EW 10)
4. Open a Web Page (EW 14)
5. Set Page Properties (EW 15)
6. Add a <Div> Tag (EW 20)
7. Add Paragraph Text (EW 23)
8. Add a Bulleted List (EW 25)
9. Complete Page Content (EW 28)
10. Save a Web Page (EW 30)
11. Use the Quick Tag Selector (EW 31)
12. Apply a Heading Style (EW 33)
13. Center Text (EW 36)
14. Change Font Color (EW 37)
15. Change Font Size (EW 39)
16. Indent Text (EW 41)
17. Italicize Text (EW 42)
18. Change a Font (EW 44)
19. Spell Check a Page (EW 46)
20. Show Code and Split Views (EW 49)
21. View the Page in the Snapshot Panel (EW 51)
22. Hide and Display Visual Aids (EW 52)
23. Preview in a Browser (EW 54)
24. Print a Web Page (EW 56)
25. Close a Web Page (EW 57)
26. Quit Expression Web (EW 58)

For current SAM information, including versions and content details, visit SAM Central (http://samcentral.course.com). If you have a SAM user profile, you may have access to hands-on instruction, practice, and assessment of the skills covered in this chapter. Since various versions of SAM are supported throughout the life of this text, check with your instructor for the correct instructions and URL/Web site for accessing assignments.

Learn It Online

Test your knowledge of chapter content and key terms.

Instructions: To complete the Learn It Online exercises, start your browser, click the Address bar, and then enter the Web address `scsite.com/ew3/learn`. When the Expression Web Learn It Online page is displayed, click the link for the exercise you want to complete and then read the instructions.

Chapter Reinforcement TF, MC, and SA
A series of true/false, multiple choice, and short answer questions that test your knowledge of the chapter content.

Flash Cards
An interactive learning environment where you identify chapter key terms associated with displayed definitions.

Practice Test
A series of multiple choice questions that test your knowledge of chapter content and key terms.

Who Wants To Be a Computer Genius?
An interactive game that challenges your knowledge of chapter content in the style of a television quiz show.

Wheel of Terms
An interactive game that challenges your knowledge of chapter key terms in the style of the television show *Wheel of Fortune*.

Crossword Puzzle Challenge
A crossword puzzle that challenges your knowledge of key terms presented in the chapter.

Apply Your Knowledge

Reinforce the skills and apply the concepts you learned in this chapter.

Modifying Text and Formatting a Web Site
Instructions: Start Expression Web. Open the Web site, Apply 1-1 Jessica's Jewels, from the Data Files for Students. See the inside back cover of this book for instructions for downloading the Data Files for Students, or see your instructor for information about accessing the required files.

The Web site you open contains an unformatted home page. Open the default.html file and modify and format the text so it looks like Figure 1–92.

Continued >

Apply Your Knowledge *continued*

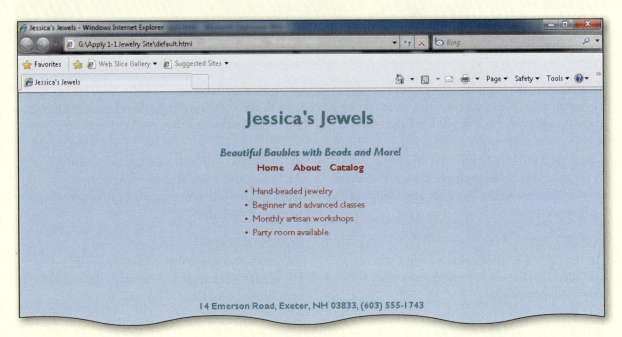

Figure 1–92

Perform the following tasks:

1. Open the Page Properties dialog box, then add the text, Jessica's Jewels, as the page title.

2. Add a page description: Beautiful Baubles with Beads and More!

3. Add the following as keywords: beads, bauble, jewels, jewelry, necklace, bracelet.

4. Change the page background to light blue (140, 240, 192), then close the Page Properties dialog box. *Hint:* Click the Custom button in the More Colors dialog box to enter the Hue, Sat, and Lum values in the Color dialog box.

5. Select the div containing the company name, Jessica's Jewels, then apply the Heading 1 <h1> style.

6. Change the font color of the <h1> tag for the company name to a teal color (42, 104, 121) by typing the values in the R, G, and B text boxes on the Font Color palette.

7. Center-align the <h1> tag for the company name.

8. Select the div containing the slogan.

9. Change the slogan div's font color to the same teal as the company name.

10. Center-align the slogan div.

11. Change the font size of the slogan div to large.

12. Apply bold and italics to the slogan div.

13. Select the div containing the navigation bar and change the font color to red (120, 0, 0) by typing the values in the R, G, and B text boxes on the Font Color palette, and then bold and center the navigation bar div.

14. Click under the div containing the navigation bar and insert a bulleted list.

15. Type the following list items, pressing ENTER after each line:
    * Hand-beaded jewelry
    * Beginner and advanced classes
    * Monthly artisan workshops
    * Party room available

16. Press ENTER a second time after the last line to end the bulleted list.

17. Select the <ul> tag of the bulleted list and change the font color to the red color used for the navigation text. Press the Increase Indent button eight times to indent the list.

18. Add a div at the bottom of the page for the footer.

19. Press ENTER twice at the beginning of the div to add some space.

20. Type the company address and phone number in the div as follows: 14 Emerson Road, Exeter, NH 03833, (603) 555-1743.

21. Select the footer div, center and bold the div, and then change the font color of the footer div to the previously used teal color, and then bold the div.

22. Select the body tag, then change the font family to Gill Sans, Gill Sans MT, Calibri, Trebuchet MS, sans-serif.

23. Save the default.html Web page.

24. Spell check the Web page.

25. Preview the site in two different browsers or resolutions.

26. Use Print Preview to view the site.

27. Print the site.

28. Change the site properties, as specified by your instructor.

29. Close the default.html Web page and the site.

30. Rename the site using the filename, Apply 1-1 Jewelry Site using Windows Explorer.

31. Submit the revised site in the format specified by your instructor.

Extend Your Knowledge

Extend the skills you learned in this chapter and experiment with new skills. You may need to use Help to complete the assignment.

Formatting a Web Site

Instructions: Start Expression Web. Open the Web site, Extend 1-1 Music Festival, from the Data Files for Students. See the inside back cover of this book for instructions for downloading the Data Files for Students, or see your instructor for information about accessing the required files.

Enhance the Web page to match the one shown in Figure 1–93.

Perform the following tasks:

1. Use Help to learn about changing the default font color and how to insert a horizontal line.

2. Print the default.html page.

3. Make notes on the hard copy as to how you will change the Web page to more closely match Figure 1–93.

4. Use the Page Properties dialog box to change the page background to orange (255, 204, 102) and the default font color to blue (0, 51, 153). (*Hint:* Click Custom in the More Colors dialog box to enter Red, Green, and Blue values.)

5. Change the font family of the masthead div using a font family containing Gill Sans (or another font family of your choice) and the font color to red. Bold and center the masthead text and change the font size to x-large.

Continued >

Extend Your Knowledge *continued*

6. Click at the end of the masthead text and press ENTER. Double-click the Horizontal Line tag in the Toolbox to insert a horizontal line under the masthead.

7. Change the font family of both the bulleted list and the paragraph to one containing Arial.

8. Increase the font size of the bulleted list text to large and apply the bold attribute.

9. Select the text, Incoming Flight, then click the Italic button on the Common toolbar.

10. On a separate piece of paper, draw a mock-up of the final page, identifying each part of the page. Make two suggestions for changes based on your own design preferences.

11. Change the site properties, as specified by your instructor.

12. Save and close the default.html page and the Web site. Using Windows Explorer, rename the Extend 1-1 Music Festival site folder as Extend 1-1 Music Site.

13. Submit the revised site in the format specified by your instructor.

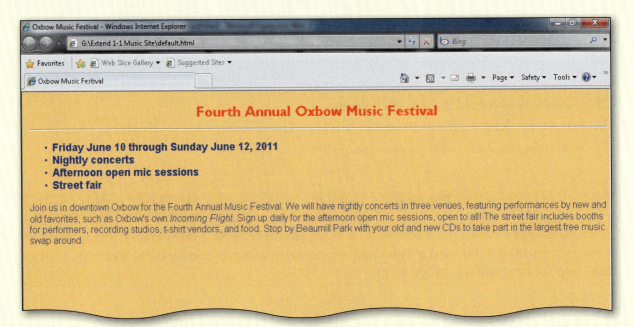

Figure 1–93

Make It Right

Analyze a site and correct all errors and/or improve the design.

Increasing Readability and Correcting Spelling Errors

Instructions: Start Expression Web. Open the Web site, Make It Right 1-1 Swim Club, from the Data Files for Students. See the inside back cover of this book for instructions for downloading the Data Files for Students, or see your instructor for information about accessing the required files.

The site's font colors and sizes do not provide enough contrast to be easily readable from the screen, and the Expression Web dictionary has flagged several words as being erroneous. Using Figure 1–94 to guide you, change the background color of the page, bullet and indent the list, change the text alignment, and then change the font sizes and colors to make the text more readable and to show a hierarchy of information. Apply a font family with Franklin Gothic Medium in it to the entire page. Correct each spelling error by right-clicking the flagged text and clicking the appropriate correction or option on the shortcut menu, then run the spelling checker to make sure there are no other errors. Change the page title in the Page Properties dialog box to Macon Waves Swim Club.

Change the site properties, as specified by your instructor. Save and close the default.html page and close the site. Using Windows Explorer, rename the Make it Right 1-1 Swim Club folder as Make it Right 1-1 Swim Club Site. Submit the revised site in the format specified by your instructor.

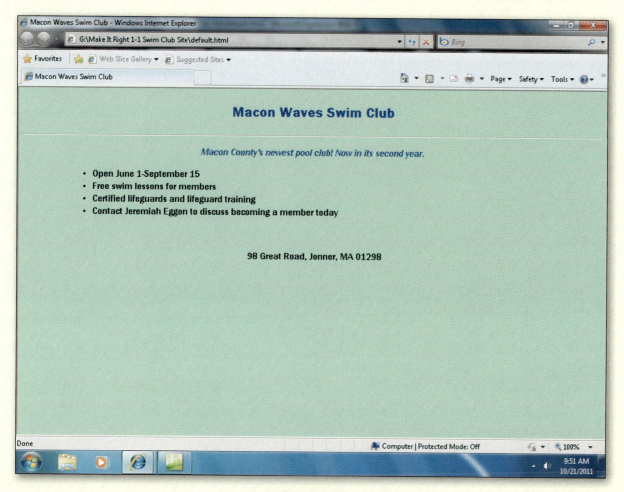

Figure 1–94

In the Lab

Design and/or format a Web site using the guidelines, concepts, and skills presented in this chapter. Labs are listed in order of increasing difficulty.

Lab 1: Creating a New Home Page

Problem: You work part-time at a small bike repair shop. Your boss, Jonas Wolfowitz, has asked you to create a home page for the shop to which he will later add more pages. Create the one-page Web site shown in Figure 1–95 based on Jonas's plan.

Continued >

In the Lab *continued*

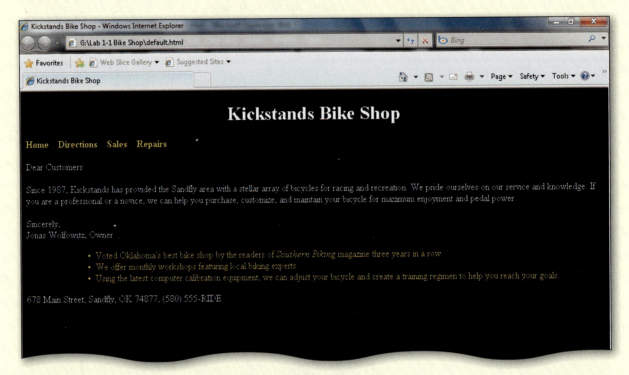

Figure 1–95

Instructions:

1. Start Expression Web.

2. Create a new one-page Web site named Lab 1-1 Bike Shop and save it on a USB flash drive.

3. Open the default.html page.

4. Enter `Kickstands Bike Shop` as the page title, `Bike Sales and Repairs` as the description, and the following keywords: `bike, bicycle, repair, Sandfly, Oklahoma`.

5. Change the page background to black and the default font color to white.

6. Add a masthead that includes the company name, Kickstands Bike Shop. Assign it the Heading 1 <h1> style and center-align the masthead text.

7. Add a div that will include a navigation bar for future pages in the site. Type `Home`, `Directions`, `Sales`, and `Repairs`, pressing TAB between each word.

8. Apply bold to the navigation bar and change the font color to bright yellow.

9. Add a new div, press ENTER, then type the following text. *Hint:* Press ENTER twice before and after the body paragraph to add line spacing.

`Dear Customers:`

`Since 1987, Kickstands has provided the Sandfly area with a stellar array of bicycles for racing and recreation. We pride ourselves on our service and knowledge. If you are a professional or a novice, we can help you purchase, customize, and maintain your bicycle for maximum enjoyment and pedal power.`

`Sincerely,`

`Jonas Wolfowitz, Owner`

10. Click below the owner name and then create a new bulleted list with the bright yellow font color. Indent the list from the left margin. Type the following list:

   - `Voted Oklahoma's best bike shop by the readers of` *Southern Biking* `magazine three years in a row.`
   - `We offer monthly workshops featuring local biking experts.`
   - `Using the latest computer calibration equipment, we can adjust your bicycle and create a training regimen to help you reach your goals.`

11. Create a new div for the footer. Type the following text:

   `678 Main Street, Sandfly, OK 74877, (580) 555-RIDE`

12. Apply a font family that includes Georgia and Times New Roman to the entire page.

13. Instruct the spell checker to ignore Wolfowitz and Sandfly.

14. View the HTML code using Split view.

15. Practice selecting text in the Code window, but do not make any changes to the HTML code.

16. Switch back to Design view.

17. Save the changes you have made to default.html, then preview the page in a browser.

18. Change the site properties, as specified by your instructor.

19. Submit the site in the format specified by your instructor, then close the site.

In the Lab

Lab 2: Formatting Fonts and Images

Problem: You own a baking business and want to enhance your home page. You finish formatting the site to create the one-page Web site shown in Figure 1–96.

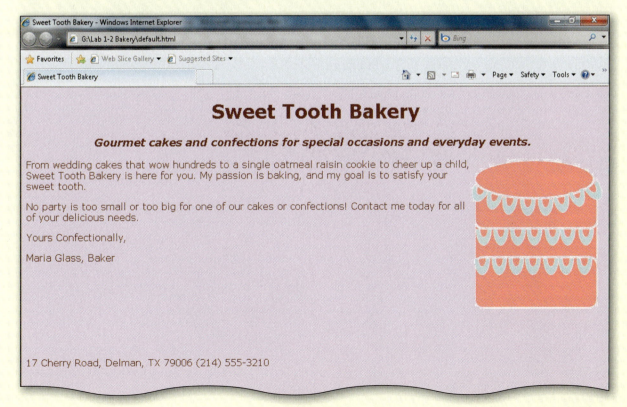

Figure 1–96

Continued >

In the Lab *continued*

Instructions:

1. Start Expression Web.

2. Open the Web site Lab 1-2 Bakery.

3. Open the default.html page.

4. Add `Sweet Tooth Bakery` as the title, `Gourmet confections for all of your events` as the page description, and the following keywords: `cake, bakery, caterer, baking, cookies`.

5. Change the page background to light pink and the default text color to dark brown.

6. Select the <body> tag on the Quick Tag Selector, then change the default font family to one containing Verdana or another font family of your choice.

7. Select the tagline paragraph tag, then apply italics and increase the font size to large.

8. Deselect all text and divs, then right-click the image of the cake to open the shortcut menu for the image.

9. Click Picture Properties on the shortcut menu.

10. Click the Appearance tab in the Picture Properties dialog box, click Right under Wrapping style, then click OK.

11. Run the spell checker and ignore all of the flagged words. Save the changes you have made to default.html, then preview the page in a browser.

12. Change the site properties, as specified by your instructor.

13. Submit the site in the format specified by your instructor, then close the site.

In the Lab

Lab 3: Creating a New Web Site

Problem: Your school's drama club has asked you to prepare a Web page for its upcoming performance. You create the one-page Web site shown in Figure 1–97.

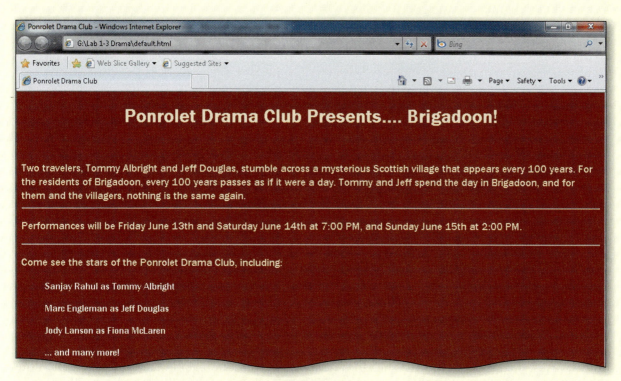

Figure 1–97

Instructions: Perform the following tasks.

1. Start Expression Web.

2. Create a new one-page Web site called Lab 1-3 Drama.

3. Open the default.html page.

4. Add `Ponrolet Drama Club` as the title, `Presenting Brigadoon!` as the page description, and the following keywords: `drama`, `Ponrolet`, `acting`, `Brigadoon`.

5. Change the page background to burgundy and the default text color to yellow (255, 255, 204). *Hint:* Enter values in the Red, Green, and Blue text boxes in the custom Color dialog box.

6. Enter the text and apply the heading, indents, and formatting as shown in Figure 1–97.

7. Change the body font family to one containing Franklin Gothic Medium (or another font family of your choice).

8. Add and position the two horizontal lines using the Toolbox.

9. Save the changes you have made to default.html, then preview the page in a browser. Change the site properties, as specified by your instructor.

10. Submit the site in the format specified by your instructor, then close the site.

Cases and Places

Apply your creative thinking and problem-solving skills to design and implement a solution.

● EASIER   ●●MORE DIFFICULT

● 1: Work with the Expression Web Window

You want to practice working with the Expression Web window. Open any site that you created in Chapter 1, then open that site's default.html page. Use the Page Properties dialog box to add a keyword. Switch to Code view, then split the view. Select text in Code view, but do not make any changes to the HTML code. Switch to Design view. Insert a new paragraph using the Toolbox. In the paragraph, create a numbered list with three items, and include one misspelled word and one name that Expression Web identifies as a misspelling. Check the spelling on the page; correct the misspelled word and ignore the name. Select one item using the Quick Tag Selector, then use the Quick Tag Selector to select the entire list. Close the default.html page without saving any changes, close the Web site, then quit Expression Web.

● 2: Design and Plan a School Web Site

You have just finished a class on Web design. The school administration of Pinkham Academy, a private high school, would like to plan a Web site that will include a home page, and eventually it will add other pages. Sketch a plan on a piece of paper for the home page of the Web site that you can present to the administration and use to gather its feedback. Include a masthead that lists the school name and a navigation bar with links to the library, administration, and calendar. The administration wants to include the school logo on the home page. Include an area for a letter from the principal and a footer for the address. The school's colors are blue and white; indicate on the Web site sketch how you will incorporate the school's colors.

●● 3: Format a One-Page Alumni Web Site

You have recently joined the Connecticut branch of your college alumni association. You have been working on a home page that can tell other local graduates of Gulliver College about upcoming alumni events. You have already entered the text for the home page. Open the site Cases and Places 3 Alumni, then open the page default.html. Use the page properties to add a title, a description, and four appropriate keywords. Use the heading style and other formatting techniques to apply italics, bold, center alignment, and indentations to make the home page easy to read.

●● 4: Create a Job Search Home Page

Make It Personal

When you are looking for a job, it is helpful to have a résumé or list of your skills that you can share with potential employers. What is your dream job? Imagine yourself a decade from now—what amazing skills and job experiences will you have collected? Will you have won any awards, made a scientific discovery, learned a foreign language, or gone to art school? Create a one-page Web site that you can use to show potential employers all of the things that you might have learned and done over the next 10 years that would qualify you for your dream job. Include a masthead, bulleted list, footer, and any other information you think is relevant. Format the Web site attractively, including adding a background color, changing the fonts, and applying effects such as bold and italics. Add a page title, a description, and keywords.

•• 5: Create a Home Page for a Sports Team

Working Together

One of your local sports teams wants to create a multi-page Web site for its fans. The site will include a home page, the calendar for the upcoming season, and biographies of the players and coaches. The home page should include a masthead, a navigation bar, a bulleted list with highlights from the previous season, and a footer with contact information. Working as a team with several of your classmates, design a Web site and create the home page. As a group, decide on the type of sport, the name of the team, and the team colors. Each team member should plan on paper the three pages (home, calendar, biographies) that will eventually be included in the site and present his or her plan to the group. As a group, decide on elements of each plan that you will incorporate into the home page, and start creating the home page using Expression Web. Add a page title, description, and keywords. Format the Web site attractively, including incorporating the team colors into the background and fonts, changing the fonts, and applying effects such as bold and italics. Run the spelling checker, use Print Preview, then print the site. Make notes as a group about any changes you need to make, then preview the site in multiple browsers and resolutions.

2 | Working with Images and Links

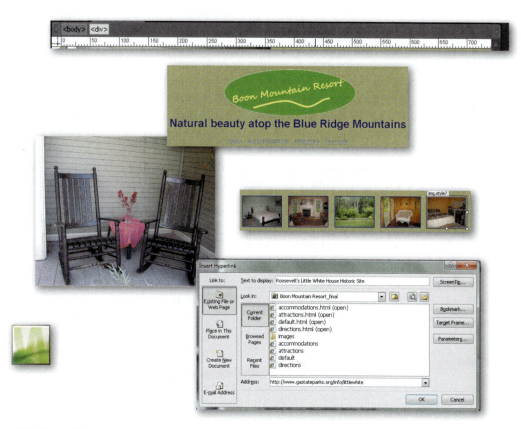

Objectives

You will have mastered the material in this chapter when you can:

- Insert and align an image
- Change the workspace
- Add borders and margins to an image
- Copy page elements to the Clipboard
- Edit an image
- Create an image thumbnail

- Create a folder for images
- Add internal links
- Add external links
- Add a bookmark
- Add an e-mail link
- Add a ScreenTip

2 | Working with Images and Links

Introduction

Text is an important part of Web site content — it describes the purpose of the site and conveys valuable details related to the site's subject matter. No matter how well written the text is, however, a site without images or that is difficult to navigate will not hold a visitor's attention for long. **Graphics** or **images** in Web pages serve a practical purpose by illustrating a product or service described in the text, displaying a company's logo, or serving as links to further information. Images also help make a site more attractive and effective by providing visual interest and continuity. **Hyperlinks**, or simply **links**, are text or graphics used to jump to another location in the same Web page, elsewhere in the site, or to another Web site. A link can also open the visitor's e-mail program that allows the visitor to send an e-mail to the site owner or other recipient. Links, in either text or graphic format, help to organize a site by providing navigation to other areas of the World Wide Web.

Project — Enhancing the Boon Mountain Resort Web Site

A Web site for a business, such as the Boon Mountain Resort, needs to inform and attract current and potential customers. Visitors to a Web site want to get an impression of the product or service very quickly. Sites that feature eye-catching images and that are easy to navigate and informative can help build a customer base, leading to increased success of the business.

A navigation bar that includes links to each of the main pages on a site usually appears on the left side or below the masthead on each page of a site. The navigation bar also might appear in both locations.

The project for this chapter uses Expression Web to add images and links to the home page for the Boon Mountain Resort Web site as shown in Figure 2–1. Additional pages and content have been added to the Web site that you created in Chapter 1, based on the site plan and feedback from site visitors and Boon Mountain Resort staff. Now you will add a logo and images so that visitors to the site can see images of the resort's various accommodations. You will also create a navigational structure, add links to other attractions near the resort, create a bookmark for a long page, and add a link that visitors can use to send an e-mail to the resort.

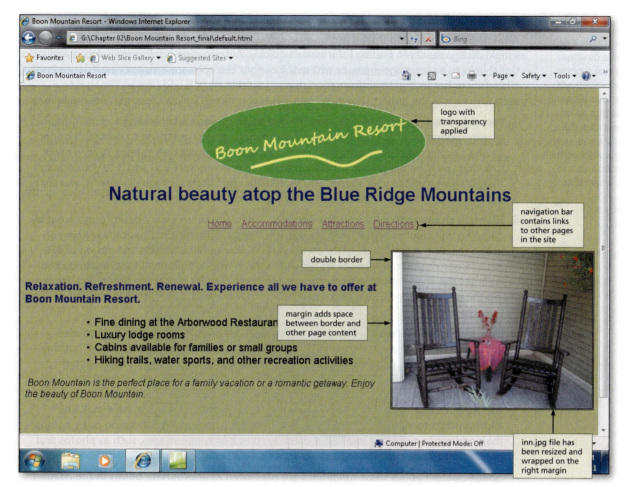

Figure 2–1

Overview

As you read this chapter, you will learn how to add images and links to the Web site shown in Figure 2–1 by performing these general tasks:

- Choose and insert images.
- Adjust the workspace layout.
- Position images in relation to text and page margins.
- Distinguish an image by modifying margins and borders.
- Make changes to the appearance and format of an image.
- Add links to other pages in the site, to other sites, and to an e-mail address.

5
- Click the Close button to close the second Open Site dialog box.
- Click the Open button to open the site (Figure 2–7).

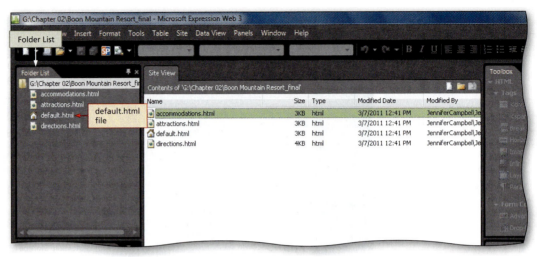

Figure 2–7

6
- Double-click the default.html page in the Site View pane to open it (Figure 2–8).

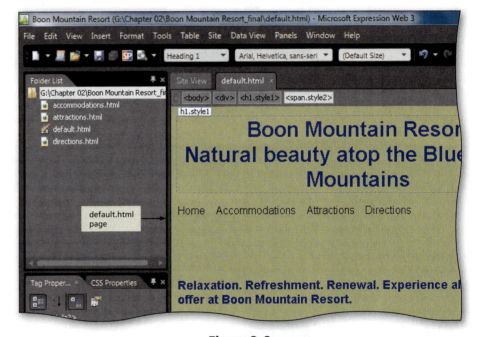

Figure 2–8

To Insert an Image

All images that you insert into a page need to be embedded into your site to make them available when your page is viewed in a browser. When you make changes to an image, you will be prompted to resave the embedded file. In the Save Embedded Files dialog box there are options to rename the image, save the image in a folder, assign an action, and change the file type.

All images used in the Boon Mountain Resort site were taken by the owner, so no credits are necessary. The following steps add a picture of the resort's main building to the home page from an external folder, assign accessibility properties, and embed the image into your site.

1

- In the Expression Web editing window, click two lines above the line beginning with the word, Relaxation, to place the insertion point in the div (Figure 2–9).

Figure 2–9

2

- Click Insert on the menu bar to open the Insert menu.

- Point to Picture on the Insert menu, then point to From File (Figure 2–10).

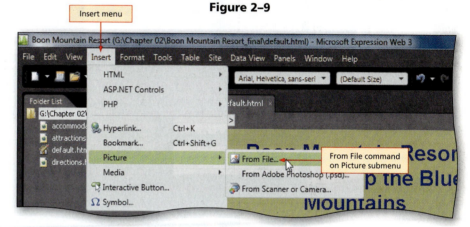

Figure 2–10

3

- Click From File to open the Picture dialog box.

- Navigate to the folder that contains your data files.

- Open the Boon Mountain Resort_images folder to access the images for this site (Figure 2–11).

Q&A

Why doesn't my files list look like the list in Figure 2–11?

If your files list looks different, then you are seeing a different files view. To make your screen match the figure, click the More options button arrow on the toolbar and then click Tiles in the menu.

Figure 2–11

1

• Click View on the menu bar to open the View menu, then point to Ruler and Grid to display the submenu.

• Point to Show Ruler on the submenu (Figure 2–20).

Q&A Why is the Ruler and Grid command dimmed on my screen?

If the Ruler and Grid command is dimmed, then you have deselected the document window. Click the inn image in the document window and repeat step 1.

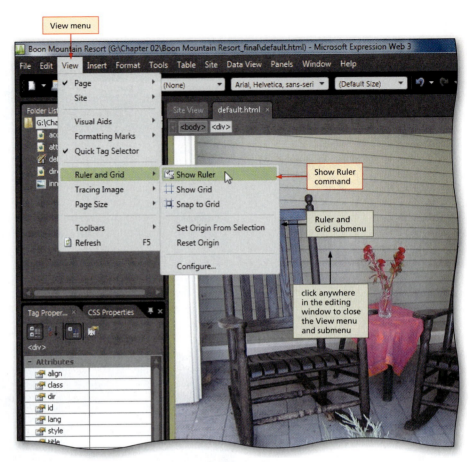

Figure 2–20

2

• Click Show Ruler on the submenu to display the rulers (Figure 2–21).

Q&A What should I do if my rulers are already displayed?

Show Ruler is a toggle command, meaning that the same steps are used to turn the rulers on and off. If your rulers were already displayed, either skip these steps or repeat them to display the rulers.

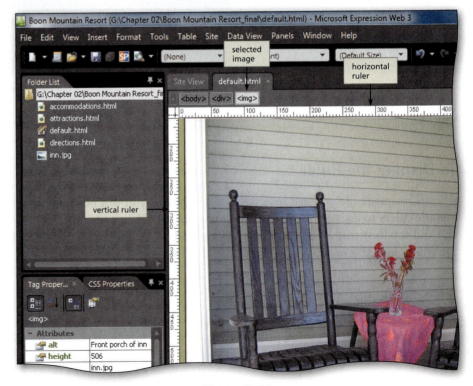

Figure 2–21

Adjusting Proportions

The relationship between an image's height and width is an image's **proportions**, or **aspect ratio**. If an image's proportions are changed, it can distort the image like a carnival funhouse mirror. To maintain the aspect ratio when resizing an image manually, press and hold the SHIFT key and then drag a corner sizing handle to adjust the height and width at the same time. When you change the height of an image in the Picture Properties dialog box, click the 'Keep aspect ratio' check box so that the width automatically adjusts proportionately, and vice versa. After you have resized an image, you should **resample** it to improve the image quality by adjusting the resolution of pixels to the new image size.

BTW

Changing Image Size
Resizing an image can make your layout more attractive but does not change the file size of the image. When you make an image larger, you risk decreasing the image quality because as you increase the size on the page, you are stretching the existing pixels in the file. Testing your site in a browser can identify problems with resized images.

To Resize an Image

Expression Web uses the actual pixel width and height of the picture as the size when it inserts the image. You can resize the physical space that the picture takes up by dragging the image using the sizing handles or by specifying the height and width in pixels in the Picture Properties dialog box. In the following steps, you will resize the image, then resample it.

1

- Verify that the image is selected and then click Format on the menu bar to open the Format menu, then point to Properties (Figure 2–22).

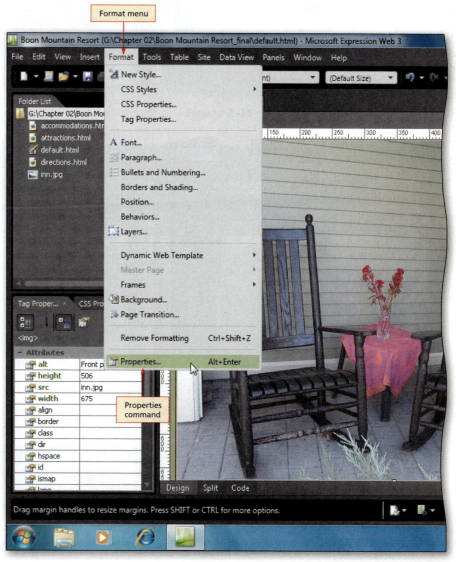

Figure 2–22

6

- Click the Resample Picture To Match Size option button to resample the image, then click outside the picture to deselect it (Figure 2–27).

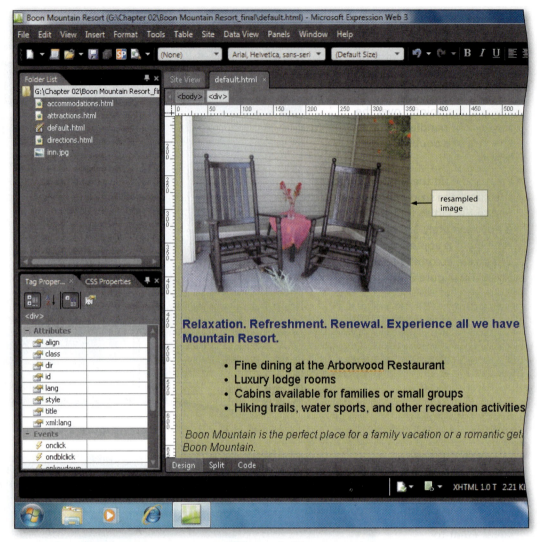

Figure 2–27

- Press CTRL+S to save the page (Figure 2–28).

- Click the OK button in the Save Embedded Files dialog box to save the embedded file.

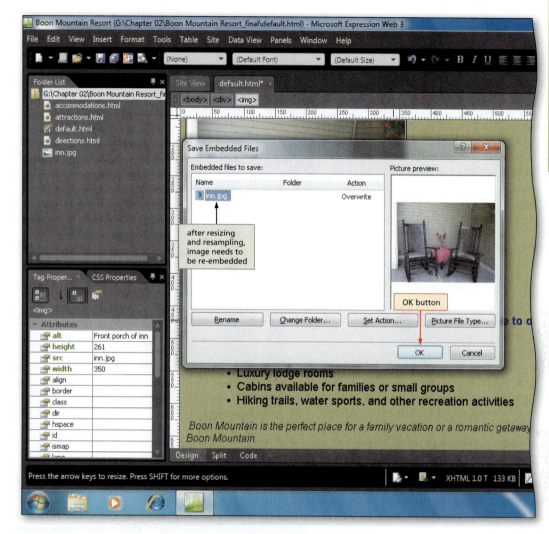

Figure 2–28

Other Ways	
1. Double-click the picture to open the Picture Properties dialog box	2. Right-click the picture, then click Picture Properties to open the Picture Properties dialog box

Positioning an Image

Changing the alignment and spacing of text and images allows you to create a flow to your page that is visually interesting and guides the reader's eye down the page. You can choose to align to the left or right margin, or to the center of the page. When you align an image that is surrounded by text, you should position the image in relation to the text. When positioning text around an image, use the **text wrapping** feature to guide how the text flows around the image. This method is preferable to using the alignment buttons on the Common toolbar, which would adjust the image and text alignment at the same time.

To Align an Image

In the following steps, you will align the image to the right margin and wrap the text around it.

1

- Double-click the image to open the Picture Properties dialog box.

- Click the Appearance tab.

- Click the Right button in the Wrapping style section of the Appearance tab (Figure 2–29).

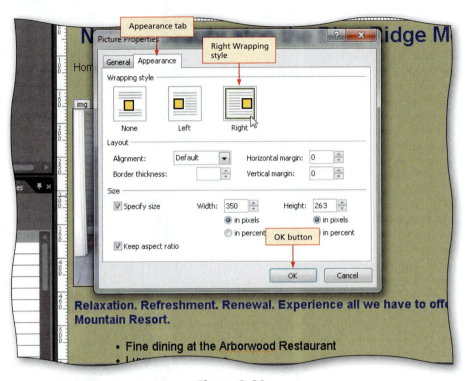

Figure 2–29

2

- Click the OK button to close the dialog box. Click anywhere outside of the image to deselect it.

- Press CTRL+S to save the page (Figure 2–30).

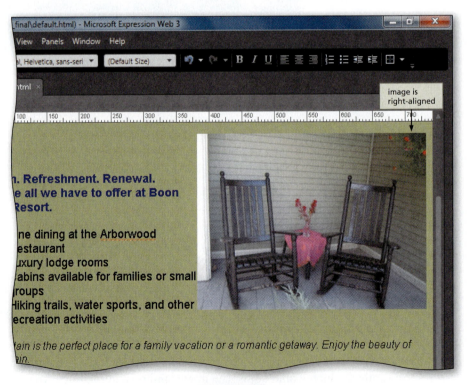

Figure 2–30

Adding Borders and Spacing

There are many different **borders** available from the Borders tab of the Borders and Shading dialog box that you can use to surround your image with lines, graphics, or effects. You can also create a custom border, or use the Borders button on the Common toolbar to add a basic border.

Image **margins** surround the top, bottom, left, and right edges of an image and separate it from adjacent text or images. Adding a margin to an image ensures that the image has sufficient spacing around it. Margins are measured in pixels.

To Add a Border to an Image

A border around an image can give it definition and distinction. As you click an option in the Style list of the Borders and Shading dialog box, the Preview pane of the dialog box changes to show you what the border will look like. The following steps add the double border style to the image.

- Click the image to select it.

- Click Format on the menu bar to open the Format menu, then point to Borders and Shading (Figure 2–31).

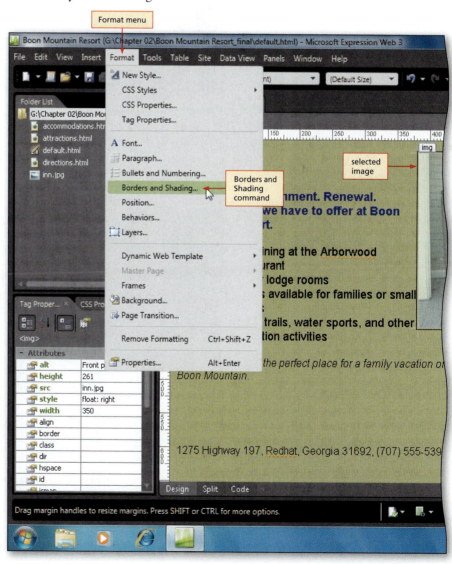

Figure 2–31

2

- Click Borders and Shading on the Format menu to open the Borders and Shading dialog box.

- Click double in the Style list to select it (Figure 2–32).

 **Experiment**

- Click other options in the Style list to view them in the Preview box, then click double to select it.

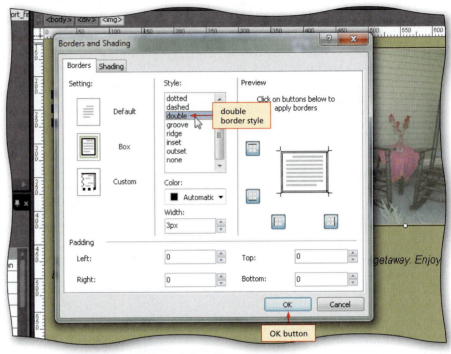

Figure 2–32

3

- Click the OK button to close the dialog box and apply the border.

Q&A How can I reverse a change to the page?

To undo the last change you have made to a page, press CTRL+Z or click the Undo button on the Common toolbar. Repeat this step to undo multiple changes that have occurred since your last save. After you save a page, you cannot undo the changes.

- Click outside the image to deselect it (Figure 2–33).

- Press CTRL+S to save the page.

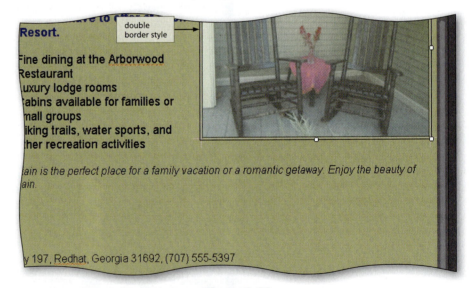

Figure 2–33

Other Ways

1. Select the image, click the Borders button arrow on the Common toolbar, then click an option from the gallery to apply it

To Modify Image Margins

Adding a margin to an image increases the space between the image and the surrounding text and helps the image to stand out. The following steps manually adjust the left and bottom image margins of the image using ScreenTips to determine the size of the margin.

 1

- Click the image to select it.

- Position the pointer over the left margin so that the double-headed arrow appears. The margin ScreenTip will appear, which should be margin-left: (0 px).

- Hold down the left mouse button and drag the left margin border to the left until the ScreenTip shows that it is 25 pixels (Figure 2–34).

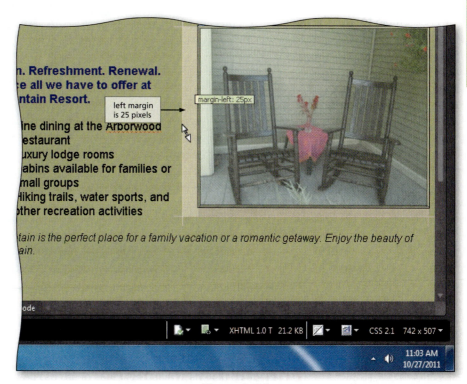

Figure 2–34

 2

- Release the mouse button to set the left margin. Using the double-headed arrow pointer, click and drag the bottom margin border down until the ScreenTip shows that it is 20 pixels (Figure 2–35), then release the mouse button.

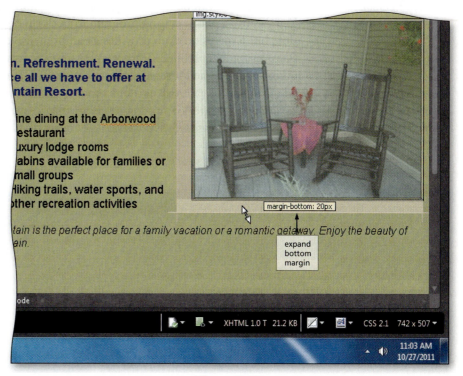

Figure 2–35

5

- Click the Insert button to open the Accessibility Properties dialog box.

- In the Alternate text text box within the Accessibility Properties dialog box, type Guest room decorated with quilts and artwork (Figure 2–56).

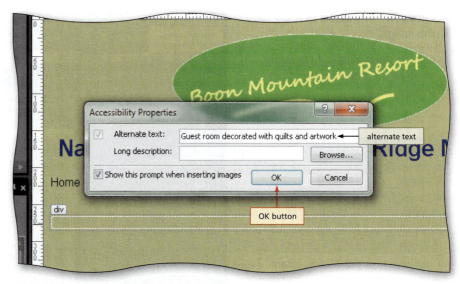

Figure 2–56

6

- Click the OK button to close the Accessibility Properties dialog box and insert the picture (Figure 2–57).

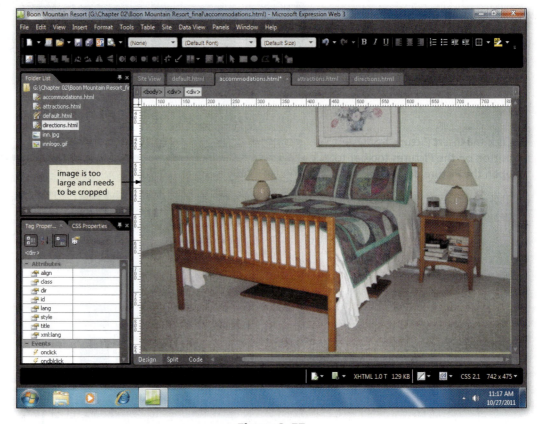

Figure 2–57

7

- Click the image to select it.

- Click the Crop button on the Pictures toolbar to display the cropping area.

- Using the double-headed arrow pointer, drag the cropping handles to adjust the cropping area so that it appears similar to Figure 2–58.

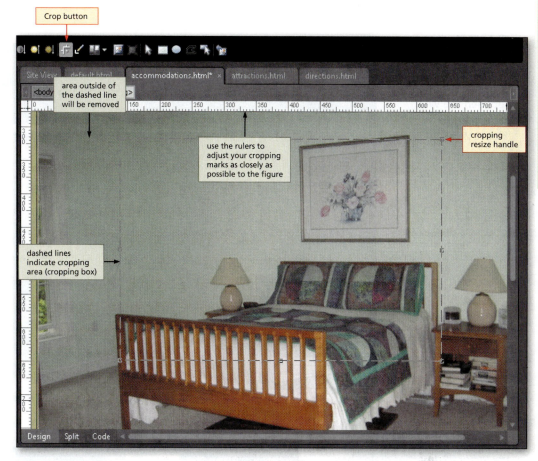

Crop button

area outside of the dashed line will be removed

use the rulers to adjust your cropping marks as closely as possible to the figure

cropping resize handle

dashed lines indicate cropping area (cropping box)

Figure 2–58

8

- Click the Crop button to accept the cropping changes you have made (Figure 2–59).

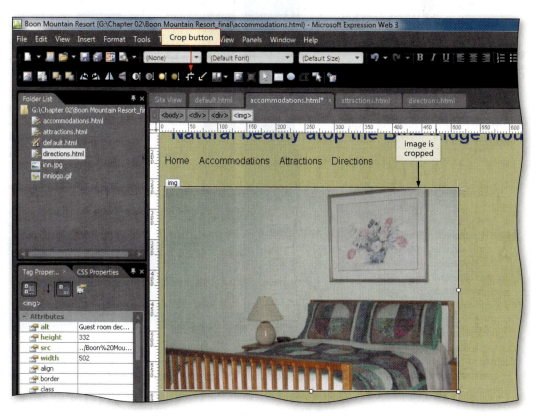

Crop button

image is cropped

Figure 2–59

10

- Press CTRL+S to save the page (Figure 2–73).

- Click the OK button to save the embedded files.

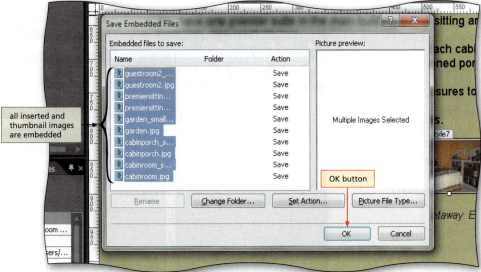

Figure 2–73

To Create a Folder for Images

To keep your site organized and help make updates easier, you should store all media files, including images and video, in a common folder. When you move an image using the Folder List, Expression Web automatically adjusts any coded references to the image file location so that the image can be found and placed appropriately on the page when viewed in a browser. You can create a separate folder for each page that includes the page and any assets, or for a smaller site, you can create one folder for all of the images. The following steps create a folder for storing files and move multiple images into it.

1

- Click anywhere in the Folder List to activate it.

- Click File on the menu bar, point to New, then point to Folder (Figure 2–74).

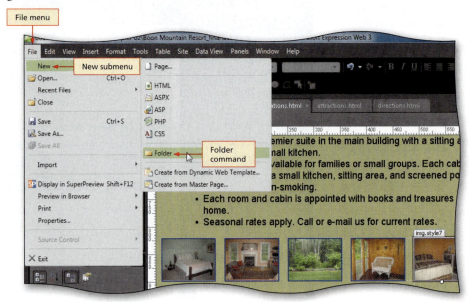

Figure 2–74

2

- Click Folder to create a new folder in the Folder List (Figure 2–75).

Figure 2–75

3

- Type images, then press ENTER to name the folder (Figure 2–76).

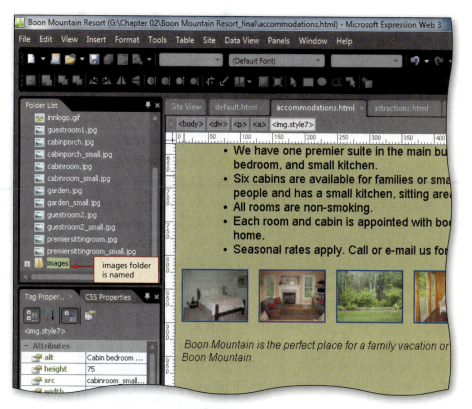

Figure 2–76

2

- Click the Preview in browser button to display the page in the browser (Figure 2–92).

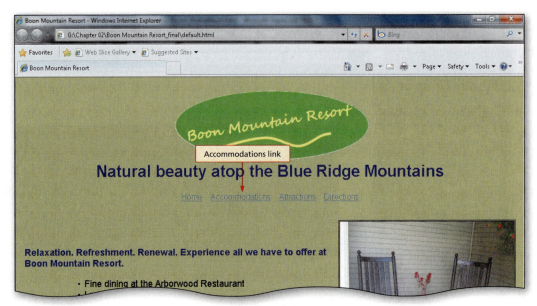

Figure 2–92

3

- Click the Accommodations link in the navigation bar to open the Accommodations page (Figure 2–93).

Q&A Why is my browser window not maximized?

Click the Maximize button in the upper-right corner of the browser window to maximize it.

- Click the browser Back button to return to the default page.

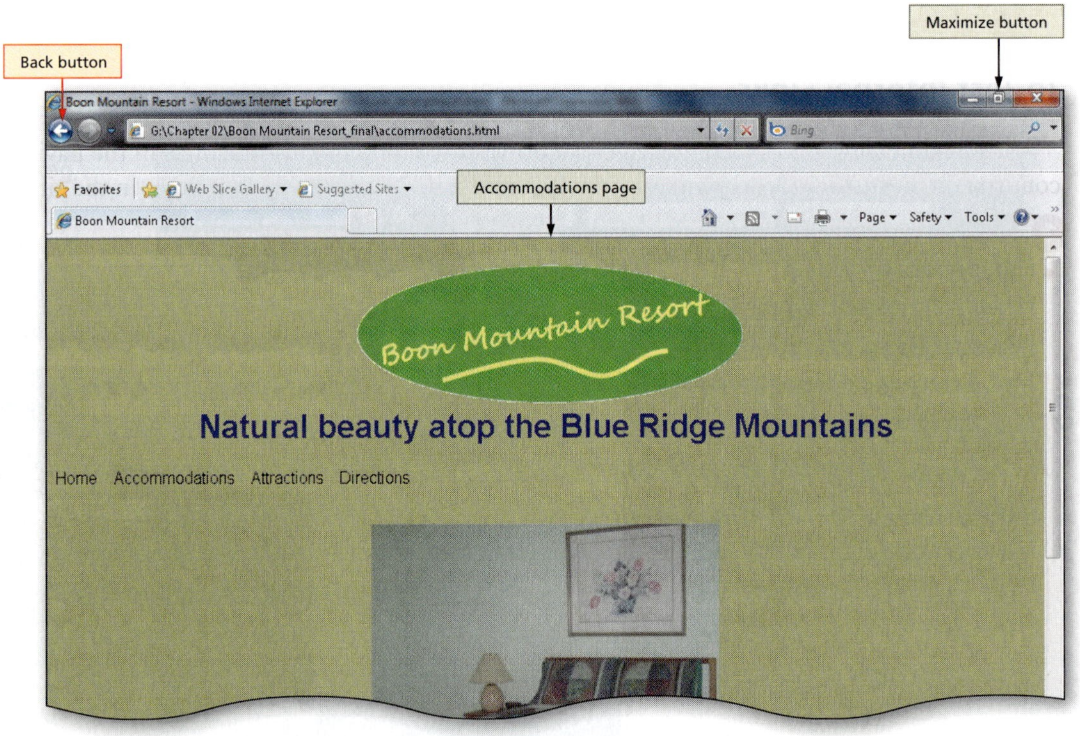

Figure 2–93

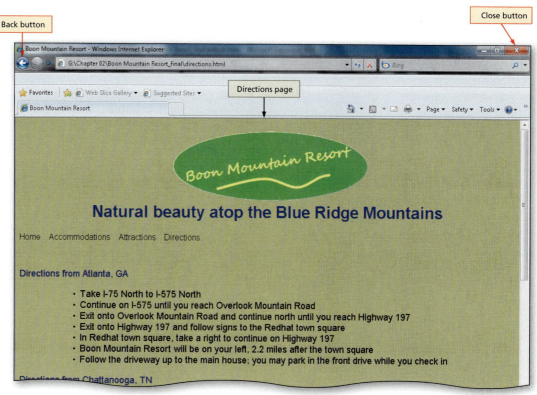

4

- Test the remaining two links; click the Attractions link, click the Back button, and then click the Directions link (Figure 2–94).

- Click the Close button to close the browser window to return to Expression Web.

Figure 2–94

To Copy and Paste Internal Links

After you have verified that the navigation bar links work, you will add it to each page in the site in the same location. For layout purposes, a placeholder navigation bar appears on each page, listing the pages but without any links. The following steps replace the placeholder navigation bar on the Accommodations, Attractions, and Directions pages.

- Select the naviga-tion div, if necessary.

- Press CTRL+C to copy the entire navigation div to the Clipboard.

- Click the attractions. html tab to make it the active Web page.

- Click the placeholder navigation bar, and then click the div. style5 tab to select the div (Figure 2–95).

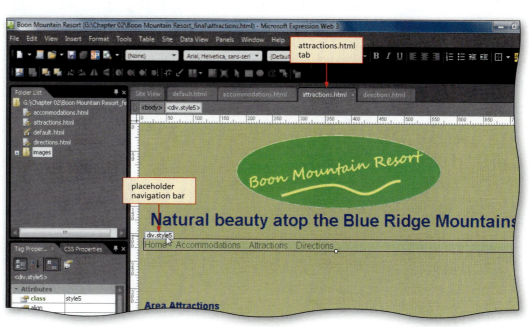

Figure 2–95

2

- Press CTRL+V to insert the navigation bar on the Attractions page (Figure 2–96).

Q&A

Why isn't my navigation bar centered?

If the pasted navigation bar isn't centered, select the div, then click the Center button on the Common toolbar.

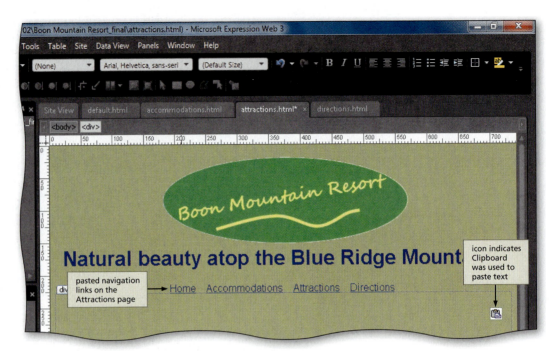

Figure 2–96

3

- Follow Steps 1 and 2 to insert the navigation bar below the masthead on the Accommodations and Directions pages (Figure 2–97).

Q&A

When I paste the navigation bar onto the accommodations.html page, the formatting does not match the page.

When copying and pasting formatting between pages, errors can occur if the page already includes a style with the same name as the one being pasted. If this occurs, reapply the formatting to the pasted text , for example, change the font family and size.

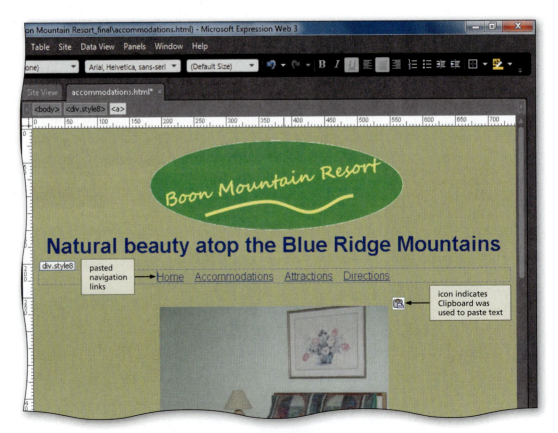

Figure 2–97

4

- Click File on the menu bar to open the File menu, and then point to Save All (Figure 2–98).

- Click Save All to save all open pages at once.

Figure 2–98

To Add an External Link

Adding external links allows you to include access to resources whose sites and content you do not control. Such links can help visitors to your site gain information that might enhance their experience on your site or with your organization or in a tab within the browser window. The following steps insert links to attractions near the Boon Mountain Resort.

1

- Click the attractions. html tab to display the Attractions page.

- Select the text in the first bulleted list item.

- Click Insert on the menu bar to open the Insert menu, and then point to Hyperlink (Figure 2–99).

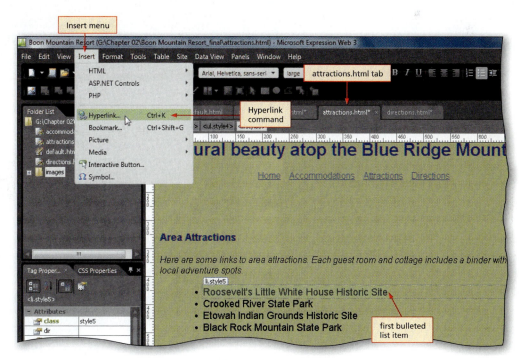

Figure 2–99

- Click Hyperlink to open the Insert Hyperlink dialog box.

- In the Address text box, type `http://www.gastateparks.org/info/littlewhite` to create a link to a page in the Georgia State Parks Web site (Figure 2–100).

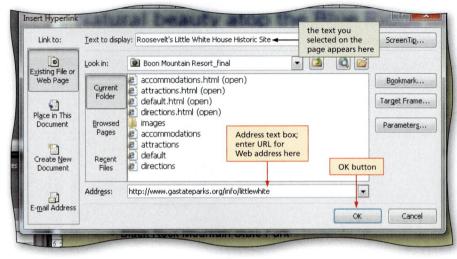

Figure 2–100

- Click the OK button to close the Insert Hyperlink dialog box (Figure 2–101).

Figure 2–101

4

- Select the text in the second bulleted list item (Figure 2–102).

Figure 2–102

5

- Press CTRL+K to open the Insert Hyperlink dialog box.

- In the Address text box, type `http://www.gastateparks. org/info/crookriv` to create a second external link (Figure 2–103).

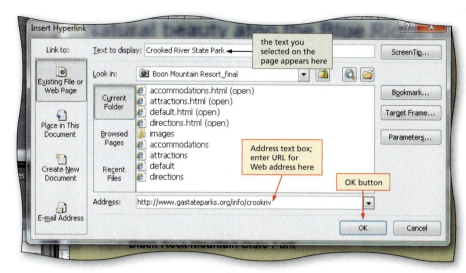

Figure 2–103

6

- Click the OK button to close the Insert Hyperlink dialog box, then click to the right of the hyperlink to deselect it (Figure 2–104).

Q&A

Why can't I add a link to the text I selected?

Make sure that you have not selected a page element, such as a line item or a div. Hyperlinks can only be added to text and images.

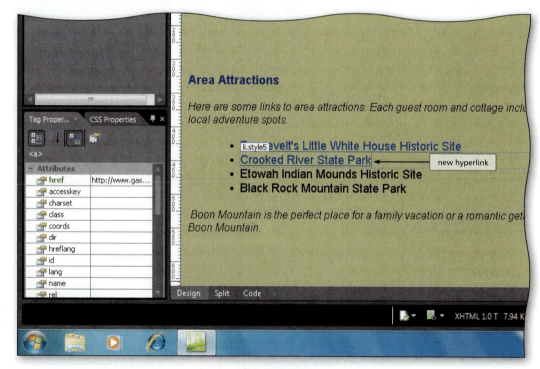

Figure 2–104

7

- Repeat Steps 4–6 to create a link from the third bullet to `http://www.gastateparks.org/info/etowah`.

- Repeat Steps 4–6 to create a link from the fourth bullet to `http://www.gastateparks.org/info/blackrock` (Figure 2–105).

- Press CTRL+S to save the page.

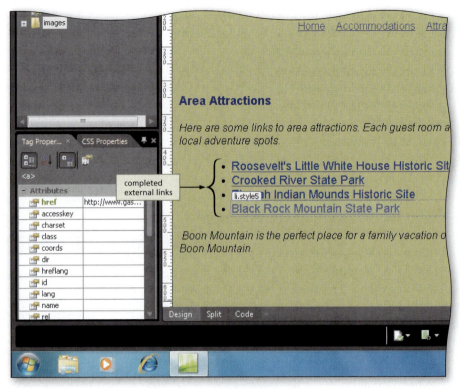

Figure 2–105

To Test External Links

The following steps open the page in a browser window, and test the links in the navigation bar.

1

- Press F12 to display the Attractions page in the browser.

- Click the first bullet link in the list to open the Little White House Web page (Figure 2–106).

Q&A Why did a new browser window or tab open when I clicked the link?

Depending on your browser and security settings, a new window or tab may open when you click an external link from a Web page saved on your computer.

Figure 2–106

2

- Click the Back button or click the Close button if your browser opened the page in a new window. Then click the second bullet link to test it, click the Back button, and repeat for the third and fourth bullet links (Figure 2–107).

Back button

Close button

if the site has been updated, your page will differ

Figure 2–107

3

- Click the Close button on the browser window.

- Click the 'Close all tabs' button, if necessary, to close the Internet Explorer dialog box (Figure 2–108).

- Click the Close button on any other open browser windows to return to Expression Web, if necessary.

if your browser uses tabbed windows, click Close all tabs in the dialog box

Figure 2–108

To Add a Bookmark

When creating a bookmark, first you assign the bookmark text or image to which you want to jump (the link's target or destination), then you can insert the bookmark hyperlink in the desired location on the page. The following steps add a bookmark link at the bottom of the Directions page that returns to the top of the page.

- Click the directions. html tab to make it the active Web page.

- Select the words, Natural beauty atop the Blue Ridge Mountains, below the logo.

- Click Insert on the menu bar to open the Insert menu, and then point to Bookmark (Figure 2–109).

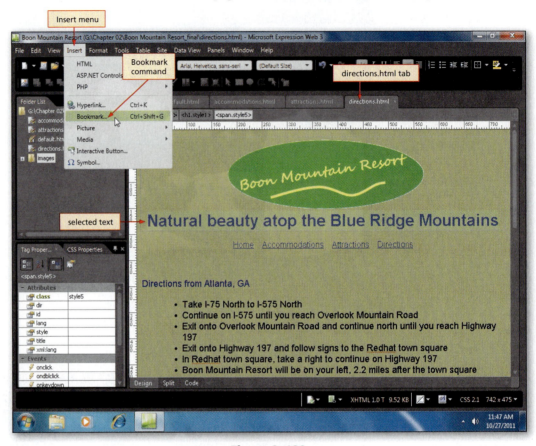

Figure 2–109

Other Ways

1. Press CTRL+G to open the Bookmark dialog box

- Click Bookmark to open the Bookmark dialog box.

- Type Top of Page in the Bookmark name text box to specify the wording that will appear as the link (Figure 2–110).

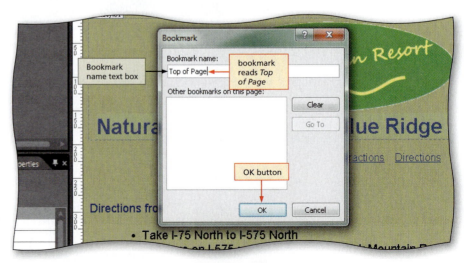

Figure 2–110

3

- Click the OK button to close the Bookmark dialog box (Figure 2–111).

Figure 2–111

4

- Scroll to the bottom of the page and then click at the end of the last bullet list item (below Directions from Redhat County Airport), then press ENTER twice to create a new paragraph tag (Figure 2–112).

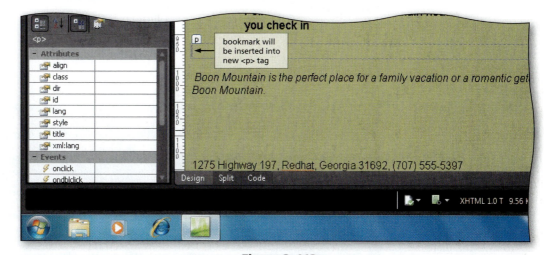

Figure 2–112

5

- Press CTRL+K to open the Insert Hyperlink dialog box.

- Click the Place in This Document button to display the list of bookmarks.

- Click Top of Page to select it as the target bookmark (Figure 2–113).

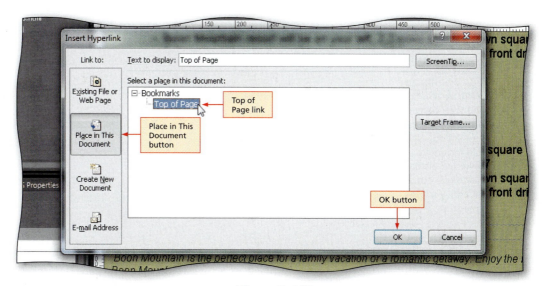

Figure 2–113

6
- Click the OK button to close the dialog box and insert the bookmark link (Figure 2–114).

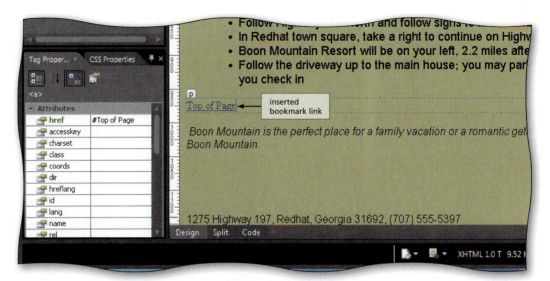

Figure 2–114

7
- Press CTRL, then click the Top of Page link to test the bookmark link (Figure 2–115).

- Click the Save button on the Common toolbar to save the page.

Figure 2–115

BTW

Forms vs. E-Mail Links
There are programs that search the Web collecting e-mail addresses to use in mass e-mailings. Some sites avoid including e-mail links and instead use forms to collect user feedback and requests for this reason.

To Add an E-Mail Link

An e-mail link opens a new, blank e-mail window using the visitor's e-mail program. In the following steps, you will add an e-mail link to your e-mail address for requests for room rates.

- Click the accommodations.html page tab so it is the active Web page tab in the editing window.

- In the last bullet item, select the word, e-mail, to make it a hyperlink.

- Press CTRL+K to open the Insert Hyperlink dialog box.

- Click the E-mail Address button.

- In the E-mail address text box, type `mailto:` followed by your e-mail address.

- In the Subject text box, type `Rooms and Rates` (Figure 2–116).

Q&A

Why is there no e-mail address in my 'Recently used e-mail addresses' text box?

The text box is empty because you are using a fresh install of Expression Web 3. Therefore, there have been no previously used e-mail addresses.

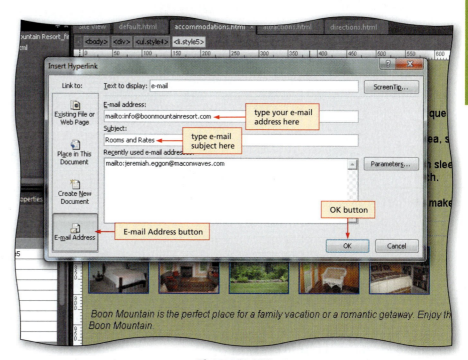

Figure 2–116

- Click the OK button to close the Insert Hyperlink dialog box and create the mailto link (Figure 2–117).

- Press CTRL+S to save the page.

Figure 2–117

3

- Press F12 to display the page in the browser.

- Scroll down and click the e-mail link to test it.

- If an Internet Explorer Security dialog box appears, click the Allow button.

- The Outlook e-mail window may appear (Figure 2–118).

- Close the e-mail window without saving changes if it opens.

- Close the browser window to return to Expression Web.

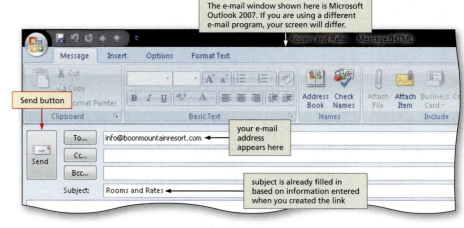

Figure 2–118

Q&A Why do I get an error message when I click the e-mail link?

Your e-mail program or browser might not be configured to process mailto links.

  Experiment

- If an e-mail window opens, click the Send button to send the e-mail to yourself.

To Add a ScreenTip

A **ScreenTip** is a window containing descriptive text that appears when you position the pointer over a button or link. Adding a ScreenTip to the e-mail address lets users know that they can contact you with any questions. The following steps add a ScreenTip to the mailto link.

1

- Select the e-mail link.

- Press CTRL+K to open the Edit Hyperlink dialog box (Figure 2–119).

Figure 2–119

2

- Click the ScreenTip button to open the Set Hyperlink ScreenTip dialog box.

- In the ScreenTip text text box, type Contact us by e-mail with any questions (Figure 2–120).

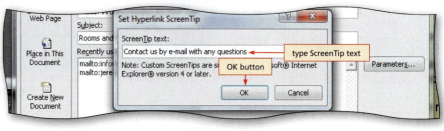

Figure 2–120

3

- Click the OK button to close the Set Hyperlink ScreenTip dialog box (Figure 2–121).

- Click the OK button to close the Edit Hyperlink dialog box.

- Press CTRL+S to save the page.

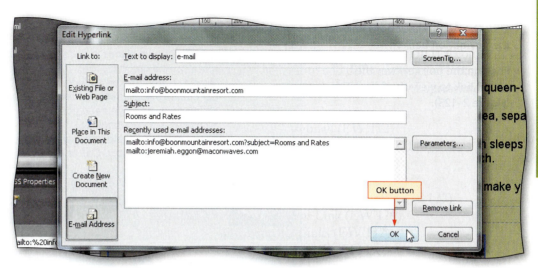

Figure 2–121

To Preview the Site

In the following steps, you will preview the site in your browser to view all of the pages and view and test the ScreenTip.

1

- Click the default. html tab to make it the active Web page.

- Press F12 to open the page in a browser (Figure 2–122).

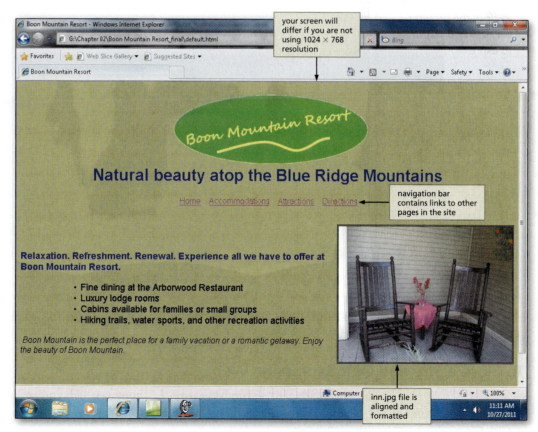

Figure 2–122

Apply Your Knowledge

Reinforce the skills and apply the concepts you learned in this chapter.

Adding Images and Links

Instructions: Start Expression Web. Open the Web site, Apply 2-1 Photography, from the Data Files for Students. See the inside back cover of this book for instructions for downloading the Data Files for Students, or see your instructor for information about accessing the required files.

The Web site you open contains a home page with formatting and text. Open the default.html file and add and format an image, create thumbnails, and add an e-mail link with a ScreenTip so that the page looks like Figure 2–125.

Figure 2–125

Perform the following tasks:

1. Open the default.html Web page.

2. Click before the words, Quiet moments.

3. Click the Insert Picture from File button on the Common toolbar.

4. Select the JPG image flowerphoto from the Apply 2-1 images folder, then click Insert.

5. Type `Lily on bush` in the Alternate text text box, then click OK.

6. Select the image, right-click the image, then click Picture Properties from the shortcut menu.

7. Click the Appearance tab, click the Left Wrapping style button, then click the OK button.

8. Press the SHIFT key and drag the lower-right sizing handle until the picture is resized to approximately 200 × 161 pixels.

9. Drag the right margin to resize the right margin to 40 pixels.

10. Drag the bottom margin to resize the bottom margin to 30 pixels.

11. Click the Bevel button on the Pictures toolbar to add a bevel to the image.

12. Save the default.html page, then click OK to save the embedded picture.

13. Click before the words, Here are some images, then press ENTER three times.

14. Click anywhere below the line that begins, Here are some images, then double-click the div tag in the Toolbox.

15. Insert the JPG image beachphoto1, then type `Two girls on a beach` in the Alternate text text box, and then click OK.

16. Select the image, then click the Auto Thumbnail button on the Pictures toolbar.

17. Click to the right of the image, then press TAB.

18. Insert the JPG image beachphoto2, type `Girl in surf` in the Alternate text text box, create a thumbnail, click next to the image, then press TAB.

19. Insert the JPG image beachphoto3, type `Girl with towel` in the Alternate text text box, then create a thumbnail.

20. Save the default.html page, then click OK to save the embedded pictures.

21. Select the words, Contact me.

22. On the Insert menu, click Hyperlink.

23. Click the E-mail Address button, then type your e-mail address in the E-mail address text box.

24. Click the ScreenTip button, type your e-mail address in the ScreenTip text text box, then click the OK button twice to close the open dialog boxes.

25. Save and then preview the site, and test the thumbnails and links.

26. Change the site properties, as specified by your instructor. Close the site.

27. In Windows Explorer, change the site folder's name to Apply 2-1 Photo Site. Submit the revised site in the format specified by your instructor.

Extend Your Knowledge

Extend the skills you learned in this chapter and experiment with new skills. You may need to use Help to complete the assignment.

Creating Links to Images and Bookmarks

Instructions: Start Expression Web. Open the Web site, Extend 2-1 Music Festival, from the Data Files for Students. See the inside back cover of this book for instructions for downloading the Data Files for Students, or see your instructor for information about accessing the required files.

You will enhance the Web page to match the one shown in Figure 2–126.

Continued >

Extend Your Knowledge *continued*

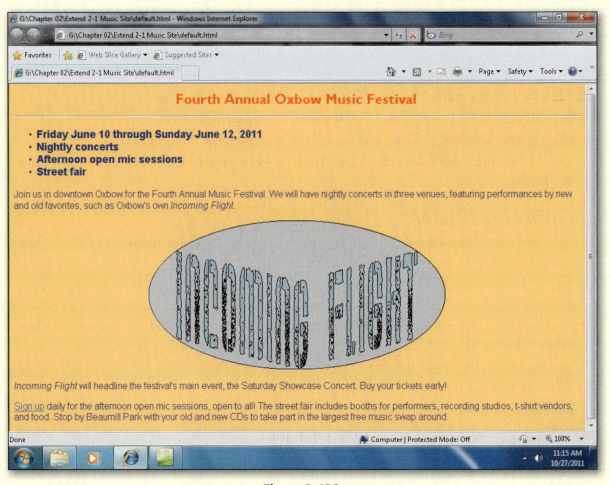

Figure 2–126

Perform the following tasks:

1. Use Help to learn about inserting a link to a file.

2. Open the default.html page, position the insertion point before the words, *Incoming Flight*, at the beginning of the second paragraph, then press ENTER.

3. Click above the words, *Incoming Flight*, to make the empty paragraph tag active. Insert the GIF image bandlogo from the folder Extend 2-1 images, and type `Incoming Flight band logo` as the Alternate text.

4. Center the image on the page.

5. Select the image, then open the Insert Hyperlink dialog box.

6. Click the Existing File or Web page button if necessary, type `http://www.incomingflight band.com` in the Address text box, then click the OK button. (*Note:* This Web page does not exist. You will get an error message when you test it.)

7. Select the words, Sign up, then open the Insert Hyperlink dialog box.

8. Click the Existing File or Web Page button if necessary, click signup_form, then click the OK button.

9. Save the default.html page and the embedded file, preview the page and test all links, then close the browser window.

10. Change the site properties, as specified by your instructor, and then close the site. In Windows Explorer, change the site folder's name to Extend 2-1 Music Site. Submit the revised site in the format specified by your instructor.

Make It Right

Analyze a site and correct all errors and/or improve the design.

Placing and Formatting Images

Instructions: Start Expression Web. Open the Web site, Make It Right 2-1 Swim Club, from the Data Files for Students. See the inside back cover of this book for instructions for downloading the Data Files for Students, or see your instructor for information about accessing the required files.

The site has one image that is large, is not aligned with the text, and has no formatting. In addition, there is no link to the second page of the Web site, which gives more information on swim lessons, and no way to contact the director by sending him an e-mail. Position the image to the right of the bulleted list, resize (approximately 300 pixels wide and maintain aspect ratio) and format it, add a link from the swim lesson text to the swim lesson page, add an e-mail link to the director's name (jeremiah. eggon@maconwaves.com), add a 5-pixel border to the image, and add two empty paragraphs before the footer, as shown in Figure 2–127.

Change the site properties, as specified by your instructor. In Windows Explorer, change the site folder's name to Make It Right 2-1 Swim Club Site. Submit the revised site in the format specified by your instructor.

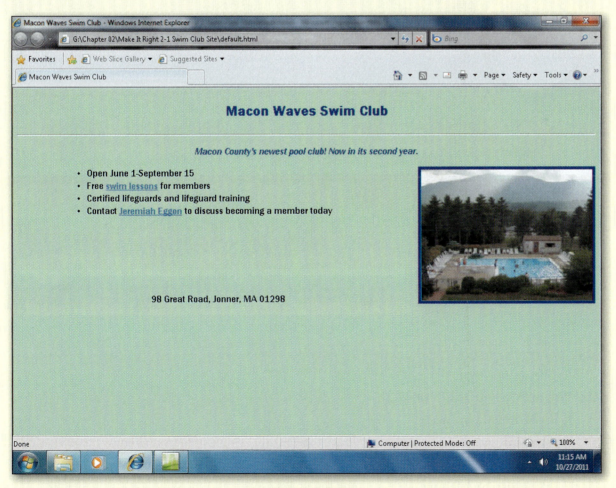

Figure 2–127

In the Lab

Design and/or format a Web site using the guidelines, concepts, and skills presented in this chapter. Labs are listed in order of increasing difficulty.

Lab 1: Creating a Navigation Bar and Inserting an Image

Problem: You work part-time at a small bike repair shop. Your boss has asked you to add images and create a navigation bar for the shop's Web site. Add images and links to the page shown in Figure 2–128.

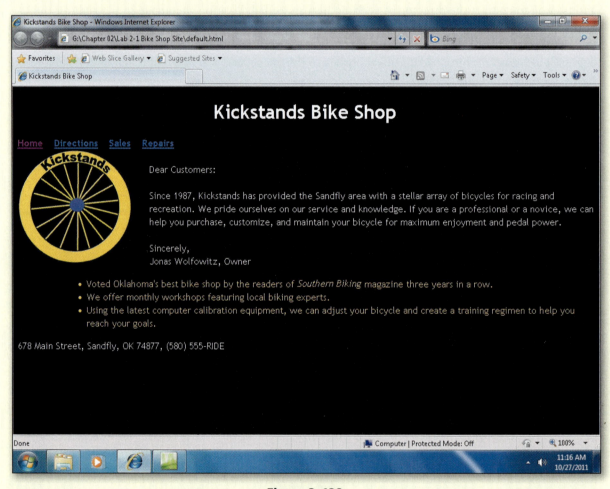

Figure 2–128

Instructions:

1. Start Expression Web.

2. Open the Web site Lab 2-1 Bike Shop.

3. Open the default.html page.

4. Position the insertion point in the line above the words, Dear Customers, then insert a new div.

5. Insert the GIF image kickstands_logo from the Lab 2-1 images folder. Do not assign alternate text.

6. Resize the logo to 200 pixels wide, keeping the image aspect ratio the same so that the height automatically adjusts, and left-align the image around the text. If necessary, drag the image up to align the text as shown in Figure 2–128.

7. Increase the right margin of the logo to 40 pixels.

8. Create a navigation bar using the text below the masthead, then copy it to each page in the site.

9. Save the changes you have made to all pages at once, then preview the site in a browser.

10. Rename the site Lab 2-1 Bike Shop Site. Change the site properties, as specified by your instructor.

11. Close the site, and then submit it in the format specified by your instructor.

In the Lab

Lab 2: Adding a Horizontal Line, Bookmark, and Link to a File

Problem: You own a baking business and want to attract customers by making your site's home page easier to navigate. On the featured recipe section of the home page, add a horizontal line at the top of the recipe and a bookmark link at the bottom to help users navigate back to the top of the page, as shown in Figure 2–129. Also add a link to an order form that users can download.

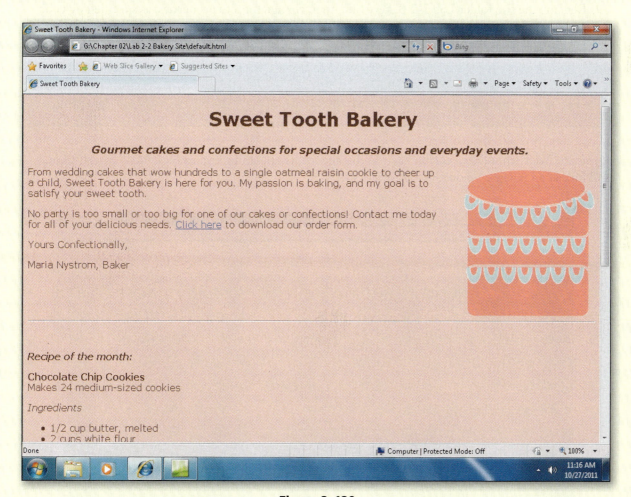

Figure 2–129

Continued >

In the Lab *continued*

Instructions:

1. Start Expression Web.

2. Open the Web site Lab 2-2 Bakery, then open the default.html page.

3. Insert a horizontal line two lines above the text, Recipe of the month. Leave two empty paragraphs before this horizontal rule so that it will not intersect with the cake.

4. Create a bookmark called Top of Page to the words, Sweet Tooth Bakery, in the masthead.

5. At the bottom of the page, between the directions and address, add a new paragraph, type the text Top of Page, and create a bookmark link from this text to the bookmark created in Step 4.

6. Add a link from the words, Click here, to the PDF file orderform.

7. Change the left margin of the cake image to 35 pixels.

8. Preview the site in a browser and test the link and bookmark.

9. Rename the site folder Lab 2-2 Bakery Site, then change the site properties, as specified by your instructor.

10. Close the site, and then submit it in the format specified by your instructor.

In the Lab

Lab 3: Formatting an Image

Problem: Your school's travel club has a Web page for its upcoming trip to New York. Insert, align, and format an image as shown in Figure 2–130.

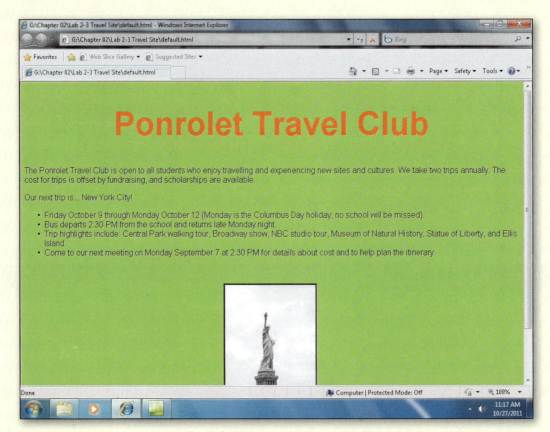

Figure 2–130

Instructions: Perform the following tasks.

1. Start Expression Web.

2. Open the Web site Lab 2-3 Travel.

3. Open the default.html page.

4. Click after the last bulleted list item, press ENTER three times, then insert the image statue.jpg from the Lab 2-3 images folder and add alternate text crediting your name as the photographer.

5. Crop the top, left, and right sides so that the image appears as shown in Figure 2–130.

6. Center-align the image.

7. Use the Borders and Shading dialog box to add a groove border around all sides. (*Hint:* To open the dialog box, click the Borders and Shading command on the Format menu.)

8. Click the More Brightness button twice.

9. Click the Color button arrow, then click Grayscale.

10. Click the More Contrast button twice.

11. Save the changes you have made to default.html and save the embedded image.

12. Preview the page in a browser.

13. Change the site properties, as specified by your instructor.

14. Close the site, rename the site folder Lab 2-3 Travel Site, and submit the site in the format specified by your instructor.

Cases and Places

Apply your creative thinking and problem-solving skills to design and implement a solution.

● EASIER   ●●MORE DIFFICULT

● 1: Add Internal and External Links

You want to practice adding links to a Web site. Open any site that you created in Chapter 1, then open that site's default.html page. Add a link to your school's Web page, add a link to your e-mail address, and create and insert a bookmark. Close the default.html page without saving any changes, close the Web site, then quit Expression Web.

● 2: Add Images and Links to a School Web Site

The administration of Pinkham Academy would like to include images and links on a Web site. If you completed the Cases and Places 2 activity in Chapter 1, you can use the sketch of the Web site as a basis for this exercise. Create a one-page Web site that has a masthead, and at least one paragraph and bulleted list describing the school's features. Next to the bulleted list, insert a right-aligned image (use a photo from an exercise in this chapter or use one of your own). Add a margin and a bevel to the image. Add an e-mail link with a ScreenTip to your e-mail address.

●● 3: Add a Gallery of Images to an Alumni Web Site

You have recently joined the Connecticut branch of your college alumni association. You have been working on a home page that can tell other local graduates of Gulliver College about upcoming alumni events. You have already entered the text for the home page. Open the site Cases and Places 2-3 Alumni, then open the page default.html. Add four images and create a gallery of thumbnails for them (use photos from an exercise in this chapter or use your own). Center-align the thumbnails and make sure to add space between each image. Save the changes to the default.html file and embed all image files, then test your thumbnails in your browser.

●● 4: Create a Personal Home Page

Make It Personal

You want to create a personal home page that you can use to link to your favorite sites and allow others to e-mail you. Create a one-page Web site and include a masthead, bulleted list, footer, and any other information you think is relevant. Format the Web site attractively. Add at least one image that you crop, size, and align with text wrapping. Add a border to the image. Insert three links to sites that you like to visit. Add a ScreenTip to each of the links that displays the name of the site or what type of information the visitor will see when he or she clicks it. Insert an e-mail link to your e-mail address.

●● 5: Enhance a Home Page for a Restaurant

Working Together

A local restaurant wants to create a multi-page Web site for its customers. The site will include a home page, a menu page, and a page with directions. All pages should include a masthead, navigation bar with links, at least one image, one or two paragraphs or lists of information, and a footer with contact information. Working as a team with several of your classmates, you are to design and create the Web site. As a group, decide on the name of the restaurant and the menu. Each team member should plan on paper the three pages (home, menu, and directions), and present his or her plan to the group. As a group, decide on elements of each plan that you will incorporate into the home page, and start creating the home page using Expression Web. Format the Web site attractively. Add the text for each page. Add images and use text wrapping, create thumbnails, and apply formatting. Create a navigation bar and copy it to each page.

3 | Working with Templates and Styles

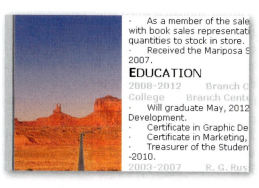

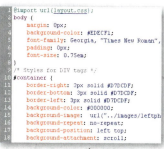

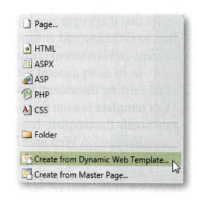

Objectives

You will have mastered the material in this chapter when you can:

- Create an Expression Web site from a template
- Rename a page
- Rename a folder
- Add and delete pages
- Add and delete folders
- Replace content in the template
- Copy and paste text from an external document

- Edit the editable regions
- Make global changes with templates
- Define styles and style sheets
- Modify a style
- Create a style
- Apply a style

BTW

Subfolders

A folder within a folder is called a subfolder.

BTW

Metadata

Metadata is information about styles and structure that is created as part of a Web site. Metadata is stored in hidden files and folders that do not appear in the Folder List, but it will be visible if you view a site's folder contents in Windows Explorer; it should not be deleted, moved, or edited.

Specifying the Structure of the Site

As you learned in previous chapters, a Web site can include folders to organize and store files. A template provides a folder for each page; each page folder includes the HTML file for the page and any embedded placeholder images or files for that page, such as the land-scape image included in Mary's portfolio. When you create a new site from a template, you will see the folders for all pages except the main default.html page, which is the home page. Because templates use style sheets to specify the formatting of the site, you will also see a folder for the style sheets. A separate folder exists for the common site images, such as the one on the left side of the page, which appears on all pages. A site created with a template includes many pages, including ones that you might not need or whose names you may want to change. You might also need to add pages to your site. Keeping a site organized includes adding new files and folders, placing newly created files or images that you embed on a page into the correct folder so that you know where to look for them when you need them, and deleting files and folders that are not needed.

Plan Ahead

Determine the folder structure of the site.

In addition to renaming files and folders generated by a template, adding and deleting pages can help you to customize a template-based site to your needs.

- **Change the file and folder names.** File and folder names should be meaningful to you, and should be unique for each folder in your site.

- **Remove extraneous pages.** Including too many pages can make your Web site difficult to navigate. Each page that a user can access should provide relevant information; if a template includes a page for which you have no need, remove it to keep your site streamlined.

- **Remove extraneous folders.** Having extra folders can make managing your Web site unnecessarily complicated. Keep the folder structure as simple as possible. If you add pages and folders to the site, a logical and easy-to-follow folder structure will help you manage the site as it grows.

- **Add necessary pages.** Sometimes templates don't provide all the pages you need. You can add a new blank page or create one based on an existing page or dynamic Web template. Choosing the appropriate method depends on the content of the new page. If you are displaying photographic images of a tree and want a separate page for each season of the year, it would make sense to create four pages that are based on the same page so that the layout for spring, summer, fall, and winter is the same, and your reader can focus on the changes in the images of the tree rather than the changes in the page layout or formatting.

- **Add necessary folders.** Adding a new folder, such as one in which to store a newly created page, can help to keep the HTML file and embedded image files for that page in one location.

To Rename a Folder

You can rename any folder or Web page within the Folder List. Folder and filenames should be lowercase and not contain spaces. Expression Web prompts you to instruct the program to update all links and references to the page or folder you are renaming so that your site contains no broken links. The following steps rename a folder.

1

- Click the about_me folder name in the Folder List, then click the folder name again to select it (Figure 3–9).

Q&A

Why did the folder's contents display in the Folder List?

Clicking a selected folder or file-name should select the name for editing. However, if you click it again too fast, it is double-clicked and its contents open. Click the folder name again, and it should select the folder name.

Figure 3–9

2

- Type about_mary, being sure to type the underscore between the two words, as the new name (Figure 3–10).

Figure 3–10

3

- Press ENTER to change the folder name (Figure 3–11).

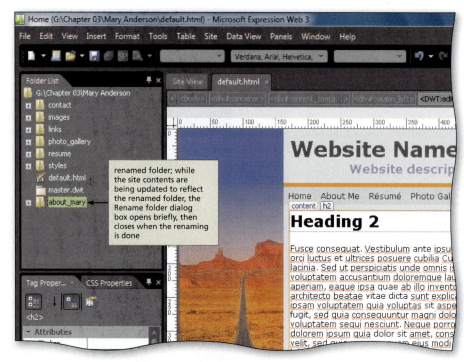

Figure 3–11

To Rename a Web Page

Renaming a Web page is done using the same steps as renaming a folder. Be sure to add the file extension to the page name. You can use either .htm or .html as the file extension, as they are both used to represent HTML files. Be sure to choose which file extension to use before development and use either .htm or .html for all pages in a Web site. Although the files work the same way, it is usually best to choose .html or .htm and be consistent within your site. The following steps rename the about_mary/default.html Web page.

1

- Click the about_mary plus button in the Folder List to expand the folder and view its contents (Figure 3–12).

Q&A

Why is there another default.html file?

When Expression Web creates a site from a template, all of the subfolders include a page called default.html. These are different from the main default.html page, and include the subfolder name in the Web page's file path (i.e., contact/default.html). Make sure when you have several default.html pages open that you are editing the correct one.

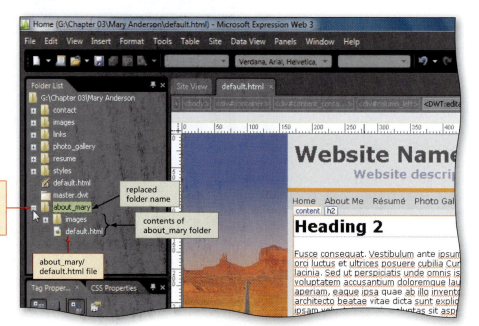

Figure 3–12

2

- Click the default.html filename in the Folder List, then click the filename again to select it.

- Type `about_mary.html`, including the underscore (Figure 3–13).

Figure 3–13

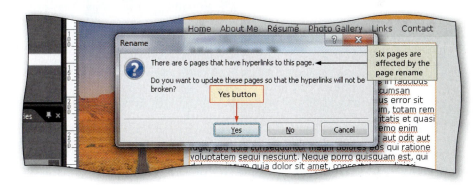

3

- Press ENTER to open the Rename dialog box (Figure 3–14).

- In the Rename dialog box, click the Yes button to update references to the page.

Figure 3–14

Other Ways

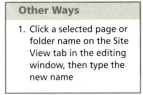

1. Click a selected page or folder name on the Site View tab in the editing window, then type the new name

Modifying the Structure of a Web Site

After determining the site's purpose, objectives, and goals, the next step in planning a site is to determine the number of pages that you will need. In Mary's case, she needs a home page, a résumé page, and a portfolio page. A site created with a template comes with a sample structure, which might not reflect the pages required for your planned site. By deleting, adding, and renaming pages, Mary can organize the structure of her site to reflect her needs, then start customizing or creating the content by adding text and images.

Even though each Web page is stored on your computer as a separate file, you should avoid deleting, renaming, or moving Web site pages or image files using Windows Explorer. When deleting or renaming pages and images with Expression Web, the software prompts you to update all relevant links and make changes within the site that reflect the page deletion. If you use Windows Explorer or another file management program, you risk creating errors, such as broken links, in your site.

BTW

Updating the Navigation Bar
When revising your site structure, you must update the navigation bar to reflect the changes by editing the master.dwt file. You will do so later in this lesson.

To Delete a Web Page

Deleting a page only deletes the HTML file; any folders and embedded files are kept in the site. Removing extra Web pages from your site also helps to reduce the file size of the entire site, increasing its usability. You cannot undo a page or folder deletion, so make sure that you do not need it before you delete it. The following steps delete a Web page, the contact/default.html page, that Mary does not need according to her site plan.

• Click the contact folder plus button in the Folder List to expand the folder and view its contents (Figure 3–15).

Figure 3–15

2

• Click the default.html filename in the Folder List to select it (Figure 3–16).

Figure 3–16

- Click Edit on the menu bar to open the Edit menu, then click Delete to open the Confirm Delete dialog box (Figure 3–17).

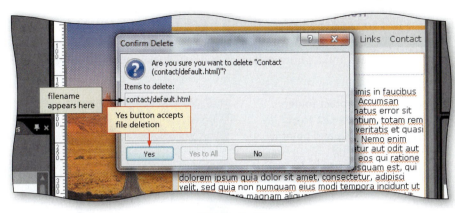

Figure 3–17

4

- In the Confirm Delete dialog box, click the Yes button to delete the file (Figure 3–18).

Figure 3–18

Other Ways

1. Right-click the page name in the Folder List, then click Delete on the shortcut menu to open the Confirm Delete dialog box

2. Click the page name in the Folder List, then press DELETE to open the Confirm Delete dialog box

To Delete a Folder

When you delete a folder, all of its contents are removed. Make sure that any files within the folder are not being used by other pages before you delete a folder and its contents. In the following steps, you will delete folders for contacts, links, and a photo gallery that Mary does not need according to her site plan.

- Right-click the contact folder name in the Folder List to display the shortcut menu, and point to Delete (Figure 3–19).

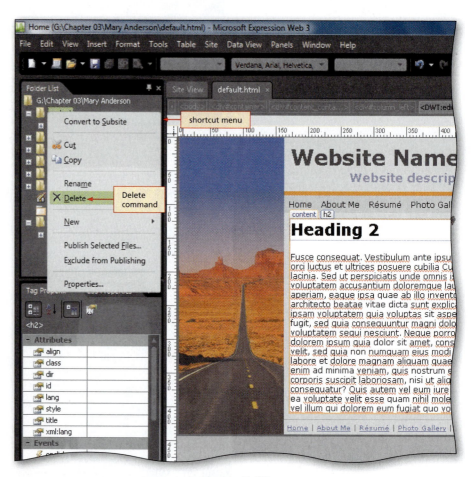

Figure 3–19

- Click Delete to open the Confirm Delete dialog box.

- In the Confirm Delete dialog box, click the Yes button to delete the contact folder (Figure 3–20).

- Repeat Steps 1 and 2 to delete the links and photo_gallery folders.

Figure 3–20

Other Ways

1. Click the folder name in the Folder List, then press DELETE to open the Confirm Delete dialog box

To Add a Folder

When adding folders to a site, it is important to insert them in the appropriate location. New folders often belong in the site's top-level folder, which stores all of the Web site files. To add a folder in this main folder, select the top folder name in the Folder List. Otherwise, your new folder might be created as a subfolder of another folder, which can be confusing and might not function as intended. The following steps add a new folder to Mary's Web site, to which she will add a newly created Web page in accordance with her site plan.

1

• Right-click the Mary Anderson folder name, which is the top folder name in the Folder List, point to New to open the New submenu, then point to Folder (Figure 3–21).

Figure 3–21

2

• Click the Folder command on the New submenu to create a new folder in the Folder List (Figure 3–22).

Figure 3–22

• Type portfolio as the new folder name (Figure 3–23).

Figure 3–23

4

• Press ENTER to rename the folder (Figure 3–24).

Figure 3–24

To Add a Web Page

When you add a page in a site created with a template, you must attach the dynamic Web template to it; otherwise, the page will be blank. You can copy and paste pages in the Folder List to create pages that have similar content and layout and determine whether you need to create a folder in which to store the page, or whether it fits logically into an existing folder. The following steps create the new page Mary needs for a new portfolio, save the page in the portfolio folder, and attach the dynamic Web template to the page so that it matches the other pages in the site.

- Click File on the menu bar to open the File menu, point to New, then point to Create from Dynamic Web Template (Figure 3–25).

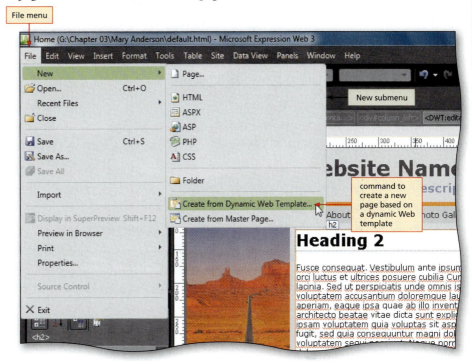

Figure 3–25

- Click Create from Dynamic Web Template to open the Attach Dynamic Web Template dialog box.

- Scroll down, if necessary, then click master to attach it to the new page (Figure 3–26).

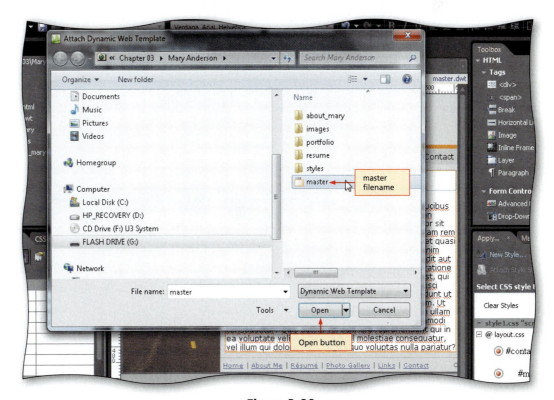

Figure 3–26

- Click the Open button to create a new, untitled Web page.
- Click the Close button to close the alert box (Figure 3–27).

Figure 3–27

- Press CTRL+S to open the Save As dialog box.
- Double-click the portfolio folder in the right pane of the dialog box to open it.
- Select any text in the File name text box, then type `portfolio.html` to name the page (Figure 3–28).

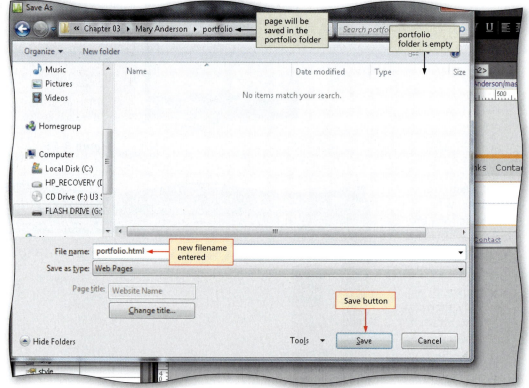

Figure 3–28

5

- Click the Save button to name the new page and save it in the portfolio folder, then click the portfolio folder plus button to view its contents (Figure 3–29).

portfolio folder plus button is now minus button

portfolio.html is saved to portfolio folder

Figure 3–29

6

- Right-click the portfolio.html page tab and point to Close (Figure 3–30).

- Click Close to close the page.

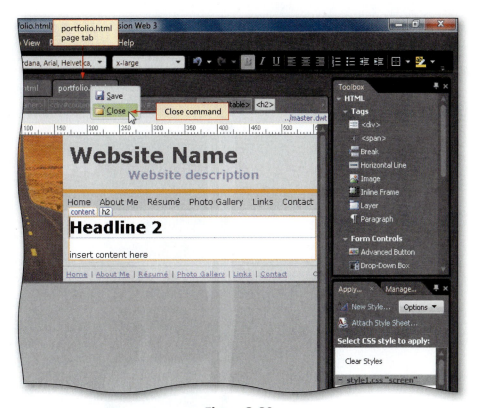

portfolio.html page tab

Close command

Figure 3–30

Entering and Editing Text

All Web pages contain content areas, called **editable regions**, including sidebars, headings, and main content areas. The editable regions are where you include the content and images specific to each page. There are two types of editable regions: headers and body text. Headers are indicated by the header level or description of the content that you should replace it with (such as Heading 1 or About Company). Body text is indicated by Latin text (such as Fusce consequat). Both headers and body text have styles attached to them, but you can modify the formatting to suit your needs.

To enter header or body content, click the area you want to edit, select the div to select all of the placeholder content, then type or paste the new text.

<table>
<tr><td>**Plan Ahead**</td><td>**Determine, accumulate, and organize the content that you will use.**

• Each page should have a header that states its purpose and has appropriate text and graphic content. Make sure to proofread your text before inserting or after typing it into the page. Reusing text from other Web pages or text files will make your work easier and reduces errors.

• Modify the dynamic Web template content on the master.dwt page that is the same for every page: the page title, footer, and navigation area.</td></tr>
</table>

To Replace Template Placeholder Text

Mary's portfolio site needs customized headings. The following steps replace heading placeholder text on the home page.

• If necessary, click the default.html page tab.

• If necessary, click in the words, Heading 2, to show the h2 tag's tab (Figure 3–31).

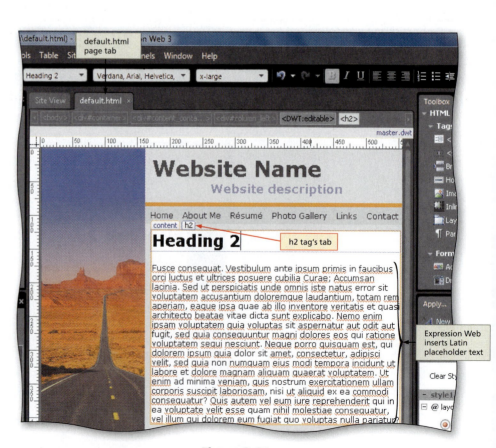

Figure 3–31

- Click the <h2> tag on the Quick Tag Selector to select the heading tag and placeholder text (Figure 3–32).

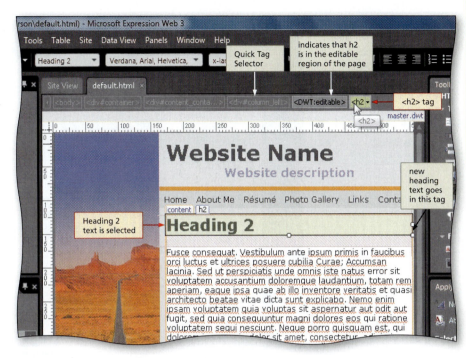

Figure 3–32

3

- Type Who am I? to customize the placeholder (Figure 3–33).

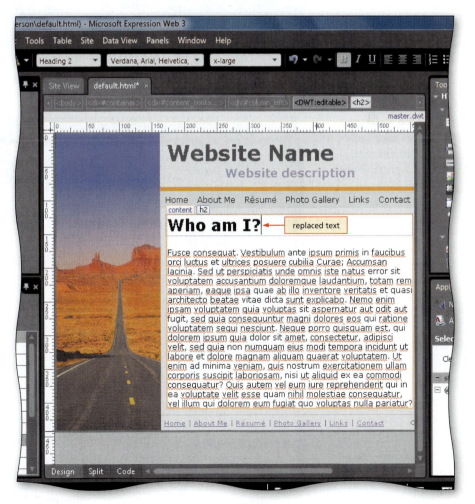

Figure 3–33

4
- If necessary, use the horizontal scroll box to move the page view to the right.
- Click in the words, Heading 4, to show the h4 tab (Figure 3–34).

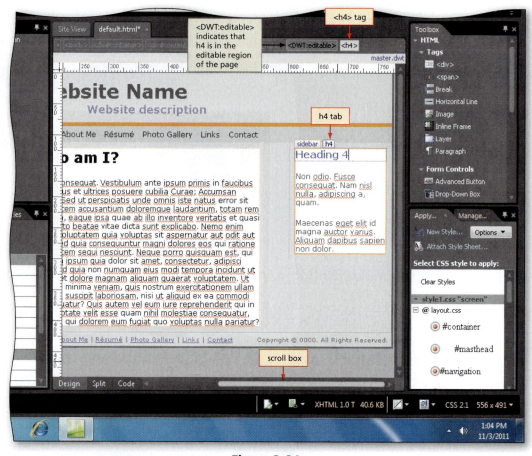

Figure 3–34

5
- Click the <h4> tag on the Quick Tag Selector to select the placeholder text and heading tag (Figure 3–35).

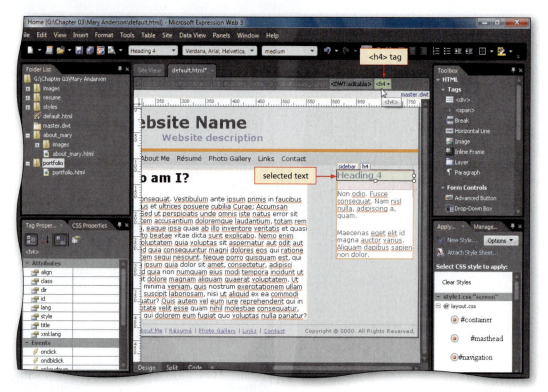

Figure 3–35

6

• Type Objective to customize the placeholder (Figure 3–36).

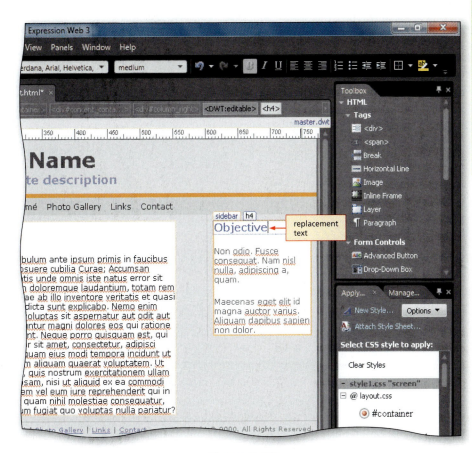

Figure 3–36

7

• Click in the paragraph below the word, Objective.

• Click the <p> tag on the Quick Tag Selector to select the placeholder text and the paragraph tags (Figure 3–37).

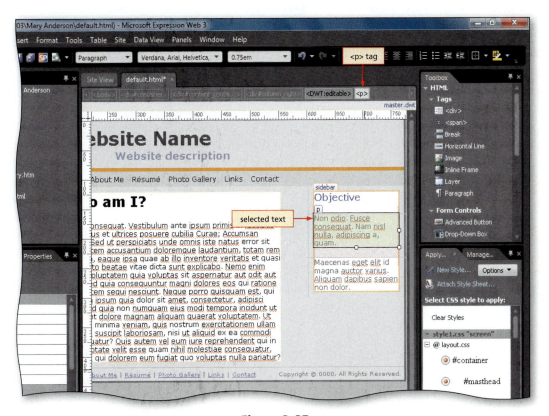

Figure 3–37

8

- **Type** To obtain a job as a Web designer in which I can combine my technical background and business knowledge to create Web sites that are attractive, easy-to-use, and meet the needs of my clients. (Figure 3–38).

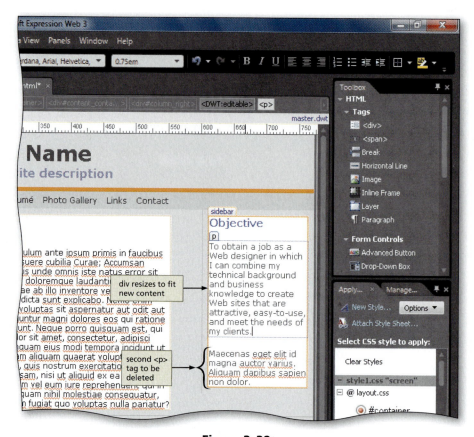

Figure 3–38

9

- Click in the paragraph below the text you just typed, click the <p> tag in the Quick Tag Selector to select the second paragraph in the sidebar, then press DELETE to delete it (Figure 3–39).

- Press CTRL+S to save the page.

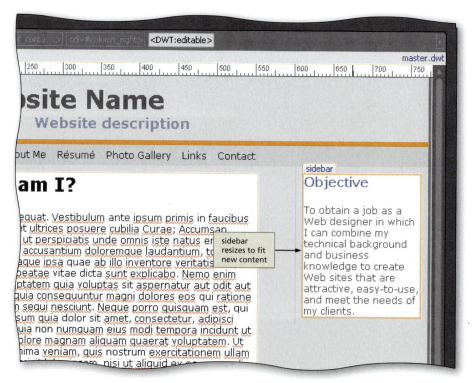

Figure 3–39

Pasting Text

To use content, including text, images, or a table, that is saved in another file or Web page, copy it to the Clipboard, then paste it into the placeholder. The Clipboard, which you used in Chapter 2 to paste text between pages in your site, is shared by other Windows programs and can be used to paste text from other programs, such as Microsoft Word, into Expression Web.

When pasting text into a Web page, it is important to remove any formatting so that it does not clash with the site's formatting. Using the Paste Text command on the Edit menu, you can choose to insert the text with or without line breaks and other paragraph formatting. All character formatting, such as boldface and italics, is removed when using the Paste Text command.

BTW

Removing Formatting
To remove formatting from text, select the text, then click Remove Formatting on the Format menu. Alternatively, you can paste the text and then use the Paste Options button that appears at the bottom of the div containing the pasted text to remove the formatting.

BTW

Extra Line Breaks
Make sure to remove all extra line breaks at the end of a document that you are selecting, or they will appear when pasted into the Web site.

To Paste Text

To insert text from another source, such as a Word document or text file, you first need to open the file in its native program and copy the text to the Clipboard. Mary needs to add her résumé to her Web site. The following steps open Microsoft Word, open a file, copy the text, paste it without formatting into the résumé page, then open another file and do the same.

- Click the Start button on the Windows 7 taskbar to display the Start menu.

- Click All Programs at the bottom of the left pane on the Start menu to display the All Programs list.

- Click the Microsoft Office folder on the All Programs list to display the Microsoft Office list.

- Click Microsoft Office Word 2007 to start Word and open a blank document (Figure 3–40).

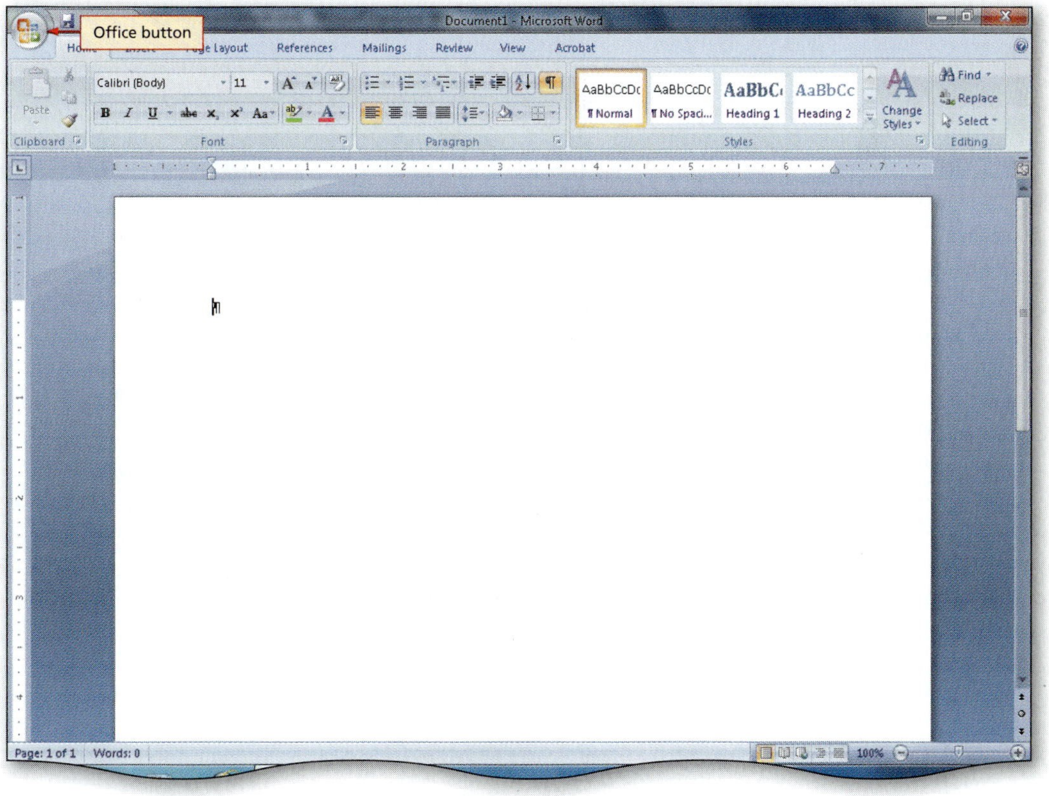

Q&A

What if I don't have Word 2007?

If you have another version of Word you can use that, or use any text editor, such as Notepad or WordPad.

Figure 3–40

● Click the Office button, then click Close to close the blank document.

● Press CTRL+O to open the Open dialog box.

● If necessary, navigate to your data files, open the mary_documents folder, and then select the hometext file (Figure 3–41).

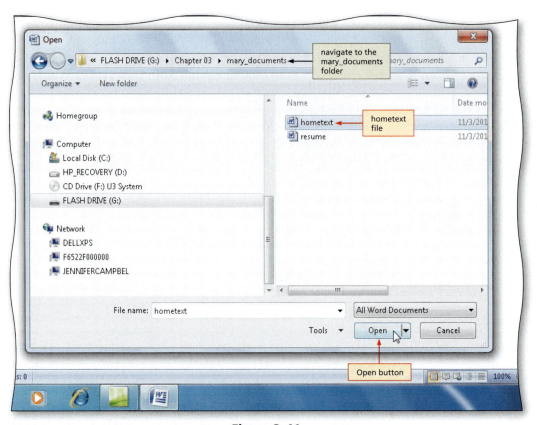

Figure 3–41

● Click the Open button to open the file in Word.

● Press CTRL+A to select all of the text in the document.

● Click the Copy button in the Clipboard group on the Ribbon to copy the selection to the Clipboard (Figure 3–42).

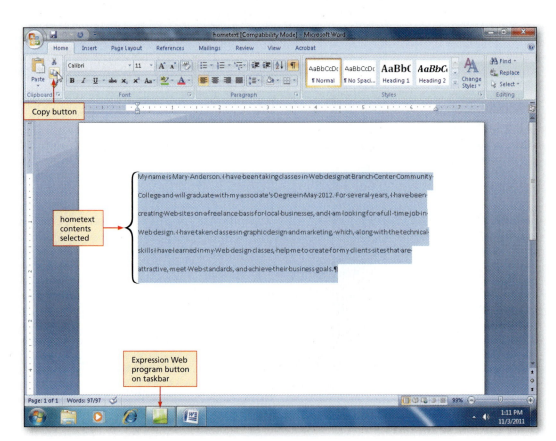

Figure 3–42

4

- Click the Expression Web button on the taskbar to return to Expression Web.

- Scroll if necessary, click in the content div below the text, Who am I?, then click the <p> tag on the Quick Tag Selector to select the paragraph tag and placeholder text (Figure 3–43).

Figure 3–43

5

- Click Edit on the menu bar to open the Edit menu, then point to Paste Text (Figure 3–44).

Figure 3–44

6

- Click Paste Text to open the Paste Text dialog box.

- Click 'Normal paragraphs with line breaks' (Figure 3–45).

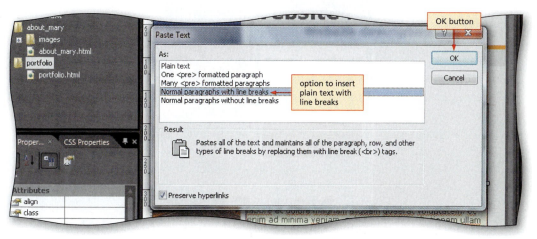

Figure 3–45

7

- Click the OK button to close the dialog box and insert the pasted text.

- Press CTRL+S to save the default. html page.

- Click the hometext Word program button on the taskbar to return to Word.

- Repeat Steps 2 and 3 to open the resume file and copy its contents to the Clipboard, and then return to Expression Web.

- Click the resume folder plus button in the Folder List to view its contents (Figure 3–46).

Figure 3–46

8

- Double-click the default.html page in the resume folder in the Folder List to open it.

- Click the content div tab to select the div tag and text (Figure 3–47).

Figure 3–47

9

- Press DELETE to remove the placeholder text from the content div.

- Click Edit on the menu bar to open the Edit menu, then click Paste Text to open the Paste Text dialog box.

- If necessary, click 'Normal paragraphs with line breaks' (Figure 3–48).

 **Experiment**

- Try pasting text with the other options in the Paste Text dialog box to see the effect.

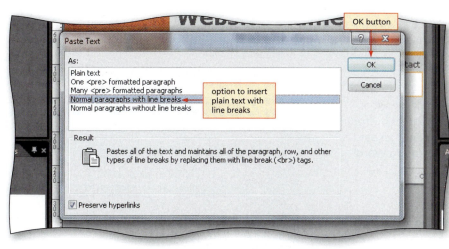

Figure 3–48

10

- Click the OK button to paste the text, then scroll up to show the top of the Web page (Figure 3–49).

- Press CTRL+S to save the default. html page.

Figure 3–49

To Close Microsoft Word

Closing files and quitting programs after you are done working with them frees up computer resources for other tasks and prevents data loss. The following steps close both Microsoft Word windows and the two files, hometext.doc and resume.doc.

- Click the Word program button on the taskbar to return to Word (Figure 3–50).

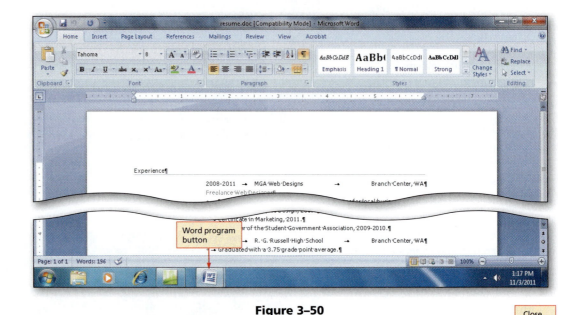

Figure 3–50

- Press CTRL+W to close the resume.doc file (Figure 3–51).

- Click the Close button on the title bar to close the hometext.doc file and the program and return to Expression Web.

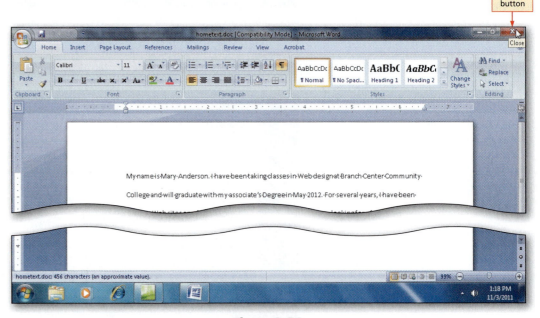

Figure 3–51

Editing Text

When you edit text, you change its content by rewording, removing, adding, or moving words. Sometimes editing requires that you change all occurrences of a word or phrase. Editing can be done directly on the Web page using skills you have likely used in a word-processing program such as Microsoft Word. To edit text by typing additional text or by using keys such as

DELETE or BACKSPACE, you must first position the insertion point (click) where your edits will take place. To delete more than one word or sentence, you must first select the text you want to remove, then delete it by pressing the DELETE or BACKSPACE key, or replace it by typing new text. Table 3–1 outlines different editing commands and shortcuts.

Table 3–1: Editing Commands and Shortcuts

Action	Effect
Double-click a word	Selects the word and the space after it
Triple-click in a paragraph	Selects the paragraph
Press BACKSPACE	Deletes text one character at a time to the left of the insertion point
Press DELETE	Deletes text one character at a time to the right of the insertion point
Press SHIFT, then the left or right ARROW on the keyboard	Selects text one character at a time to the left or right of the insertion point
Press SHIFT and CTRL, then press the left or right arrow on the keyboard	Selects text one word at a time from the left or right of the insertion point

BTW

Quick Reference
For a table that lists how to complete the tasks covered in this book using the mouse, shortcut menu, and keyboard, see the Quick Reference Summary at the back of this book, or visit the Expression Web 3 Quick Reference Web page (scsite.com/ew3/qr).

You can also find and change all instances of a word or phrase using the Find and Replace tools. For instance, to change a person or company's name, you use the Find tool to locate each instance of the name, then replace or ignore each instance individually, or replace all at once.

To Edit Text

The heading of the sidebar is, by default, the page name, Résumé. The sidebar text and heading on the resume page need to be revised to reflect Mary's contact information. When entering lines of text into a paragraph <p> tag, pressing ENTER automatically inserts a new <p> tag for the next line and adds space between the tags. To create multiple lines of text within one paragraph tag, press SHIFT+ENTER instead of ENTER to insert a line break that moves the insertion point to the next line but keeps it in the tag. The following steps edit text using the keyboard to delete and type text and using the mouse to select text.

1
- Use the vertical and horizontal scroll bars, if necessary, to view the sidebar.

- Drag to select the sidebar heading, Résumé, then type Contact Me to replace the placeholder text (Figure 3–52).

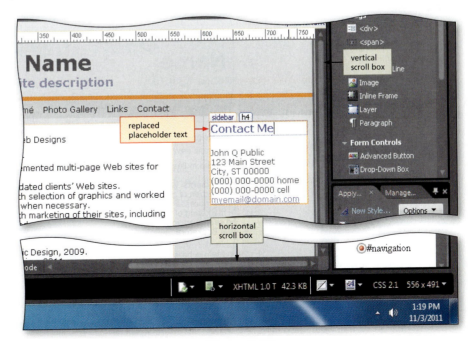

Figure 3–52

6

- Double-click the word, Freelance, which is the first word on the fourth line of the content div, to select it.

- Press BACKSPACE to delete the word (Figure 3–57).

- Press CTRL+S to save the page.

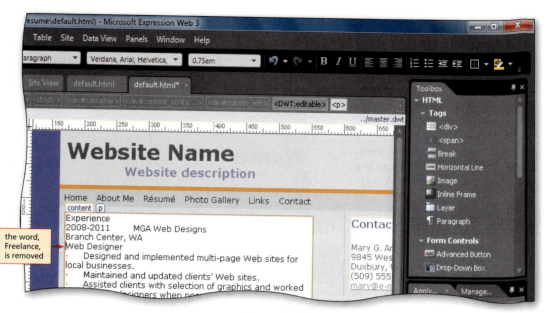

Figure 3–57

To Find and Replace Text

You can use the Find and Replace commands to locate and change single instances or all occurrences of a word or phrase, or use the Replace command on its own to replace words or phrases without first using the Find command. The bookstore where Mary has been working has recently changed its name from Caterpillar to Mariposa. Mary is not sure whether the name change occurred before or after she last saved her résumé, so she will first use the Find command, then the Replace command. The following steps find all instances of the word, Caterpillar, and replace them with Mariposa.

1

- Click Edit on the menu bar to open the Edit menu, then point to Find (Figure 3–58).

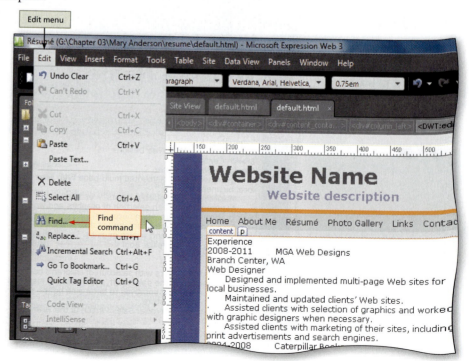

Figure 3–58

- Click Find to open the Find and Replace dialog box.

- If necessary, select any text in the Find what text box and type Caterpillar (Figure 3–59).

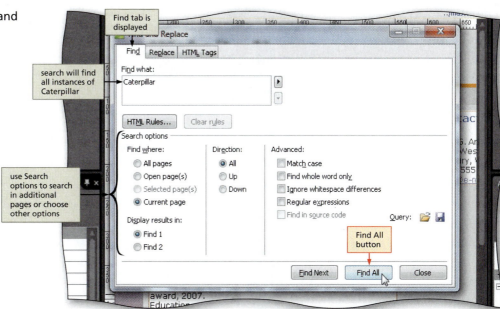

Figure 3–59

❸

- Click the Find All button to display the search results in the Find 1 panel at the bottom of the editing window (Figure 3–60).

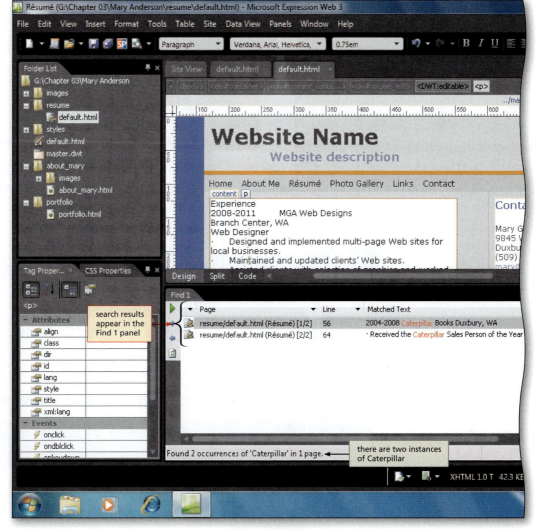

Figure 3–60

4

- Click Edit on the menu bar to open the Edit menu, and then click Replace to open the Find and Replace dialog box.

- If necessary, select any text in the Find what text box and type `Caterpillar`, click in the Replace with text box, and then type `Mariposa` (Figure 3–61).

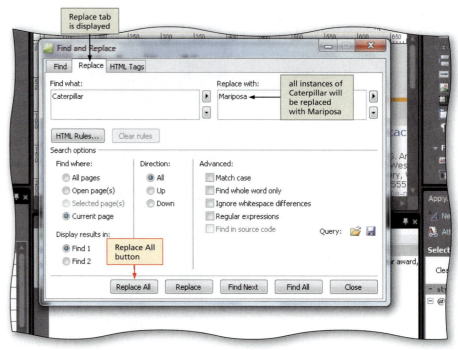

Figure 3–61

5

- Click the Replace All button to replace the text and open an alert box (Figure 3–62).

Figure 3–62

6

- Click the OK button in the alert box to confirm the replacement (Figure 3–63).

 **Experiment**

- Open the Find and Replace dialog box, click the HTML Tags tab, and try searching for tags such as `<div>` and `<p>`.

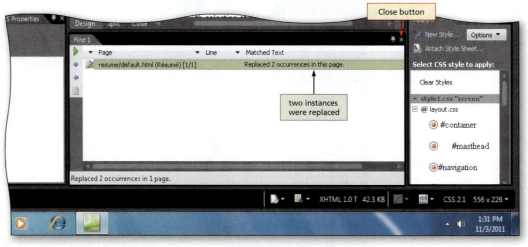

Figure 3–63

7

- Click the Close button on the Find 1 panel to complete the find and replace operation.

- Press CTRL+S to save the résumé page (Figure 3–64).

- Click the Close button on the resume/default.html page tab to close the page.

Q&A What if I get an alert box?

If you get an alert box telling you that you will not be able to undo the Replace command, click Yes or OK, depending on the type of alert you receive. You are still able to undo the replace if necessary.

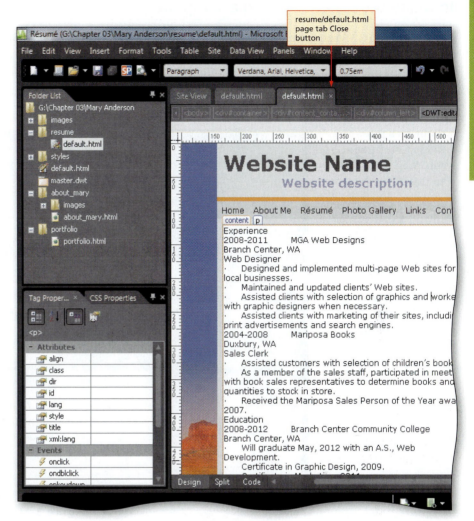

Figure 3–64

Dynamic Web Page Template Pages

Each page in a site contains common text or image elements that relate general information about the site. This information can include a masthead with a company name or logo, a footer with copyright information or the company's address, and a navigation bar with links to the main pages of the site. The dynamic Web template uses placeholders for this information; these placeholders can only be edited from the master.dwt page. Placeholders on the master.dwt page describe the type of information that you need to add, such as Website name or Website description.

To edit master page information, such as the Web site title or description, you must edit the dynamic Web page master file, master.dwt. You should save and close all open pages prior to opening the master.dwt page. When you make edits to the master page, you must save the master page before the changes are applied to the affected pages. You will be prompted to accept the changes for all pages, or you can accept them individually.

BTW

Creating Templates
You can also create a dynamic Web template from an existing page to create additional pages that share the same formatting and layout. To do so, you need to remove all text and define the editable regions.

To Make Global Changes to a Template

All of Mary's Web pages should include a name for her Web site (in this case, her name), a description, and copyright information. The following steps edit the master.dwt page to add text to the masthead and footer. You will also edit the navigation bar on the master.dwt page to reflect the pages you have added and deleted by deleting, renaming, and reassigning the hyperlinks. These changes will be made to all pages that are attached to the template.

- Right-click the default.html page tab, then click Close to close the page.

- Double-click the master.dwt page in the Folder List to open it in the editing window.

- Select the text in the Website Name heading (Figure 3–65).

Figure 3–65

- Type Mary G. Anderson to customize the site name.

- Select the text in the Website description heading, then type Web Design to reflect the site's purpose.

- Scroll right if necessary, click in the Copyright paragraph, select 0000, then type 2011 to update the year (Figure 3–66).

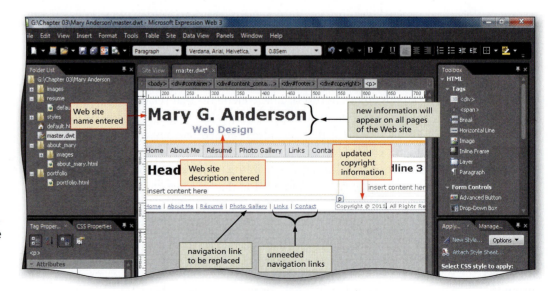

Figure 3–66

3

- In the footer, double-click the word, Contact, to select it.

- Press DELETE to remove the link.

- Select the word, Links, and the vertical lines before and after it, then press DELETE to remove the link and the pipe characters.

- Select the words, Photo Gallery, then type `Portfolio` to change the link name (Figure 3–67).

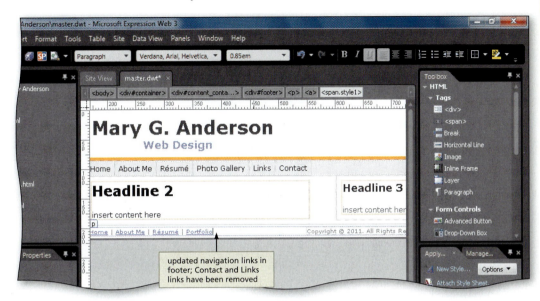

Figure 3–67

4

- In the navigation bar below the Web Design header, click in the word, Contact.

- Click the <a> tag on the Quick Tag Selector bar to select the tag (Figure 3–68).

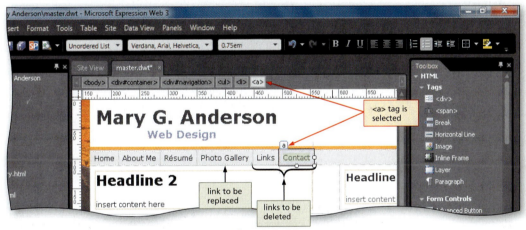

Figure 3–68

5

- Press DELETE to remove the Contact link.

- Select the Links tag, then press DELETE to remove the link.

- Select the words, Photo Gallery, then type `Portfolio` to change the link name (Figure 3–69).

Figure 3–69

6

- Drag to select the word, Portfolio.

- Click Insert on the menu bar to open the Insert menu, then click Hyperlink to open the Edit Hyperlink dialog box (Figure 3–70).

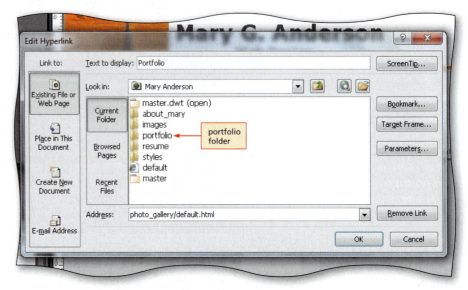

Figure 3–70

7

- Double-click the portfolio folder to open it.

- Click the portfolio file to select it (Figure 3–71).

- Click the OK button to update the hyperlink.

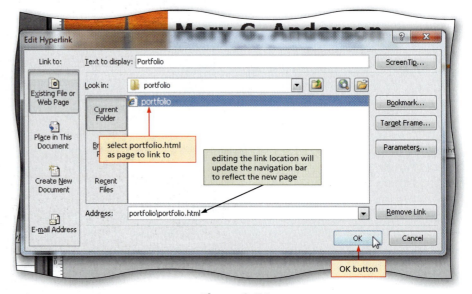

Figure 3–71

8

- Repeat Steps 6 and 7 to update the portfolio link in the bottom navigation bar.

- Press CTRL+S to save the master.dwt page and open an alert box confirming that the changes will be made to all site pages (Figure 3–72).

Figure 3–72

9

- Click the Yes button in the alert box to update the four attached files (Figure 3–73).

Figure 3–73

10

- Click the Close button to close the alert box.

- Click the Close button on the master .dwt page tab to close the master template.

- Double-click the main default.html file in the Folder List to open the default. html page and see the changes you made on the master.dwt page (Figure 3–74).

- Click the Close button on the default.html page tab to close the page.

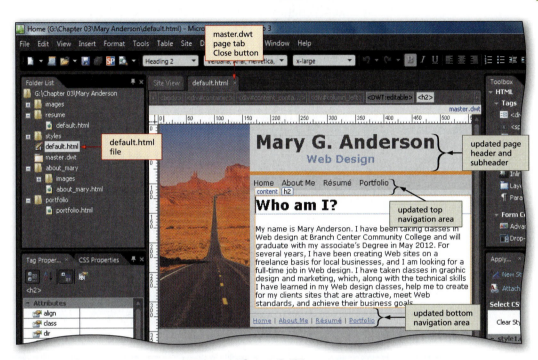

Figure 3–74

Defining Styles and Style Sheets

In a Web page created using an Expression Web template, the layout and formatting are saved to cascading style sheet (CSS) files. You can customize the look of your site by creating, modifying, and applying styles that use a combination of formatting attributes, and that can be used to create consistency across all pages.

A style is a formatting attribute or group of attributes applied to a single character, a word, a section, or an entire Web site. A **style sheet** is a collection of style rules that are applied to specific elements. CSS is a type of style sheet. The style rules list the properties, such as formatting and layout, that apply to an element. Using style sheets ensures consistency of styles among elements. For instance, to change all bulleted lists from round to square bullets, you can simply change the style in the style sheet, and the change is applied to all bulleted lists in your site. Style sheets separate the content of a page (written in HTML) from the formatting. **Cascading** refers to the weighting, or prioritizing, of potential style conflicts. Priority is determined by **specificity**, which generally means that the rule that is higher in the priority is used if there is a conflict. A site can have several style sheets, each of which controls different aspects of formatting and layout. Expression Web templates come with embedded styles saved to style sheets, which are stored in the styles folder.

BTW

Expression Web Help
The best way to become familiar with Expression Web Help is to use it. Appendix A includes detailed information about Expression Web Help and exercises that will help you gain confidence in using it.

BTW

Web Standards
For more information on Web standards, see Appendix B.

Style Sheet Types

Style sheets can be internal, which means they are associated with a page or site, or external, which means they are saved as a separate file that can be applied to multiple pages or sites. By storing styles in a separate file, called an **external style sheet**, you can control the formatting of a site and also apply that style sheet to other pages or sites. Styles can also be saved as an **internal style sheet** by embedding them into the header of an XHTML page; an internal style sheet can only be used on the page in which it is embedded, however. An **inline style** is used to format a section of text and is defined by including a tag in the body of the document. An inline style only applies to the exact section of text or element to which you apply it and cannot be reused for other elements or pages. When style conflicts arise, inline styles have first priority and are applied first, followed by internal styles, then external styles.

BTW

CSS Versions
All browsers support slightly different features of CSS. It is important to test your site using various browsers before publishing it to make sure that the formatting appears the same on all browsers.

Style Rule Syntax

In general, syntax refers to a set of rules; for instance, to specify wording and punctuation in HTML or CSS code. A style rule's syntax has three parts: a **selector** (the element to which the rule applies, such as h1), a **property** (how the element will be changed, such as font style or font size), and a **value** (the specific change or degree of change, such as bold or large). Selectors can refer to a specific element, a class of element, or a single instance of an element.

As with HTML, you do not need to know how to code a style when creating it, but it is important to understand the **syntax**, or the order of the rules. The first part of a style is the selector, followed by the property and value, which together make up the **declaration** (Figure 3–75). Proper use of punctuation, such as braces, semicolons, and colons, ensures that your styles are interpreted correctly by a browser. Make sure to enter a semicolon to separate each style rule, and do not move or delete braces or other punctuation marks, unless you are sure that they are unnecessary.

Figure 3–75

> **Distinguish the site using styles.**
> When deciding on the styles to use in your site, note that you can modify an existing style, create element-based styles that can apply to all instances of an element, or format a specific element or text area by creating a class-based style rule.

Plan Ahead

To Modify a Style

To apply, create, and modify styles and style sheets, you can use the Apply Styles and Manage Styles panels, located below the Toolbox. When you add or edit a style, the style sheet file opens and needs to be saved along with the page that you are modifying.

Mary would like to modify the look of her site by revising the appearance of the links. The following steps change the style of the navigation bar.

- Double-click the master.dwt page in the Folder List to open it.

- In the Apply Styles panel, point to the #navigation style, click the arrow to open the menu, and then point to Modify Style (Figure 3–76).

Figure 3–76

Apply Your Knowledge *continued*

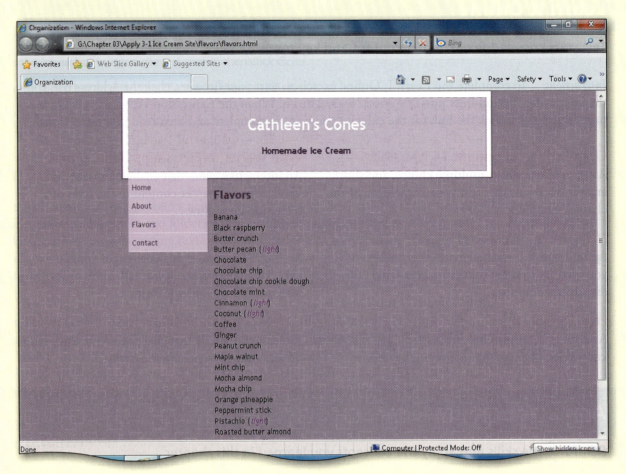

Figure 3–93

Perform the following tasks:

1. Create a new site called Apply 3-1 Ice Cream Site using the Organization 4 site template.

2. Open the faq folder.

3. Delete the faq/default.html file.

4. Delete the faq, information_links, news, photo_gallery, and calendar folders.

5. Add a new folder named menu to the top folder in the site (the one that lists the drive and folder name).

6. Insert a new page into the menu folder and attach the master.dwt file to it.

7. Save the new page as flavors.html in the menu folder.

8. Change the name of the menu folder to flavors.

9. If necessary, open the flavors.html page.

10. Open Microsoft Word 2007.

11. Open the document flavors.doc from the Apply 3-1 documents folder in your data files folder.

12. Select the list and copy the text to the Clipboard, then close Word.

13. Return to Expression Web.

14. Select the text in the paragraph tag below Heading 2.

15. Click Edit on the menu bar, then click Paste Text.

16. Click the 'Normal paragraphs with line breaks' option, then click OK.

17. Replace all instances of lowfat with light.

18. Select the Heading 2 tag, then type `Flavors`.

19. Save the flavors page, then close it.

20. Open the master.dwt page.

21. Change the left navigation bar to have four links: `Home`, `About`, `Flavors`, and `Contact`.

22. Change the hyperlink of the Flavors link to link to `flavors.html`.

23. Select the paragraph tag containing the bottom navigation bar and delete it. Then, delete the footer div.

24. Change the main heading (Organization) to `Cathleen's Cones` and the subheading (Organization Description) to `Homemade Ice Cream`, then save and close the master.dwt page, updating attached pages.

25. Create a new class-based style called `.light` in the style1.css file.

26. Assign the Purple font color and the italic font style to the .light style.

27. Open the flavors.html page, then apply the .light style to the four instances of the word, light.

28. Save the style1.css style sheet and the flavors.html page.

29. Preview the site and test the links, then close the browser.

30. Change the site properties, as specified by your instructor, then close the site. Submit the revised site in the format specified by your instructor.

Extend Your Knowledge

Extend the skills you learned in this chapter and experiment with new skills. You may need to use Help to complete the assignment.

Modifying a Template

Instructions: Start Expression Web. Create a new site based on a template, and then modify the text and styles in the master.dwt file to make the default.html page match the one shown in Figure 3–94.

Continued >

Extend Your Knowledge *continued*

Figure 3–94

Perform the following tasks:

1. Use Help to learn about adding an editable region to a dynamic Web template.

2. Use the Organization 2 template to create a Web site named Extend 3-1 Softball Site, then open the master.dwt page.

3. Click before the Home link in the footer, press ENTER, then click the blank paragraph above the footer.

4. Point to Dynamic Web Template on the Format menu, then click Manage Editable Regions.

5. In the Editable Regions dialog box, type `fact` in the Region name text box.

6. Click the Add button, then click the Close button.

7. Create a new style named `.fact`.

8. Choose the medium font size, the italic font style, and the Maroon color, then click the OK button.

9. Drag to select the fact paragraph placeholder text, then apply the .fact style.

10. Replace ORGANIZATION with `THE LASALLE SHARKS`, then replace Organization Description with `Girls' Softball`.

11. Save the master.dwt page, update all attached pages, close the master.dwt page, then open the main default.html page.

12. Replace the contents of the Heading 2 tag with `The 2011 Season is here!`.

13. Replace the contents of the paragraph tag under the heading with `Players, parents, and fans... Get ready for another great year of Sharks softball`.

14. Change the sidebar heading to 2010 League Champions.

15. Change the sidebar caption to Congratulations to the 2010 Sharks, who won the Tri-County League Champion game 10-8.

16. Delete the sidebar photo.

17. Replace the contents of the fact paragraph with Shortstop Katie Yang has a 3.9 GPA and plays the viola.

18. Save the default.html page, preview the page, then close the browser window.

19. Change the site properties, as specified by your instructor. Submit the revised site in the format specified by your instructor.

Make It Right

Analyze a site and correct all errors and/or improve the design.

Placing and Formatting Images

Instructions: Start Expression Web. Open the Web site, Make It Right 3-1 Tools, from the Data Files for Students. Additional files needed for this activity are located in the Make It Right 3-1 Files folder. See the inside back cover of this book for instructions for downloading the Data Files for Students, or contact your instructor for information about accessing the required files.

   The site needs to be revised to match Figure 3–95. In the master.dwt page, change the contact information, remove the Calendar link from the two navigation bars, and change the copyright information in the footer. Update the links in the bottom navigation bar by deleting those not on the side navigation bar, making sure the order matches the side navigation bar, and that the links in the bottom navigation bar all appear on one line. One of the unneeded links should be changed to the Contact link which links to the contact/contact.html page. Also insert and apply the tool_logo.gif to the master. dwt page, change the size of the logo, and apply transparency to the logo's background color (*Hint:* to change the logo image, right-click the Logo placeholder, then click Picture Properties on the short-cut menu, then click Browse and open tool_logo from the Make It Right 3-1 Files folder in your Chapter 03 data files). After the image is inserted, use the Appearance tab on the Picture Properties dialog box to change the width to 150. Use the Pictures toolbar to make the background color of the logo transparent. Delete the msfp_smbus2_01.jpg image. On the main default.html page, delete the msfp_smbus2_01.jpg image, change the headline, description, and subheading as shown in Figure 3–95. Insert the New Sales Opportunity subheading and then copy and paste the contents of the tool_sales .doc file from the Make It Right 3-1 Files folder into the paragraph placeholder. Delete the remaining placeholder text and tags. Create a new style on the style1.css style sheet called .highlight that uses bold, italics, Navy font color, and small font size, and apply it as shown in Figure 3–95. Delete the extra content folders (*Hint:* keep the images and styles folders).

   Change the site properties, as specified by your instructor. Rename the site folder, Make It Right 3-1 Tools Site. Submit the revised site in the format specified by your instructor.

Continued >

Make It Right *continued*

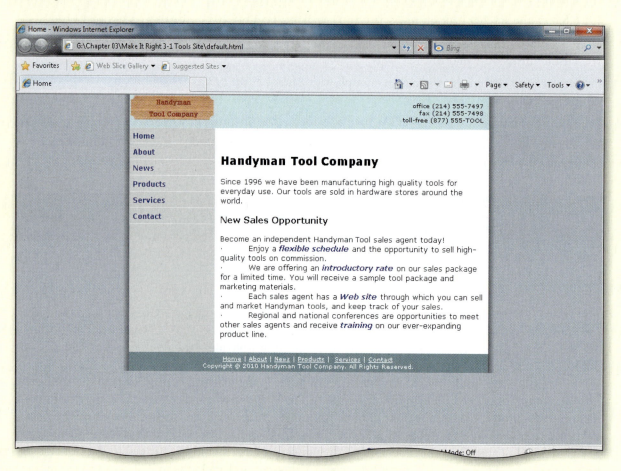

Figure 3–95

In the Lab

Design and/or format a Web site using the guidelines, concepts, and skills presented in this chapter. Labs are listed in order of increasing difficulty.

Lab 1: Creating a New Site from a Template

Problem: You have been hired to create a Web site for a local park. As part of creating the site, you are to add and edit page content. Use a template to create the new site, and insert and edit text to create the site shown in Figure 3–96.

Figure 3–96

Instructions:

1. Start Expression Web.

2. Create a new Web site called Lab 3-1 Park Site using the Organization 1 template.

3. Open the master.dwt page. Replace the word, ORGANIZATION, with FOREST EDGE PARK. Replace the words, Organization Description, with Mitcheltown, Delaware.

4. Save and close the master.dwt page, and update all associated pages.

5. In the Folder List, click the about plus button. Change the about/default.html filename to about .html and update links.

6. Open the about.html page. Change the Heading 2 About placeholder to About Forest Ridge Park.

7. Start Word and open the about_park.doc file from the Lab 3-1 documents folder. Select and copy the text, then close the file and Word.

8. Paste the text as normal paragraphs without line breaks into the paragraph under About Forest Ridge Park. If necessary, delete any empty paragraphs that follow the pasted text.

9. Use the Replace command to replace all instances of the word, Ridge, with Edge. Close the Find and Replace dialog box.

10. In the right sidebar, replace the words, Additional Resources, with Natural Beauty. In the paragraph below Natural Beauty, replace the placeholder text by typing Forest Edge Park was created to preserve the area as an open space for Mitcheltown residents and to protect the wildlife and plant life that call it home.

11. Save the changes to the about.html page, preview the site in a browser, then close the browser and the page.

12. Close the site, then submit the site in the format specified by your instructor.

In the Lab

Lab 2: Replacing Template Text and Modifying the Dynamic Web Template

Problem: You are the owner of an interior design company. You want to create a Web site you can use to attract new clients. Use a template to create a new site, modify the site contents, and modify styles to create the site shown in Figure 3–97.

Figure 3–97

Instructions:

1. Start Expression Web.

2. Create a new Web site called Lab 3-2 Interior Design Site using the Personal 7 template.

3. Change the contact folder name to `clients`, and change the contact/default.html filename to `clients.html`, updating links.

4. Open the master.dwt page. In both navigation bars, change the Contact link name to `Clients`. Verify that the hyperlinks for both link to the clients.html page and edit if necessary.

5. Replace the words, My Website, with `Beachfront Design`. Replace the words, Website description, with `by Maggie Waterson`.

6. Add the styles as noted in Table 3–2 below. The styles should be defined in the current page. The #masthead h3 style already exists and therefore can be modified.

Table 3–2

Style Name	Affects	Values
#masthead h1	Beachfront Design	Navy; bold; Times New Roman, Times, serif; xx-large
#masthead h3	by Maggie Waterson	Black; italic; Times New Roman, Times, serif; large
#navigation	Top navigation bar	Navy; bold; Times New Roman, Times, serif
h2	Headline 2	Navy; bold; Times New Roman, Times, serif; x-large
a	Bottom navigation bar	Navy; Times New Roman, Times, serif

7. Save and close the master.dwt page, and update all attached pages. Save and close the style3.css file.

8. In the Folder List, click the about_me plus button. Change the about_me/default.html filename to about_me.html.

9. Open the about_me.html page. Change Heading 2 to About Me.

10. Start Word, and open the aboutme.doc file from the Lab 3-2 documents folder. Select and copy the text, then close the file and Word.

11. Select the placeholder text in the paragraph under About Me, then paste the copied text as normal paragraphs without line breaks. If an empty paragraph appears below these new paragraphs, delete it.

12. Delete the bottom sidebar div. In the right sidebar, type "Our beach cottage is a fun, casual retreat." (Sarah M., Nantucket).

13. Save the changes to the about_me.html page, then preview the site in a browser.

14. Change the site properties, as specified by your instructor.

15. Close the site and then submit the site in the format specified by your instructor.

In the Lab

Lab 3: Creating and Applying Styles

Problem: Your client owns a coffee shop and has asked you to add a page with a menu to a site he has created using a template. Create a new page, add links to it, and create and apply styles to format the page as shown in Figure 3–98.

Figure 3–98

Continued >

In the Lab *continued*

Instructions: Start Expression Web. Open the Web site, Lab 3-3 Coffee, from the Data Files for Students. An additional file needed for this activity is located in the Lab 3-3 documents folder of the Data Files for Students. See the inside back cover of this book for instructions for downloading the Data Files for Students, or see your instructor for information about accessing the required files.

Perform the following tasks.

1. Create a new folder in the main site folder called `menu`.

2. Create a new page from a dynamic Web template, using the master.dwt page from the site. Save the page as `menu.html` in the menu folder.

3. Select the text, Headline 2, then type `Menu`.

4. Open Word. Open the file menu.doc from the Lab 3-3 documents folder. Select all of the text, then copy it to the Clipboard. Close the document and quit Word.

5. Use the Paste Text command to insert the copied text into the paragraph under the Menu heading using normal paragraphs without line breaks.

6. Create a new style called `.category` and define it in the existing style0.css style sheet. Format the style with the large font size, bold font weight, and small-caps font variant. Click the underline and overline check boxes in the text-decoration section, then click OK to complete the new style.

7. Create a new style called `.item` and define it in the style0.css style sheet. Format the style with the medium font size, italic font style, and Silver color. Click OK to complete the new style. Attach the style0.css style sheet to the menu.html page. (*Hint:* Open the menu.html page. Click the Attach Style Sheet link in the Apply Styles task pane. Click the Browse button, navigate to and click style0. css, click the OK button, then click the OK button to attach the style sheet.)

8. Apply the .category style to the following lines: JUST FOR BREAKFAST, MUFFINS, SCONES/ BISCUITS/CROISSANTS, FOR THE YOUNG AT HEART, and DRINKS.

9. Apply the .item style to the following lines: Sandwich, Parfait, Morning Glory, Blueberry Bran, Corn, Lowfat Raspberry, White Chocolate Ginger, Cheddar Chive Biscuit, Croissant, Strawberry Tart, Blueberry Turnover, and Cinnamon Twist.

10. Save and close the menu.html page and the style sheet, if necessary.

11. Open the master.dwt page and create a link in both navigation areas from the word, Menu, to the menu.html page. Save and close the master.dwt page and update attached files.

12. Preview the main default.html page in a browser.

13. Change the site properties, as specified by your instructor.

14. Close the site, rename the site folder Lab 3-3 Coffee Site, then submit the site in the format specified by your instructor.

Cases and Places

Apply your creative thinking and problem-solving skills to design and implement a solution.

- • Easier   •• More Difficult

• 1: Changing a Site Structure

Practice adding and removing pages and folders to and from a Web site by first creating a site using any template. Delete a folder and its contents. Open a folder that contains a page and delete the page, then delete the folder. Rename a file and folder. Add a new folder to the main directory, then add a new page based on the master.dwt page to the new folder. Close the site without saving any changes, then quit Expression Web.

• 2: Make Global Changes to a Web Site

Create a new site for your book club using a template. Delete at least one page and its folder. Open the master.dwt page, and add a title and description for your site. Update the navigation area by deleting references to the pages you deleted. Change other information, such as copyright or logo, as necessary. Save and close the master.dwt page. Open the default.html page and view the changes you made.

•• 3: Paste and Edit Text

Using one of the Small Business templates, create a site for a travel agency. Use Word to create an itinerary for a trip you have taken or would like to take. Include a word that you will later replace with another after you have pasted the text into your Web site. Copy and paste the text into a page in your Web site. Use the Replace command to find and replace at least one word in the text. Practice selecting words and characters and deleting text. Enter text into the other editable regions on the page, then save and close the page. Open the master.dwt page, then edit the placeholder text. Save and close the master.dwt page, then close the site.

•• 4: Create a Personal Home Page

Make It Personal

You want to create a site that includes your résumé and information about you. Create a new site using one of the Personal templates. Enter information on the master.dwt page and the default.html page, then save and close the pages. Use Word to create a résumé, open a previously created résumé, or open the résumé file from the project in this chapter. Copy the résumé to the Clipboard. Open the résumé page, then paste the résumé from the Clipboard. Create at least two styles and apply them to the résumé page to format it. Save the pages and style sheets, then close the site.

•• 5: Enhance Text Using Styles

Working Together

Your local pizzeria wants to create a site for its business with three pages: home, menu, and directions. Working as a team with several of your classmates, plan and create the Web site. As a group, decide on the name of the restaurant and the menu. Each team member should create the text for the three pages in Word. As a group, decide on an Expression Web template for the pizzeria site. Add, delete, and rename pages as necessary so that your site contains the appropriate pages. Edit the text and navigation area(s) on the master.dwt page as necessary. Modify two of the existing styles in the style sheet. On each of the three pages, edit the placeholder text and insert the Word files you have created. On the menu and directions pages, create and apply at least two styles. Preview the site, test the navigation bar, and make sure that your site is readable and attractive. Save and close the pages and style sheet, then close the site.

Expression Web Design Feature

Web Design Basics

Objectives

You will have mastered the material in this special feature when you can describe how to:

- Identify a Web site's purpose, target audience, and structure

- Plan a site's navigation system

- Use color and page layout to unify the look and feel of a Web site

- Write and format effective Web page text

- Select and format appropriate Web page images, animation, and multimedia elements

- Perform pre- and post-publishing testing

Identifying Your Site's Target Audience

Potential visitors to a site are called its **target audience**. A site might have more than one target audience. Identifying the target audience requires developing a general profile for audience members. While the target audience for a small personal site might be well known to the site's owner, a small business owner or the management of a large commercial enterprise will likely find it necessary to research the demographic characteristics (age, gender, educational level, income, and so forth) and psychographic characteristics (social group affiliations, purchasing preferences, political affiliations, and so forth) that define their sites' target audience in order to build a satisfactory profile.

Good sources of material for developing a target audience profile include the U.S. Department of Labor, the Census Bureau, and the Small Business Administration Web sites and publications. After creating a target audience profile to identify who will likely visit your site, you should determine the types of pages to be featured at your site and each page's general content.

Types of Web Pages

Your site will have a starting page, called its home page. Because the home page is generally the primary page at a site — and often a visitor's entry point to the site — it is important that the home page content answers three important questions:

- *Who* owns and publishes the site?
- *What* information is available at the site?
- *Where* is specific information located at the site?

Figure SF 1–2, the Harry & David site home page, illustrates content that adequately answers visitors' Who?, What?, and Where? questions. The owner's name, graphic logo, and similar identifying content elements on the home page identify the site's owner. Text and images on the home page tell visitors what information or features can be found at the site, while links tell visitors where the information or features are located at the site.

Figure SF 1–2

The type and number of additional pages, called **subsidiary pages**, vary depending on a site's purpose. While a personal Web site might include only a home page and one or two subsidiary pages, a commercial Web site is likely to have a much more complex set of subsidiary pages. For example, Figure SF 1–3 illustrates just three subsidiary pages of the many pages at the Harry & David site: a product catalog page, a shopping cart page, and an About Us page. Each of these subsidiary pages can be quickly viewed by clicking a link on the Harry & David home page.

BTW

Adding Contrast
Choose font colors that contrast strongly with the page background. Only use light-colored fonts on very dark backgrounds. When selecting a background color, keep in mind that it should be either very dark or very light to allow for enough font contrast to be readable.

Color Schemes

Color is an important design tool that you can use to ensure the unity and overall look and feel of your Web site's pages. To create an attractive and appropriate color scheme, you can choose three or four colors; for example, from the primary or secondary colors on the traditional color wheel (Figure SF 1–8). Choose colors that both set the mood — energetic and fun, competent and trustworthy, or crisp and businesslike — for your site and also help communicate its message. Figures SF 1–9 and SF 1–10 illustrate the different color schemes that support the very different Web site messages at the TD Waterhouse home page and Ben & Jerry's Fun page for kids.

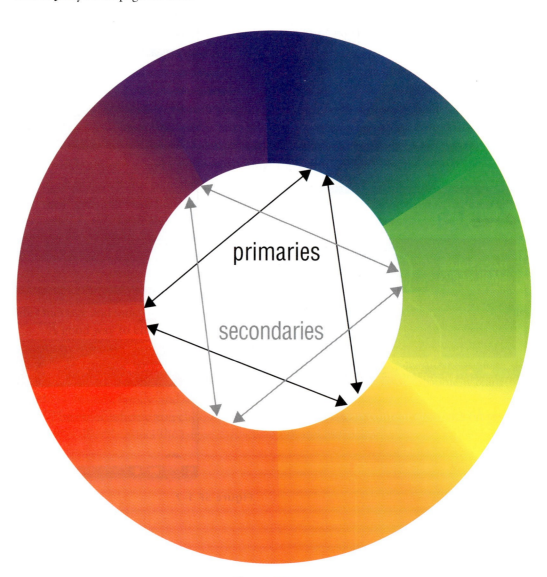

Figure SF 1–8

calm, business-like color scheme invokes feelings of confidence and trust

Figure SF 1–9

lively color scheme sets the mood for fun and play

Figure SF 1–10

BTW

Web-Safe Palette
The Web-safe palette consists of 216 of the 256 colors that can be displayed by an 8-bit computer screen. Because most Web site visitors today use computer screens that can display millions of colors, many Web designers no longer adhere to the Web-safe palette.

Additionally, you should choose background and foreground colors that provide adequate contrast. For example, the light-colored background, dark text, and complementary accent colors in the TD Waterhouse site's color scheme provide an appropriate background and foreground contrast, as do the more vibrant colors in the Ben & Jerry's Fun page color scheme.

Colors have significant psychological and cultural traits that you must consider when choosing your Web site's color scheme. To learn more about color traits and designing with color, visit **scsite.com/ew3/websources** and click a link under Special Feature 1, Designing with Color.

Page Length and Content Positioning

Web site visitors characteristically dislike scrolling Web pages either vertically or horizontally, so you should create a logical layout for each of your site's pages that keeps page length as close to a single screen's viewing area as possible while also positioning the most important content elements so that visitors can easily see and access them. For example, consider positioning identifying information, such as a logo or name, in the upper-left corner of each page, major navigational elements near the top and/or on the left side of each page, and important text and image content in one or two columns in the center of the page below and to the right of the identifying and navigational elements — all within a single viewing screen, if possible.

The Our Food: Food Facts page at the Taco Bell Web site (Figure SF 1–11) successfully limits page length to a single screen (when viewed at the common 1024 × 768 screen resolution). Additionally, critical navigational and identification content are effectively positioned at the top of each page.

Figure SF 1–11

The screen resolution at which visitors view your Web pages will vary and can affect their need to scroll pages either vertically or horizontally (or both) to view the pages' content. To learn more about designing Web sites to accommodate different screen resolutions, visit **scsite.com/ew3/websources** and click a link under Special Feature 1, Screen Resolution.

Arranging individual elements on a page so that the page conveys the correct message and evokes the desired mood requires that you combine the basic design concepts of balance, proximity, alignment, and focus in positioning page content elements.

BTW

Legal and Privacy Issues

Certain types of content related to legal and privacy issues, such as a copyright statement or links to pages that contain the site owner's privacy policy statement or its disclaimer of liability statement, are generally positioned at the bottom of a site's pages.

Balance, Proximity, Alignment, and Focus

Balance refers to the symmetric (in balance) or asymmetric (out of balance) arrangement of elements in relationship to each other. Like color, balance can set the mood of a Web site. For example, the U.S. House of Representatives site's home page (Figure SF 1–12) uses a symmetric arrangement of content elements to evoke a profes- sional, conservative mood. On the other hand, an educational site directed at children, such as the Discovery Kids site (Figure SF 1–13), can effectively use an asymmetric arrangement of elements to create a mood of excitement, enthusiasm, and fun.

a calming, symmetric arrangement of content

Figure SF 1–12

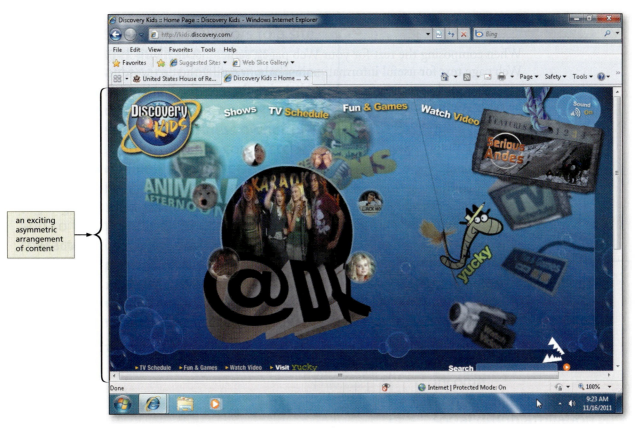

an exciting asymmetric arrangement of content

Figure SF 1–13

Placing related content elements near each other — for example, an image and its caption — uses **proximity** to visually link the related elements. **Alignment** of page elements horizontally and/or vertically gives a page a well-organized, professional look. The most dominant element, or **focal point**, on a page is the element upon which visitors concentrate their attention when they view a page. Photographs or other striking images, such as those in the center column in Figure SF 1–12, are commonly used as a page's focal point. The U.S. House of Representatives home page illustrates the effective use of balance, proximity, alignment, and focus to grab visitors' attention and reinforce the site's message: Check out the Congressional resources available here!

One of the most important content elements at your site is the text you use to convey accurate and current information. How you write and organize your site's textual content plays an important role in enhancing your site's usability.

BTW

Layout Tables and Frames
Although Web standards support using CSS to control element positioning and page layout, most modern WYSIWYG editors, including Expression Web, also provide tools for using layout tables to control element positioning. Using frames to display multiple Web pages on the same screen is, like layout tables, considered to be an outdated layout approach.

4 | Creating Styles and Layouts with CSS

Objectives

You will have mastered the material in this chapter when you can:

- Create ID-based styles
- Position content with CSS
- Format text with CSS
- Identify CSS syntax
- Use the CSS Properties panel
- Create a font family
- Create an external style sheet

- Modify a style sheet using code
- Attach a style sheet
- Add a Web page using CSS layouts
- Copy and paste elements among pages
- Organize style sheets
- Create a CSS report

4 | Creating Styles and Layouts with CSS

Introduction

Styles are rules used to control the formatting and layout of pages as well as individual elements and text in a Web page. The goal of using styles is to create consistently formatted pages that can be easily updated. You can apply styles directly to text or an element to format it individually, or you can save groupings of styles to a file called a **style sheet**. When a style sheet is **attached** to a Web page or pages, or to all pages in a Web site, it formats all like elements the same way. You can apply multiple style sheets to a single Web page: one for layout and one for text formatting, for instance.

Expression Web uses **Cascading Style Sheets (CSS)**, a style sheet language, to store style rules. CSS is the W3C preferred method for page layout and font. Expression Web is a great tool for using CSS to define formatting and layout. Expression Web will even create styles for you based on changes that you make to your page content, and uses panels and dialog boxes to create, modify, and apply styles. The actual styles are saved to style sheets as CSS files, which can be viewed and edited by using the style language to enter and modify the style code.

Project — Gallery Web Site

Galisteo Art Gallery in Goldstream, California, has a Web site that is in need of enhancing. The site currently consists of a few pages of simple text and images. The owner would like the site to look more professional and have the page elements consistent within the site. She also wants to add a new page that has a different layout and use CSS to make the new page's formatting consistent with the other site pages.

The project in this chapter uses Expression Web to create, modify, and apply formatting and layout guidelines using CSS to enhance the content and images of the unformatted Web site. The consistently formatted elements will appear on each page. You will create a new style sheet and define style rules while viewing the style sheet code. You will also add a page that uses CSS to define its layout and run a report to check for unused or incorrect CSS codes. The enhanced site is shown in Figure 4–1.

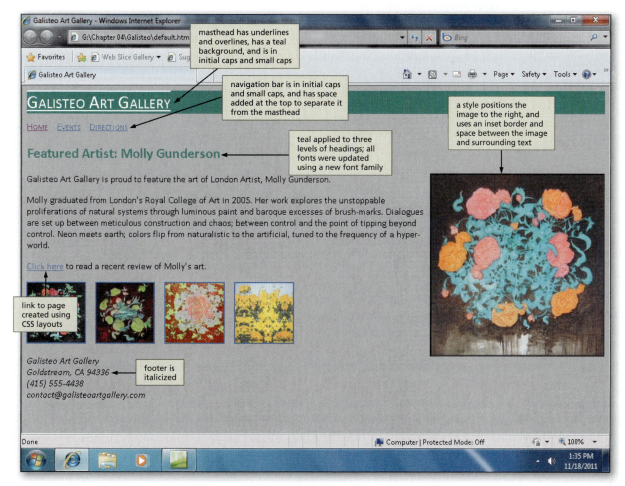

Figure 4–1

Overview

As you read this chapter, you will learn how to create the Web site shown in Figure 4–1 by performing these general tasks:

- Use CSS to format and lay out Web pages
- Create and modify styles
- Create a new font family
- Create an external style sheet
- Modify style sheet codes
- Attach a style sheet to pages in a Web site
- Add a Web page using CSS layouts
- Create a CSS report

Plan Ahead

General Project Guidelines

When formatting a Web site with CSS, you should keep in mind the purpose of using styles: to create consistent, accessible Web sites that are easy to maintain.

As you plan to enhance a Web site using styles, such as the one shown in Figure 4–1, you should follow these general guidelines:

1. **Define formatting and layout using styles.** Formatting and layout are two ways to enhance and organize your site. With CSS, you can use and create style rules that define the appearance (formatting) and position (layout) for each element on your Web site.

2. **Create your own styles and style sheets.** Saving the styles you create in Expression Web to a style sheet allows you to edit the style sheet(s) to make modifications to your site by rewriting the code or using panels and dialog boxes. When saving styles, you must specify whether the styles are part of an inline style that is used for only one instance of one element, as an embedded or internal style sheet that is applied only to the current page, or as an external style sheet that you can apply to other Web pages. Viewing the CSS style rules in Expression Web's Code view allows you to see text-based code that you can modify, copy, and reprioritize. Attaching the same style sheet to multiple pages ensures style consistency.

3. **Evaluate style sheets.** You can test the compatibility of your site with its associated style sheet(s) by running a CSS report. A CSS report alerts you to areas that you may need to fix, such as unused or conflicting style rules.

Using CSS to Control Formatting and Layout

A style sheet is a file that stores style rules using a coded stylesheet language. CSS is the type of stylesheet language used with Expression Web. There are three ways to save styles using CSS: external, internal, and inline. Table 4–1 defines and distinguishes the three ways to save styles.

Table 4–1 CSS Style Saving Options

Storage option	Stored in	Used for
External style sheet	A file that contains only the CSS code and that is saved with the extension .css	Applying styles to a page, a site, or multiple site pages
Internal style sheet	The Head section of the XHTML file for the page	Formatting the document in which it is created
Inline style	The Body section of the XHTML file for the page	Applying formatting to a single instance of an element or selection

CSS Syntax

A CSS rule has three parts: a selector (the "what," such as h1), a property (the "how," such as font-size), and a value (the "how much," such as xx-large). There are three main types of selectors: a specific element, a class of element, or an ID selector, which affects a single instance of an element. You can even assign a style rule to multiple selectors. There are also three selectors that are used when creating internal and external CSS styles: element, class, and ID. A selector defines the target to which a style rule is applied; an inline style only applies to one instance, which is the selector. When viewing the style rules in a CSS file, the selector appears before the bracketed information.

Figure 4–2 shows a style sheet from the Galisteo Web site. Expression Web uses color coding to distinguish the different parts of the style rules. Gray is used to show comments or headings that give information about the styles or style sheets, but that do not contain code. Line breaks and indentations help differentiate rules and parts of rules. Braces are used to show beginnings and endings of rules.

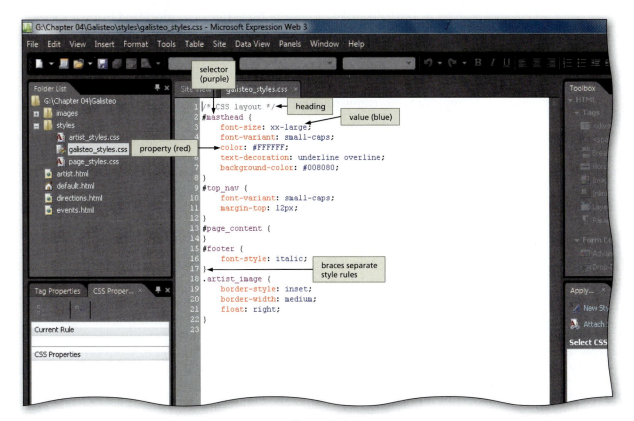

Figure 4–2

An **element-based style rule** affects an HTML page element, such as paragraphs, lists, or body text, and applies that rule to all instances of that element. When you create an element-based style rule, it uses **inheritance**, which means that it affects not only the element to which you apply the rule but also any elements contained within that element — for instance, the body element, which can contain paragraphs, lists, and so on. A **class-based style rule** is used to format a specific instance of an element or a part of an element. When you create a class-based style rule, you must manually apply it to page content, as opposed to an element-based style rule, which automatically is applied to all instances of that element. An **ID-based style rule** is used to format a specific element that only appears once per page, such as in the footer. An ID-based style rule must be applied directly to the element for it to take effect. Table 4–2 defines and distinguishes the three CSS types.

Table 4–2 CSS Style Types		
Style type	**Used for**	**Example**
Element	A rule that you want applied for every instance of an HTML element, such as defining the margins that surround every p tag	h1 {font-size: xx-large}
Class	A rule that you want to repeat several times in a page or site, such as to format headings within a block of text that contains a résumé	.jobtitle {color: red; font-size: large}
ID	A rule that you want applied to a single instance that will appear only once per page, such as a footer or masthead	#footer {color: blue; font-variant: italic}

Using CSS to Prioritize Rules

Because a single page might have multiple CSS rules and style sheets associated with it, CSS applies styles in a specific order of priority. Style rules are prioritized by their specificity or locality. Inline styles take precedence over internal styles, and internal styles take precedence over external styles. ID style rules are applied over conflicting class or element style rules.

If a portion of a rule is overruled, such as font size, by the precedence of a higher priority rule, any other non-conflicting portions of the rule, such as font color, will still be applied. For example, an inline style that formats header fonts as extra-large will take precedence over an internal style sheet that formats header fonts as large and navy blue. The navy blue font color is still applied. Within a style sheet, conflicts are resolved by giving precedence over whichever rule is furthest down in the list of rules.

Plan Ahead

Define formatting and layout using styles.
When enhancing a Web page, you should consider the types of elements you need to format and the type of CSS rule that best fits each element. Keep in mind the goal of achieving consistency within the site.

- Use direct formatting sparingly, doing so only to emphasize certain words or phrases that are not repeated.
- Create ID-based style rules to easily update like page elements, such as the masthead or footer on all pages at once.
- Create class-based style rules to change the style of headings or paragraphs, or to reposition or add a border to an image.
- Use a combination of panels, dialog boxes, and Code view to create and modify styles.

BTW

Storing Color Information
Although Expression Web prompts you to select colors by their names, the specification for colors can also be coded using the # sign followed by numbers and/or letters (a hex value) that indicate the exact color to the browser.

To Start Expression Web and Reset the Workspace Layout

If you are using a computer to step through the project in this chapter, and you want your screens to match the figures in this book, you should change your computer's resolution to 1024×768. For information about how to change a computer's resolution, read Appendix G.

You may need to ask your instructor how to start Expression Web for your computer. The following steps, which assume Windows 7 is running, start Expression Web based on a typical installation and reset the panels in the workspace to the default.

Note: If you are using Windows XP, see Appendix E for alternate steps. If you are using Windows Vista, see Appendix F for alternate steps.

1 Click the Start button on the Windows 7 taskbar to display the Start menu.

2 Click All Programs at the bottom of the left pane on the Start menu to display the All Programs list.

3 Click Microsoft Expression on the All Programs list to display the Microsoft Expression list.

4 Click Microsoft Expression Web 3 to start Expression Web.

5 Open the Panels menu, and then click Reset Workspace Layout.

6 Click View on the menu bar, point to Ruler and Grid, then click Show Ruler to turn on the rulers, if necessary.

To Open a Web Site and Web Page

The following steps open the Galisteo Web site and the default.html page.

1

• Click Site on the menu bar to open the Site menu, then point to Open Site (Figure 4–3).

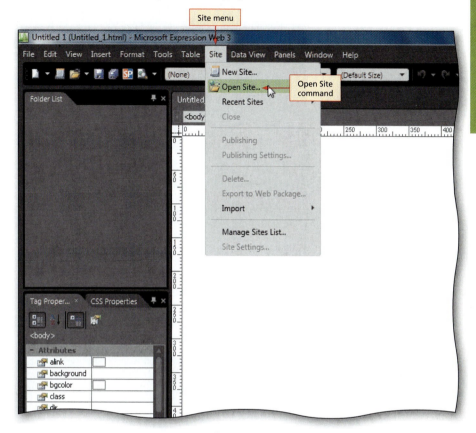

Figure 4–3

2

• Click Open Site to open the first Open Site dialog box, then click Browse to open the second Open Site dialog box.

• Navigate to and open the folder where you keep your data files (Figure 4–4).

Q&A

Why is the left column in my window narrower?

You can widen the left column in Windows Explorer by pointing to the right side of the column's border, then when the pointer with the left and right pointing arrows appears, drag the column border to the right.

Figure 4–4

3

• Click the Galisteo folder, click the Open button to close the second Open Site dialog box, then click the Open button to open the site in Expression Web (Figure 4–5).

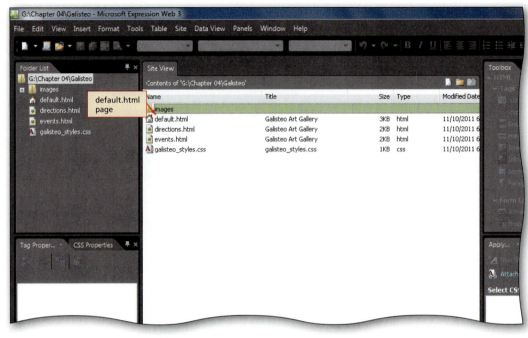

Figure 4–5

4

• Double-click the default.html page in the Site View panel to open it (Figure 4–6).

• Scroll through the page to view the current layout and formatting.

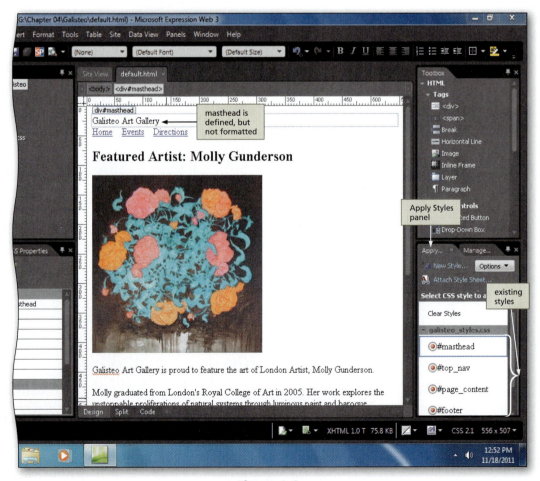

Figure 4–6

To Define an ID-Based Style

When creating an ID-based style, you must define the element to which it will apply, such as the masthead or the footer. The Galisteo Web pages were created using a CSS layout, which means that ID-based styles for the four page elements were created when the page was created. These styles appear in the Apply Styles panel, but no formatting has been assigned, so the elements look very plain. Using the Modify Style dialog box, the following steps modify the ID-based styles to format the masthead and footer elements for all pages.

- Place the pointer over the #masthead style in the Apply Styles panel so that the style arrow appears, click the arrow to view the menu, then point to Modify Style (Figure 4–7).

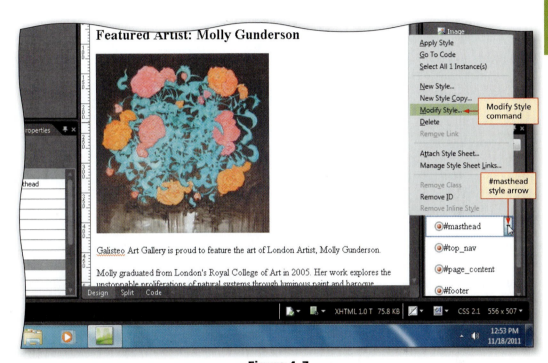

Figure 4–7

- Click Modify Style to open the Modify Style dialog box.

- Click the font-size box arrow to display the font size options (Figure 4–8).

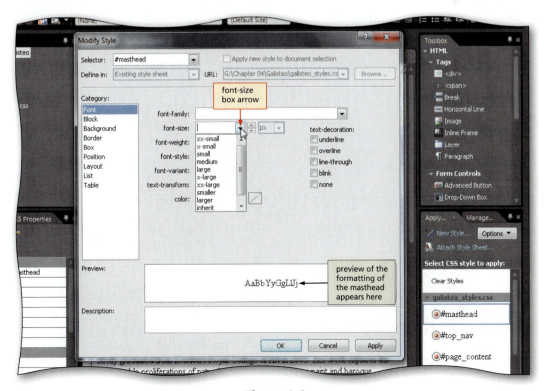

Figure 4–8

3

- Click xx-large to change the masthead text size.

- Click the font-variant box arrow, then click small-caps to change the masthead text style.

- Click the color box arrow, then click White to change the masthead text color.

- Click the underline and overline check boxes in the text-decoration section to further customize the masthead (Figure 4–9).

Experiment

- Select other font-color, font-size, and font-variant options to view their effects in the Preview box. Change your dialog box selections back to match Figure 4–9.

Q&A Why is the Preview box blank?

The white font color cannot be seen on a white background. Steps 4 and 5 change the background color of the masthead to contrast with the white font color.

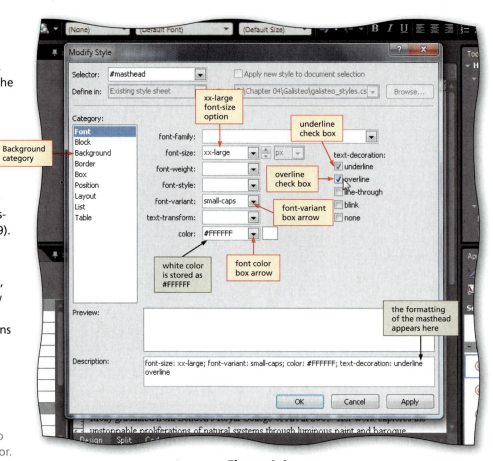

Figure 4–9

4

- Click Background in the Category list to display background formatting options.

- Click the background-color box arrow to display the color palette (Figure 4–10).

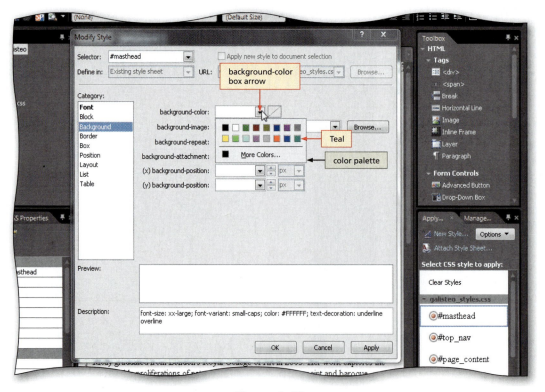

Figure 4–10

5

- Click Teal to make the masthead background teal (Figure 4–11).

Figure 4–11

- Click the OK button to close the Modify Style dialog box (Figure 4–12).

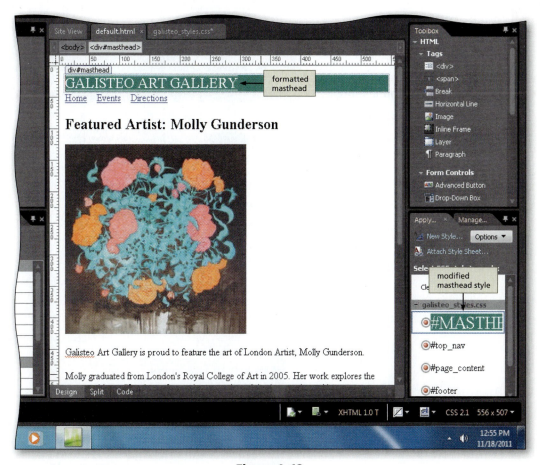

Figure 4–12

6

- Click the #footer style arrow in the Apply Styles panel to view the menu, then point to Modify Style (Figure 4–13).

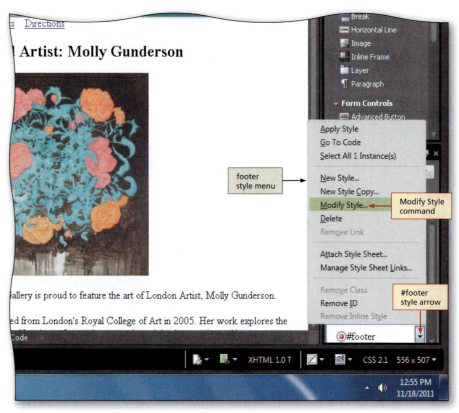

Figure 4–13

7

- Click Modify Style to open the Modify Style dialog box.

- Click the font-style box arrow, then point to italic (Figure 4–14).

- Click italic to change the footer font style.

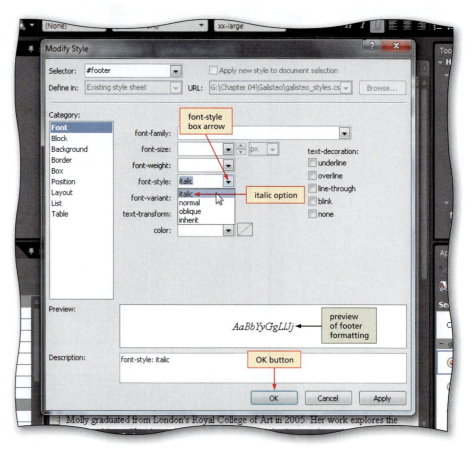

Figure 4–14

8
- Click the OK button to close the Modify Style dialog box.

- If necessary, drag the vertical scroll box to scroll down the page and view the changes in the footer (Figure 4–15).

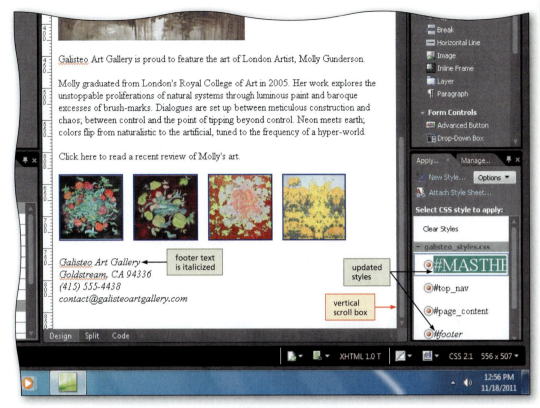

Figure 4–15

9
- Click File on the menu bar, then point to Save All (Figure 4–16).

- Click Save All to save changes to all open pages.

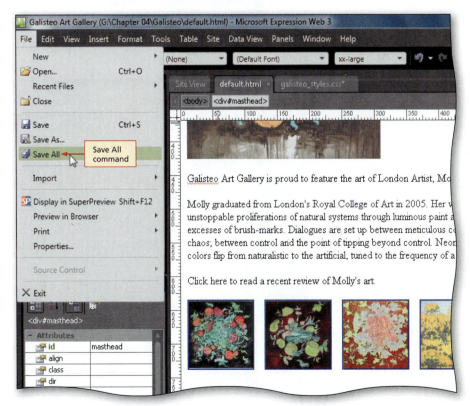

Figure 4–16

To Position Content Using a Class-Based Style

Using CSS, you can specify the position of elements such as images. The following steps create a class-based style for the main image on the home page by specifying its position and defining a margin.

- Click the New Style link on the Apply Styles panel to open the New Style dialog box (Figure 4–17).

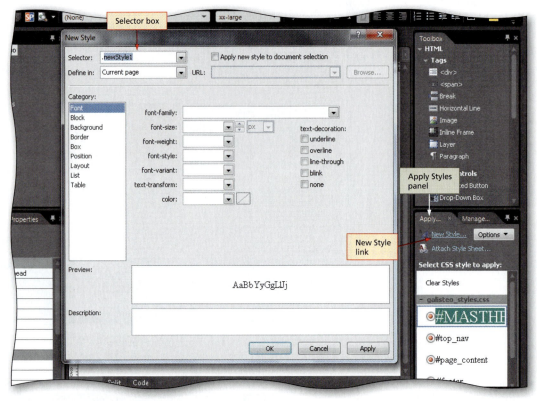

Figure 4–17

- In the Selector box, type `artist_image` to name the new style. Be sure the initial period remains in the text box.

- Click the Define in box arrow, then click Existing style sheet to activate the URL box.

- Click the URL box arrow to display a list of existing style sheets.

- Click galisteo_styles. css to select the location where the new style will be saved (Figure 4–18).

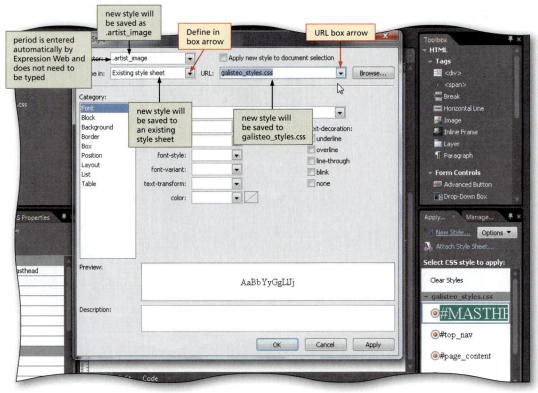

Figure 4–18

3

- Click Layout in the Category list to display layout formatting options.

- Click the float box arrow, then point to right (Figure 4–19).

- Click right to align the element to which the style will be applied with the right page margin.

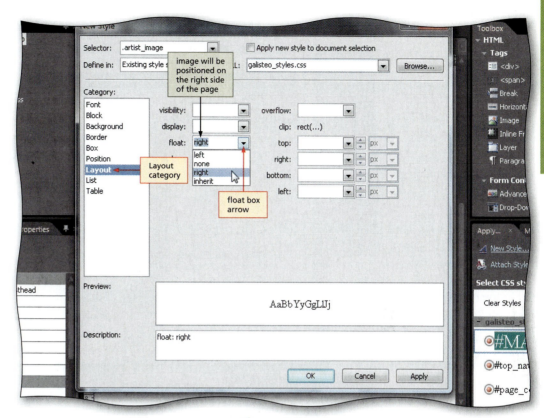

Figure 4–19

4

- Click Border in the Category list to display border formatting options.

- Click the top border-style box arrow to display the menu, then click inset from the menu.

- Click the top border-width box arrow, then point to medium (Figure 4–20).

- Click medium to add a medium-width border to the element to which the style will be applied.

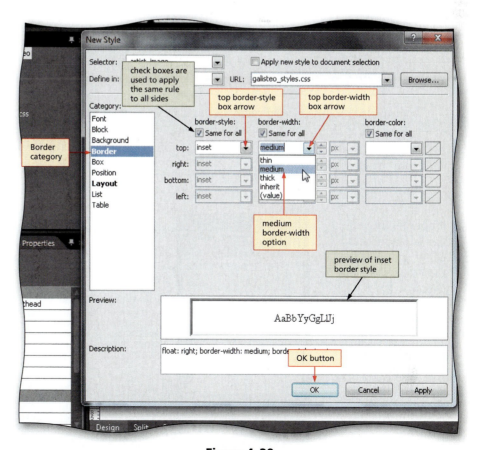

Figure 4–20

• Click the OK button to close the New Style dialog box.

• If necessary, drag the vertical scroll box up to view the image at the top of the page.

• Click the image at the top of the page to select it.

• If necessary, scroll down in the Apply Styles panel and click .artist_image to apply the new style to the image (Figure 4–21).

• Save all open files and click the OK button to save the embedded file, if necessary.

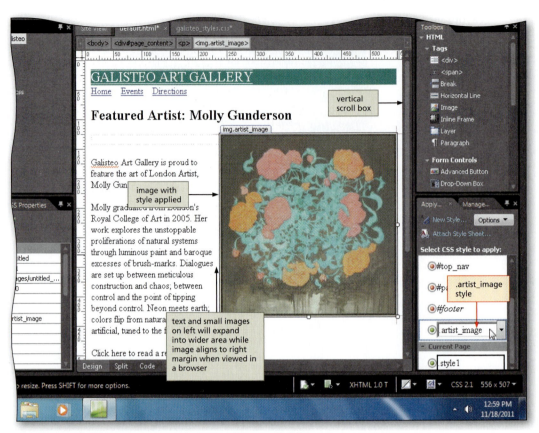

Figure 4–21

To Use the CSS Properties Panel

You can also modify styles directly in the CSS Properties panel instead of opening the Modify Style dialog box. Changes you make in the CSS Properties panel are applied automatically. The following steps use the CSS Properties panel to apply small caps to the navigation bar and to add a space at the top of the navigation bar to separate it from the masthead.

• Click the CSS Properties tab in the Tag Properties panel to display the CSS Properties panel (Figure 4–22).

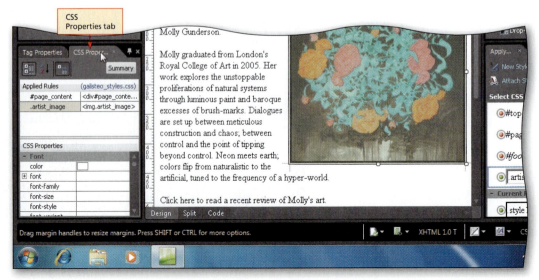

Figure 4–22

2

- Scroll up in the editing window, if necessary, and click in the navigation bar to display the style properties in the CSS Properties panel (Figure 4–23).

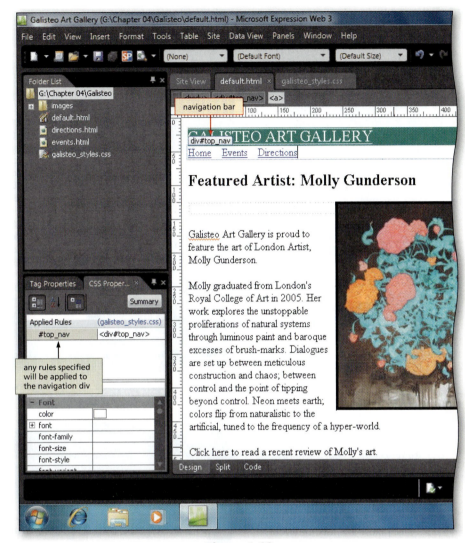

Figure 4–23

3

- If necessary, scroll down in the CSS Properties panel and click in the font-variant box to display the arrow.

- Click the font-variant box arrow, then point to small-caps (Figure 4–24).

- Click small-caps to apply small caps to the navigation bar.

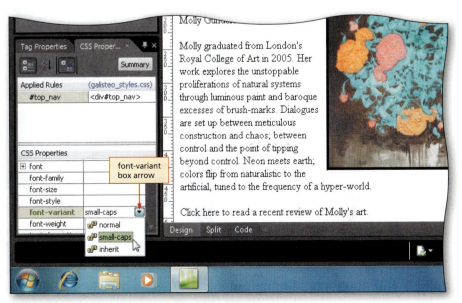

Figure 4–24

Plan Ahead

Create your own styles and style sheets.

A style sheet can be used to group certain styles so that they can be applied to Web sites as a collection of specific formats. For example, you can apply styles for the font family and page background by creating a style sheet that specifies just those elements. You can then apply the style sheet to pages that may use different layouts.

When creating style sheets, plan for the following:

- **The number of style sheets for your site.** Do you need one for layout and one for formatting? Are there pages that require their own style sheets?

- **The priority of styles.** Are there styles that may be conflicting? How will you ensure the priority of rules?

- **The organization of style sheets.** How will you name the sheets to ensure that you know what each includes? Will you store your style sheets in a folder or series of folders?

BTW

User-Defined Style Sheets

Another accessibility feature of CSS is that a user can instruct his or her browser to override a site's CSS styles and apply a local CSS file, which will present the Web site in a format that fits the user's needs.

To Create an External Style Sheet

A style sheet that you create in Expression Web is a blank file with the extension .css. To specify styles, you must enter code by typing it in the file or assign styles to the CSS file in the New Style dialog box. The following steps create a new, blank style sheet in the Galisteo Web site. You will later enter code into the style sheet for all of the general page specifications, then attach it to all site pages.

1

- Open the File menu, then point to New to open the New submenu (Figure 4–28).

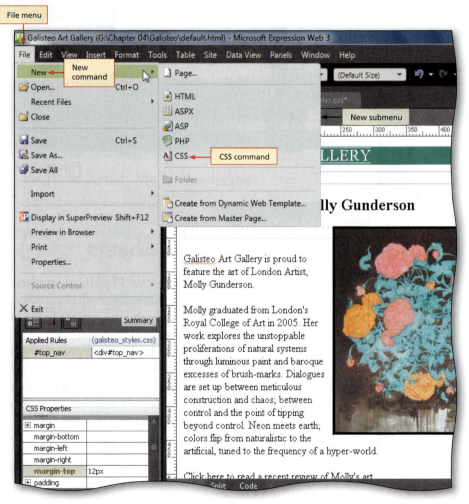

Figure 4–28

2

- Click CSS to open a new, untitled CSS file (Figure 4–29).

Figure 4–29

3

- Press CTRL+S to open the Save As dialog box.

- Type page_styles.css in the File name box (Figure 4–30).

Q&A Do I have to type .css at the end of the filename?

Yes. The default file type for new Expression Web files is HTML, so you must specify that the file is a style sheet by including the file extension .css.

Figure 4–30

- Click the Save button to name the new CSS file (Figure 4–31).

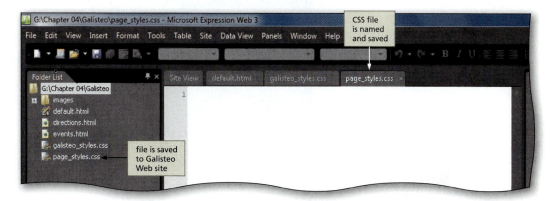

Figure 4–31

Font Families

Using a consistent font family in your site provides visitors with a common experience, regardless of the fonts they have installed on their computer. A **font family**, or font set, is a collection of similar font styles that a browser applies to text on a Web page. Expression Web includes three default font families, and you can also create your own. Specifying font families increases the usability of your site by providing a default font, then providing alternative fonts and font styles in case the font you specify isn't available on the Web page visitor's system. Font families, like other formatting characteristics, can be applied as a style. You can specify the default font or font family for a Web page by including it in the body section of a style sheet.

There are three types of fonts that are preferred according to CSS specifications, due to availability on users' systems and also readability on the screen: serif, sans-serif, and mono-space. Serifs refer to the strokes at the ends of a letter's lines; **serif** fonts have strokes, and **sans-serif** fonts do not. **Monospace** fonts resemble old-style computer fonts, and are not as commonly used as serif and sans-serif fonts. Two other types of fonts, cursive (or script) and fantasy fonts, should be avoided because they are not considered Web-safe as they are difficult to read online and not available on all users' systems.

When creating a font family, first decide whether to use all serif or all sans-serif fonts, then choose two or three fonts of that type that are generally available in most browsers. Lastly, include a generic font type, such as serif, sans-serif, or monospace, in your font family. Including a generic font type as part of your font family ensures that a browser can display a substitute font type in the event that your site's specific fonts are not available on the site visitor's system.

To Create a Font Family

The following steps create a font family using two sans-serif fonts and the generic sans-serif font type. You will later use this font family to define the body font in a style sheet, then apply the style sheet to all of the pages in the Galisteo site.

- Click Tools on the menu bar to open the Tools menu (Figure 4–32).

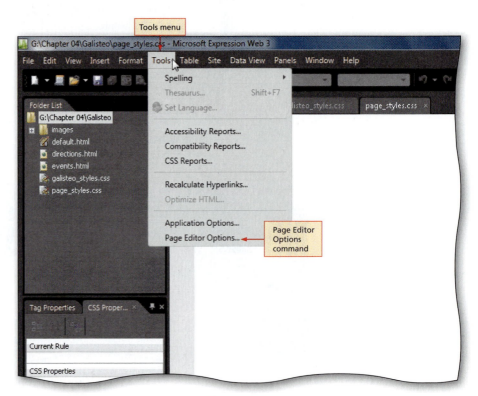

Figure 4–32

2

• Click Page Editor Options to open the Page Editor Options dialog box (Figure 4–33).

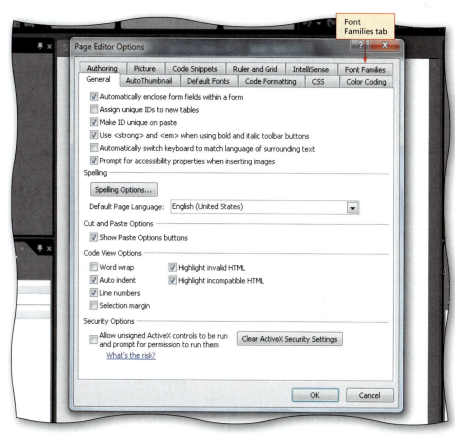

Figure 4–33

3

• Click the Font Families tab to display font family options.

• If necessary, click (New Font Family) in the Select font family list to start creating a new font (Figure 4–34).

Q&A

How do I know what fonts look like and what type they are?

If you don't have a specific font in mind or are not sure what font type a font is, click the Font list arrow in the Expression Web window to view fonts available on your system and see a preview of each font. Make a list of the fonts you would like to use, then do an Internet search for Web-safe fonts and see if yours comply.

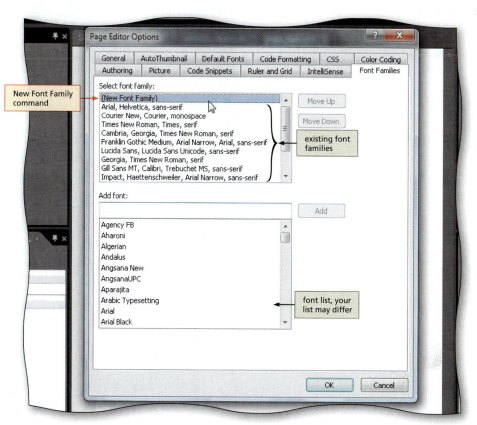

Figure 4–34

4

- Scroll to and click Calibri in the Add font list.

What if Calibri isn't available?

Fonts can vary based on the software installed on your computer. If Calibri is not available, then find another sans-serif font to include, such as Verdana.

- Click the Add button to create a new font family with Calibri as the main font (Figure 4–35).

 Experiment

- Scroll through the list of available fonts to view all of the possible options.

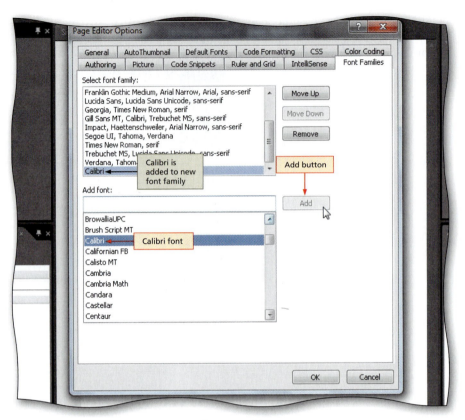

Figure 4–35

5

- Scroll to and click Gill Sans MT in the Add font list, then click the Add button to add Gill Sans MT as the second font in the new font family (Figure 4–36).

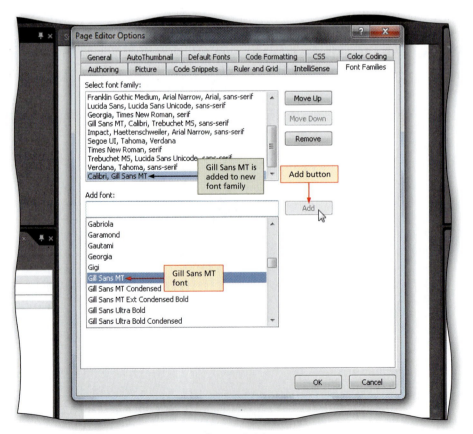

Figure 4–36

6

- Scroll to and click sans-serif in the Add font list, then click the Add button to include a generic sans-serif font to the font family (Figure 4–37).

- Click the OK button to close the Page Editor Options dialog box.

Q&A Will the font family I create be available for me when I am working with other Web sites?

Yes. Font families that you create are stored on your computer and are available when you are using your version of Expression Web.

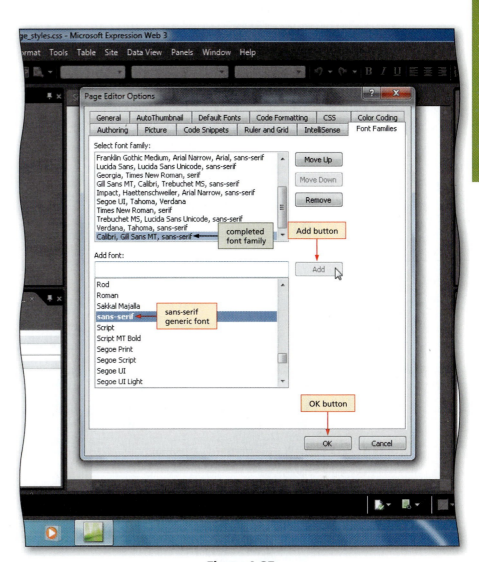

Figure 4–37

Entering CSS Code

When entering code into a style sheet, it is good design practice to include headings and comments that explain the background of the sheet and its rules. As you enter CSS code in a style sheet, Expression Web uses a feature called **IntelliSense** to prompt you by displaying shortcut menus of suggested selectors and options based on what you type. When a shortcut menu appears, double-click an option, press ENTER to accept the highlighted option, or continue typing to narrow your choices.

BTW

Comments in a CSS File
Comments are added to a document using the /*comment text*/ syntax. Adding comments to a CSS file can help you and others understand the CSS code by pointing out the effects the styles will have on a Web page, or by noting changes that you have made to the CSS code.

To Modify a Page in Code View

When creating an element-based style rule, you can use multiple selectors, such as different heading levels, to apply the same rule, such as font-color, to each of them by separating them with commas.

Remember to enter code very carefully, as your styles will not be properly applied if the code contains typing errors. Using the IntelliSense shortcut menus can help eliminate errors. The following steps use Code view to enter a heading and define style rules for the Galisteo Web site body font and page background color, then enter code to change three levels of headings to teal.

- Click in the new CSS file, type /*External Style Sheet to define page content by Your Name*/ (type your own name) to add a title to the page_styles.css page, then press ENTER twice (Figure 4–38).

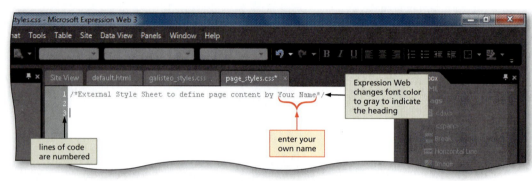

Figure 4–38

- Type bo to display the shortcut menu (Figure 4–39).

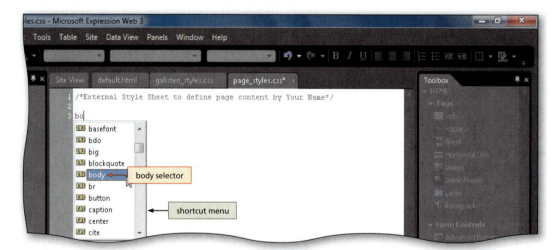

Figure 4–39

- Double-click body on the shortcut menu to start defining the styles for the body of the page.

- Press the SPACEBAR, then type { to start a declaration block for the body content.

- Type f to display the shortcut menu, then point to the font-family option (Figure 4–40).

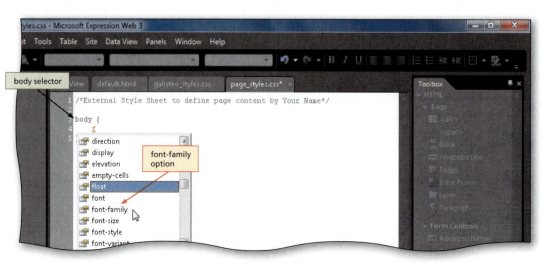

Figure 4–40

4

- Double-click font-family to select it and open the font-family shortcut menu (Figure 4–41).

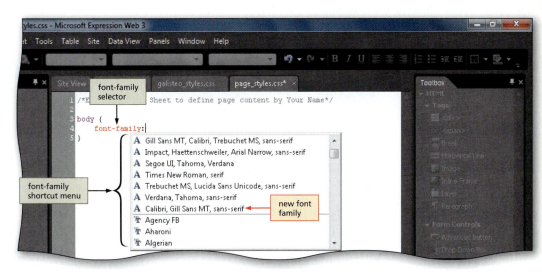

Figure 4–41

5

- Scroll down if necessary, then double-click Calibri, Gill Sans MT, sans-serif to specify this font family (Figure 4–42).

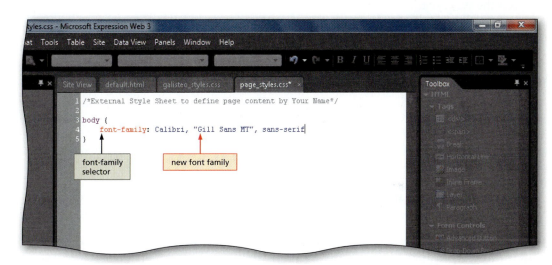

Figure 4–42

6

- Type ; then press ENTER to start a new line of code.

- Double-click background-color on the shortcut menu to select it.

- Scroll down and double-click silver on the shortcut menu to select silver as the color for the page background, then type ;.

- Press ESC, press DOWN ARROW, then press ENTER to start a new line of code (Figure 4–43).

Figure 4–43

- Type h1,h2,h3 { to start a new rule that will be applied to three heading levels, then press ENTER.

- Scroll down and double-click color on the shortcut menu to select color as the property.

- Scroll down and double-click teal on the shortcut menu to select teal as the value, then type; .

- Press the ESC key to close the shortcut menu (Figure 4–44).

- Press CTRL+S to save the style sheet.

Figure 4–44

Other Ways

1. When the shortcut menu appears and the word you want to insert is selected, press ENTER to insert it

To Attach a Style Sheet

When attaching a style sheet, you can attach it to a single page or to all pages in the site. The following steps open the events.html page, attach the page_styles.css style sheet to all pages in the Galisteo Web site at once, and view the changes.

- Double-click events.html in the Folder List to open the page (Figure 4–45).

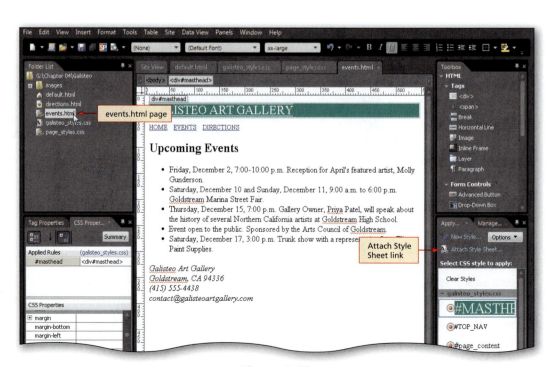

Figure 4–45

2

- Click the Attach Style Sheet link in the Apply Styles panel to open the Attach Style Sheet dialog box.

- Click the All HTML pages option button to select it (Figure 4–46).

- Verify that the Link option button is selected.

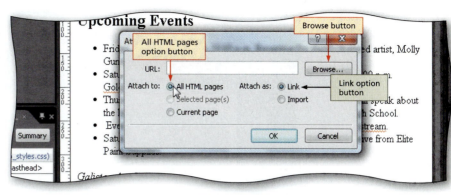

Figure 4–46

3

- Click the Browse button to open the Select Style Sheet dialog box.

- Click page_styles to select it (Figure 4–47).

Q&A Why do the icons next to my style sheets appear different?

Depending on the default program your system recognizes for CSS files, these icons may be different. This is OK.

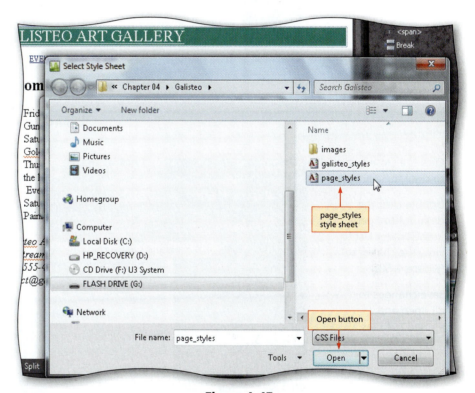

Figure 4–47

- Click the Open button to close the Select Style Sheet dialog box (Figure 4–48).

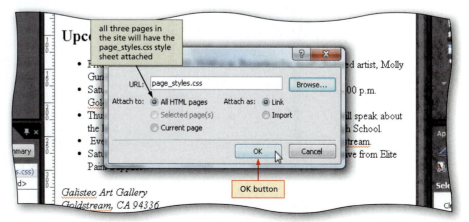

Figure 4–48

4

- Click the OK button to close the Attach Style Sheet dialog box (Figure 4–49).

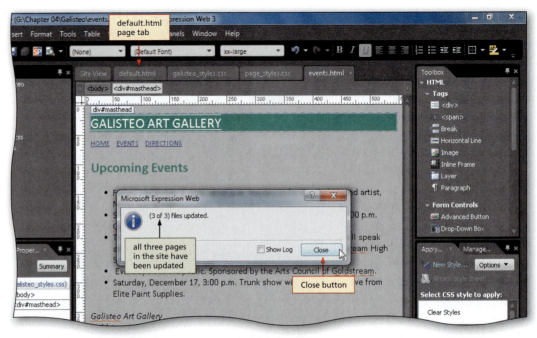

Figure 4–49

5

- Click the Close button to close the alert box.

- Double-click the default.html page in the Folder List to view the changes (Figure 4–50).

- Save changes to all open and embedded files.

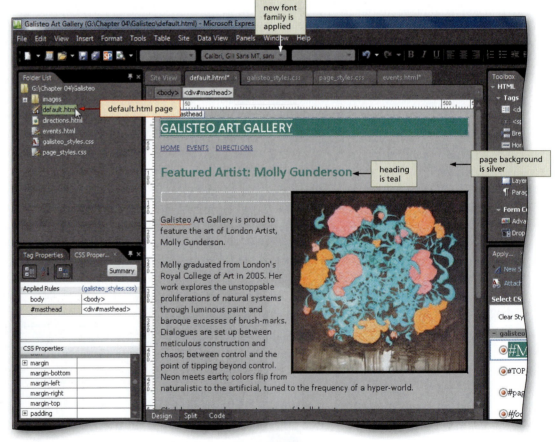

Figure 4–50

Pre-Built CSS Layouts

Expression Web provides blank pages that use a CSS layout that includes divs for all of the page elements (masthead, content area, footer, columns, and so on) that are defined by using ID-based styles. When you use a CSS layout to create a new page, two files will open: an HTML page and a style sheet that includes the ID-based styles, which are blank. You can attach additional style sheets to the new Web page to apply formatting consistent with other pages in your site.

To Use Pre-Built CSS Layouts

The owner of the Galisteo Web site needs a new page added with a different layout. The following steps create and save the new page and the style sheet.

1

• Open the File menu, point to New, then click Page to open the New dialog box (Figure 4–51).

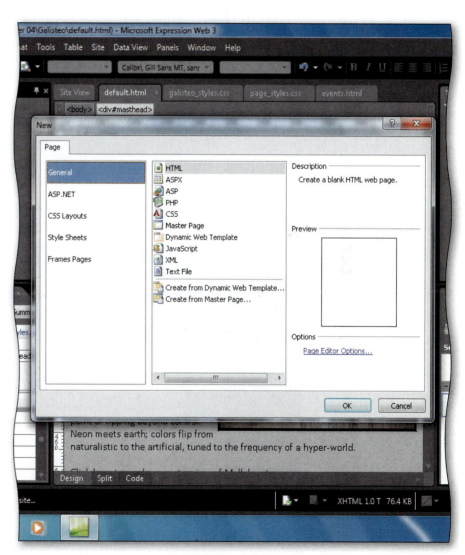

Figure 4–51

2

- Click CSS Layouts in the left pane to display CSS layout options.

- Click 'Header, nav, 2 columns, footer' in the middle pane to select it as the new page layout and view the page preview thumbnail (Figure 4–52).

  🔍 **Experiment**

- Click the other CSS layout options to view them in the Preview box, then click 'Header, nav, 2 columns, footer.'

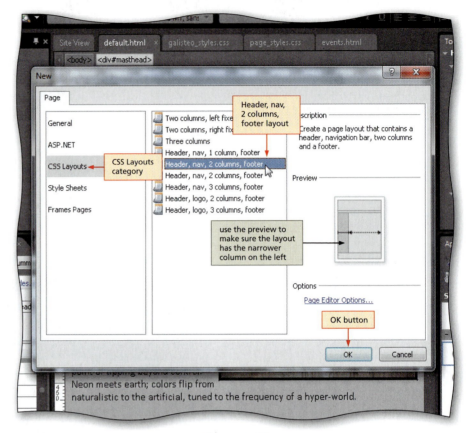

Figure 4–52

3

- Click the OK button to close the New dialog box and open the blank page and style sheet (Figure 4–53).

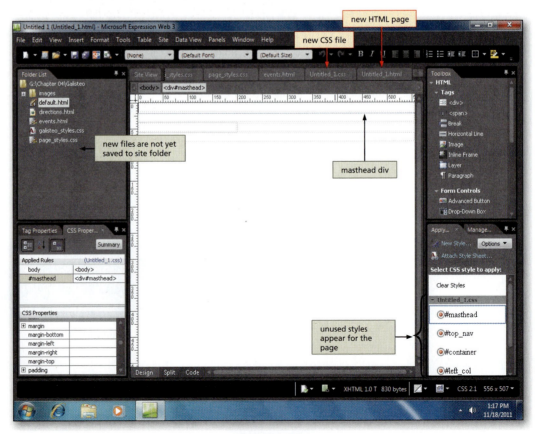

Figure 4–53

4

- Press CTRL+S to open the Save As dialog box.

- Type `artist.html` in the File name text box (Figure 4–54).

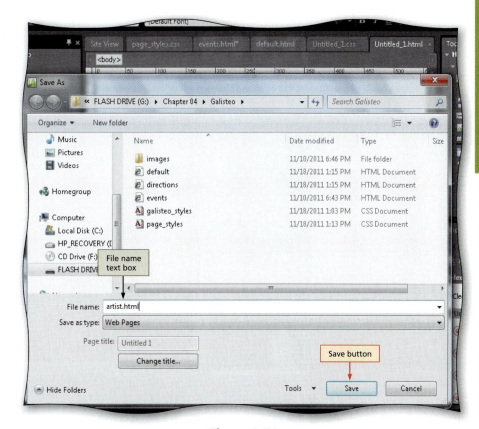

Figure 4–54

5

- Click the Save button to open the Save As dialog box for the CSS file.

- Type `artist_styles.css` in the File name text box (Figure 4–55).

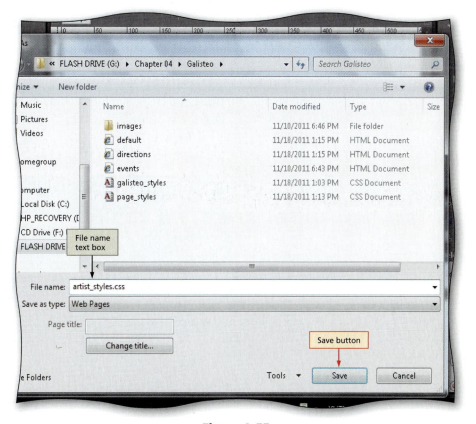

Figure 4–55

- Click the Save button to save the CSS file to the site folder (Figure 4–56).

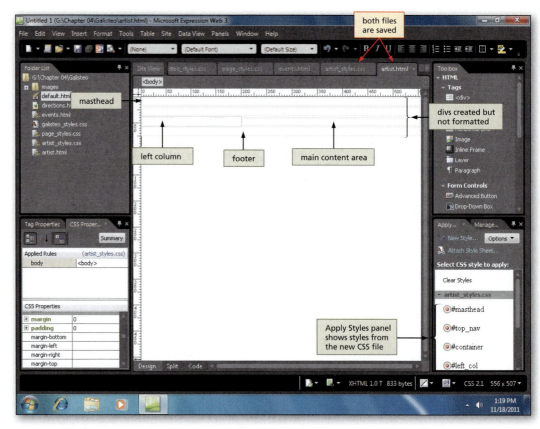

Figure 4–56

To Copy and Paste Elements

The following steps add content to the new artist page by copying and pasting text from other pages. Later in this chapter you will attach style sheets to the artist.html page to make the formatting consistent with the other site pages.

- Click in the masthead, then type Galisteo Art Gallery as the masthead text (Figure 4–57).

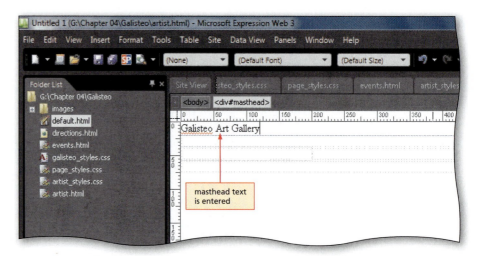

Figure 4–57

2

- If necessary, click the left scroll arrow so the default.html page is in view, then click the default. html page tab to display the default.html page.

- Click in the navigation bar, then click div#top_nav on the Quick Tag Selector to select the entire div (Figure 4–58).

Figure 4–58

3

- Press CTRL+C to copy the navigation div to the Clipboard.

- If necessary, click the right scroll arrow until the artist.html tab is in view, click the artist.html page tab to display the artist.html page.

- Click in the navigation div, then click <div#top_nav> on the Quick Tag Selector to select the div (Figure 4–59).

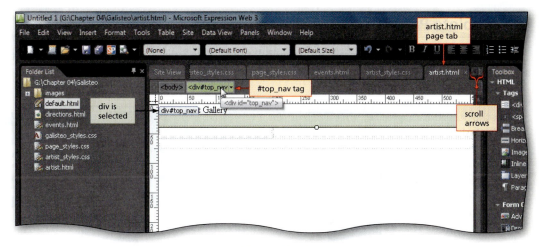

Figure 4–59

4

- Press CTRL+V to replace the existing div with the copied navigation bar (Figure 4–60).

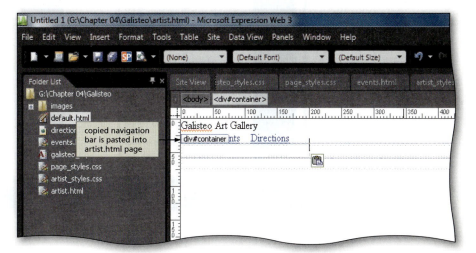

Figure 4–60

4
- Press CTRL+A to select all of the content.
- Press CTRL+C to copy the content to the Clipboard (Figure 4–65).

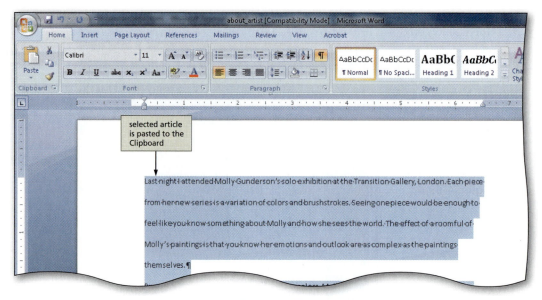

Figure 4–65

5
- Click the Close button on the title bar to close the file and quit Microsoft Word.
- Click in the #page_ content div to position the insertion point (Figure 4–66).

Figure 4–66

6
- Click Edit on the menu bar and then point to Paste Text (Figure 4–67).

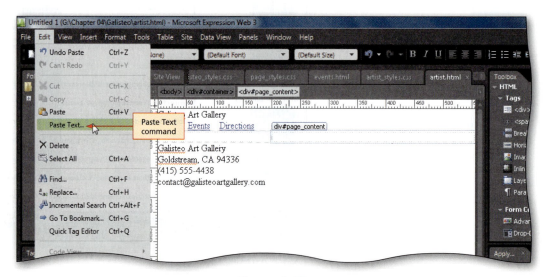

Figure 4–67

- Click Paste Text to open the Paste Text dialog box.

- Click 'Normal paragraphs without line breaks' (Figure 4–68).

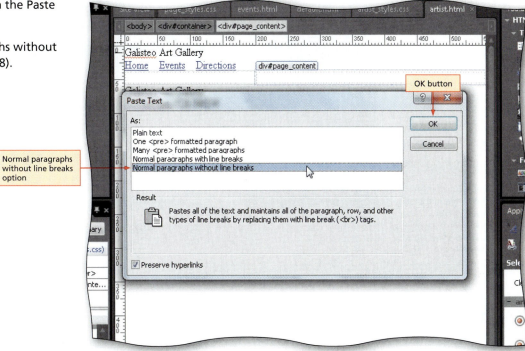

Figure 4–68

- Click the OK button to insert the text.

- Click in the #left_col div to position the insertion point.

- Type by Xi Lu, then press ENTER.

- Type London Art Weekly, then press ENTER.

- Type July, 2011 (Figure 4–69).

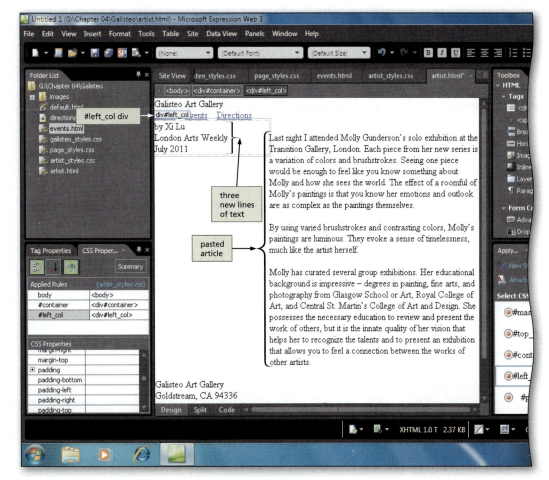

Figure 4–69

- Select the words, London Art Weekly, then click the Italic button on the Common toolbar to italicize the text (Figure 4–70).

- Press CTRL+S to save the artist.html page.

Other Ways

1. Click the Copy button on the Common toolbar (Expression Web) or the Ribbon (Word) to copy selected text or images to the Clipboard

Figure 4–70

To Attach Multiple Style Sheets

To format the artist.html page so that it is consistent with the other site pages, you will attach two style sheets to the page. The galisteo_styles.css file was created when the default.html page was created, and it contains the styles for the masthead and other page elements, which you updated earlier. You created a new style sheet, page_styles.css, to define styles for the page background and headers. The artist_styles.css file was created when the artist.html page was created. It defines the page objects, such as the masthead, navigation bar, and footer, but there are no formatting style rules associated with that style sheet. When you attach the galisteo_styles.css file, the style rules for the masthead, footer, and navigation bar will be applied to those objects on the artist.html page. Because no formatting is defined in the artist_styles.css file, no conflicts will occur. The following steps attach the page_styles.css and the galisteo_styles.css style sheets to the new page.

- Click the Attach Style Sheet link in the Apply Styles panel to open the Attach Style Sheet dialog box (Figure 4–71).

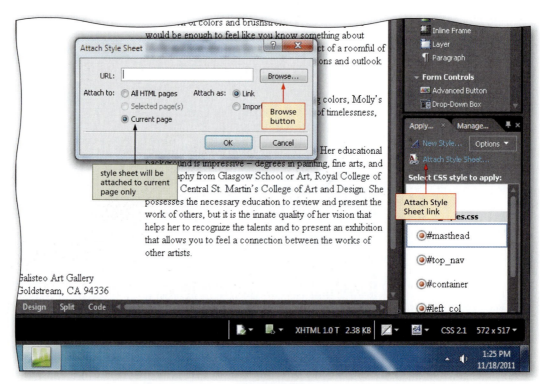

Figure 4–71

2

- Click the Browse button to open the Select Style Sheet dialog box.

- Click the page_styles file to select it (Figure 4–72).

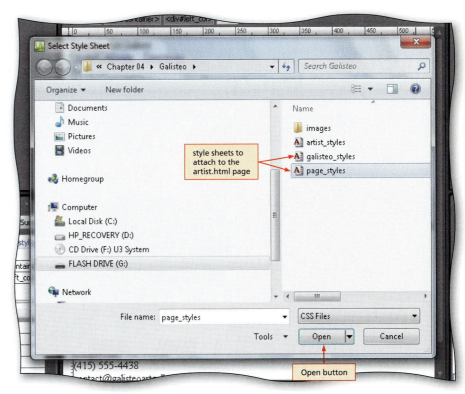

Figure 4–72

3

- Click the Open button to close the Select Style Sheet dialog box (Figure 4–73).

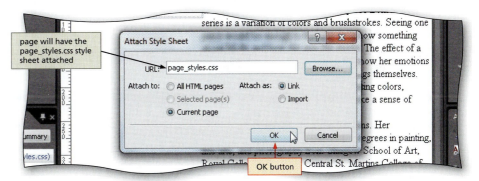

Figure 4–73

4

- Click the OK button to close the Attach Style Sheet dialog box and attach the page_styles.css style sheet to the new Web page (Figure 4–74).

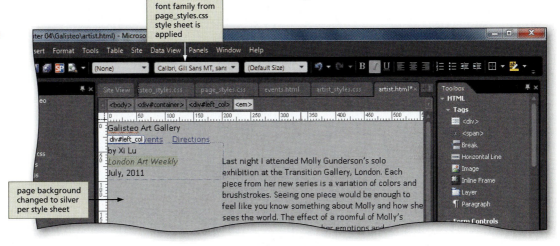

Figure 4–74

- Repeat Steps 1 through 4 to attach the galisteo_styles.css style sheet from the Galisteo site folder to the artist.html page (Figure 4–75).

- Press CTRL+S to save the page.

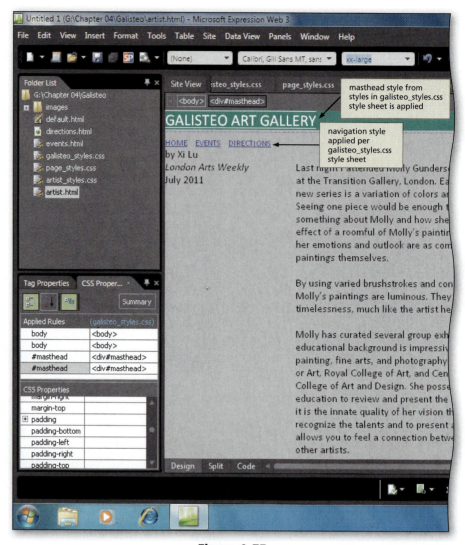

Figure 4–75

To Add a Hyperlink

The following steps create a link from the default.html page to the artist.html page.

1

- Double-click the default.html page in the Folder List to return to the default.html page.

- If necessary, scroll down and select the words, Click here (Figure 4–76).

Figure 4–76

2

- Press CTRL+K to open the Insert Hyperlink dialog box, then click the Existing File or Web Page button, if necessary.

- Scroll if necessary, then click artist to select it as the link target (Figure 4–77).

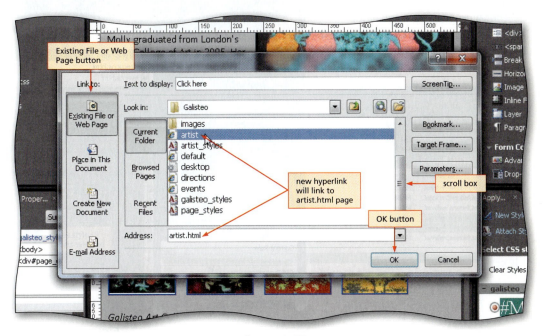

Figure 4–77

Extend Your Knowledge

Extend the skills you learned in this chapter and experiment with new skills. You may need to use Help to complete the assignment.

Modifying a Template

Instructions: Start Expression Web. Create a new Web site with one page that uses a CSS layout and styles to make the default.html page match the one shown in Figure 4–91.

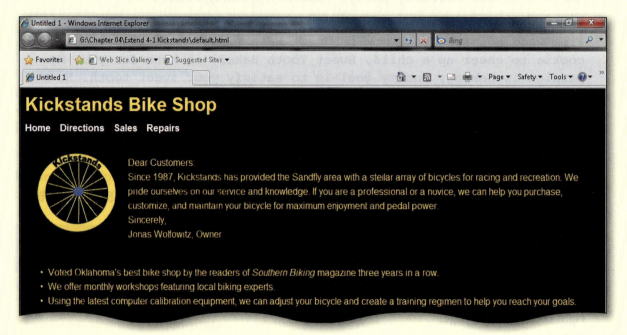

Figure 4–91

Perform the following tasks:

1. Click Site on the menu bar, then click New Site.

2. Click Empty Site in the General category.

3. Click the Browse button and navigate to the folder where you save your data files and open the folder. Type `Extend 4-1 Kickstands` after the path in the Location box, then click the OK button.

4. Click File on the menu bar, point to New, then click Page.

5. Click the CSS Layouts category, click 'Header, nav, 1 column, footer,' then click the OK button.

6. Save the HTML page as default.html and the CSS as kickstand_styles.css.

7. Type `Kickstands Bike Shop` in the masthead div.

8. Type `Home`, `Directions`, `Sales`, and `Repairs` in the navigation div, pressing TAB between each word.

9. Click in the page_content div, then type:

`Dear Customers:`

`Since 1987, Kickstands has provided the Sandfly area with a stellar array of bicycles for racing and recreation. We pride ourselves on our service and knowledge. If you are a professional or a novice, we can help you purchase, customize, and maintain your bicycle for maximum enjoyment and pedal power.`

`Sincerely,`

`Jonas Wolfowitz, Owner`

10. Press ENTER twice. Insert a paragraph tag.

11. Click the Bullets button on the Common toolbar.

12. Type the following list:

· Voted Oklahoma's best bike shop by the readers of *Southern Biking* magazine three years in a row.

· We offer monthly workshops featuring local biking experts.

· Using the latest computer calibration equipment, we can adjust your bicycle and create a training regimen to help you reach your goals.

13. Delete any empty paragraph tags after the bulleted list, if necessary. Click in the footer div, then type 678 Main Street, Sandfly, Oklahoma, 74877, (580) 555-RIDE.

14. Save the default.html page, then display the kickstand_styles.css file.

15. Click after the first line of code (/* CSS layout */), then press ENTER.

16. Type the following, using the shortcut menu as necessary:

```
body {
background:black;
font-family:Arial, Helvetica, sans-serif;
color:yellow
}
```

17. Save the kickstand_styles.css file, then display the default.html page.

18. In the Apply Styles panel, click the arrow next to #masthead, then click Modify Style.

19. Apply the following rules: font-size: xx-large; font-weight: bold; text-transform: capitalize. Then click the OK button.

20. Click in the top_nav div, click <div#top_nav> on the Quick Tag Selector, then display the CSS Properties panel.

21. Use the CSS Properties panel to apply the following styles to the navigation bar: color: white; font-weight: bold; margin-top: 12 px; margin-bottom: 12 px.

22. In the Apply Styles panel, click the arrow next to #page_content, then click Modify Style.

23. Click the Block category, click the line-height box arrow, click (value), type 24, then click the OK button.

24. Click in the footer, click the footer div on the Quick Tag Selector, then use the CSS Properties panel to apply the following rules: color: white; font-style: italic; text-align: center; margin-top: 24.

25. Click in the page_content div before Dear Customers, press ENTER, then press the UP ARROW.

26. Click Insert on the menu bar, point to Picture, then click From File.

27. Insert the image kickstands_logo.gif from the Extend 4-1 Image folder. Do not enter text in the Accessibility Properties dialog box.

28. Open the Picture Properties dialog box, click the Appearance tab, verify that the 'Keep aspect ratio' check box is checked, enter 140 for the width, then click OK.

29. Click the New Style link on the Apply Styles panel.

30. Create a new style called .image and define it in kickstand_styles.css. Apply the following rules: float: left; margin: 20px. Then click the OK button. (*Hint:* The float property is in the Layout category of the New Style dialog box.)

31. Select the image, then apply the .image style to it. Attach the kickstand_styles.css style sheet to the default.html page. Save all files.

32. Preview the page, then close the browser window.

33. Change the site properties as specified by your instructor. In Windows Explorer, rename the Web site folder Extend 4-1 Kickstands Site. Submit the revised site in the format specified by your instructor.

Make It Right

Analyze a site and correct all errors and/or improve the design.

Placing and Formatting Images

Instructions: Start Expression Web. Open the Web site, Make It Right 4-1 Drama, from the Data Files for Students. See the inside back cover of this book for instructions for downloading the Data Files for Students, or see your instructor for information about accessing the required files.

Create and apply an external style sheet using panels, dialog boxes, and Code view to format the Web page while keeping in mind the guidelines for this chapter to create the home page shown in Figure 4–92.

Figure 4–92

1. Create and save a new CSS file called drama_styles.css.

2. Add a comment to the CSS page by typing /*Page Styles created by Your Name*/.

3. Define the body styles by typing:

   ```
   body {
        background-color:maroon;
        font-family:Arial, Helvetica, sans-serif;
        color:#FFFF99
   }
   ```

4. Save the drama_styles.css file, then attach it to the default.html page.

5. Create a new style called .cast_list and save it to the drama_styles.css page. The style should have font-style: italic and list-style-type: square.

6. Apply the .cast_list style to the bulleted list of cast members.

7. Change the site properties as specified by your instructor. Save all pages, preview the default.html page in the browser, then close the site.

8. Using Windows Explorer, rename the site folder as Make It Right 4-1 Drama Site. Submit the revised site in the format specified by your instructor.

In the Lab

Design and/or format a Web site using the guidelines, concepts, and skills presented in this chapter. Labs are listed in order of increasing difficulty.

Lab 1: Creating a New Style Sheet

Problem: You are a photographer, and you want to update your business's home page by creating a style sheet that you can apply to future pages. Create styles and a style sheet to create the page shown in Figure 4–93.

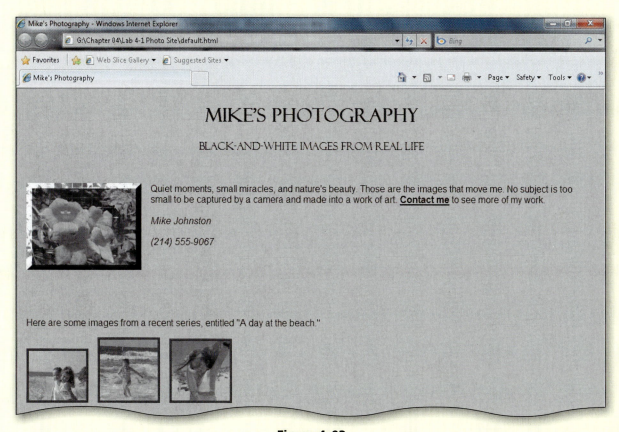

Figure 4–93

Instructions:

1. Start Expression Web.

2. Open the Web site, Lab 4-1 Photo, from the location in which you store your data files.

3. Create a new CSS file and save it as photo_styles.css.

4. Type the following comment at the top of the CSS file: /*External Style Sheet to define page content by Your Name*/.

5. Use the shortcut menu to apply the Arial, Helvetica, sans-serif font-family and the silver background color to the body tag.

6. Save the changes to the style sheet, then attach it to the default.html page.

Continued >

In the Lab *continued*

7. Select the flower image, then use the CSS Properties panel to add a 16-pixel margin to the right of the image.

8. Create a new style called .thumbnail in the photo_styles.css style sheet. Click the Border category. Specify that the border is the same for all sides, and use the ridge style, medium width, and black color.

9. Apply the .thumbnail style to each of the three thumbnails at the bottom of the page.

10. Create a new style called .e-mail in the photo_styles.css style sheet. Specify that the font weight is bold and the color is black, and apply underline. Save the changes to the style sheet.

11. Select the e-mail link, Contact me, and apply the .e-mail style.

12. Save the changes to the default.html page, preview the page in a browser, then close the site. Using Windows Explorer, rename the site folder Lab 4-1 Photo Site.

13. Submit the site in the format specified by your instructor.

In the Lab

Lab 2: Creating and Applying Styles

Problem: You have volunteered to update the Web site for the Connecticut branch of the Gulliver College Alumni Society. Modify the styles to format the site as shown in Figure 4–94.

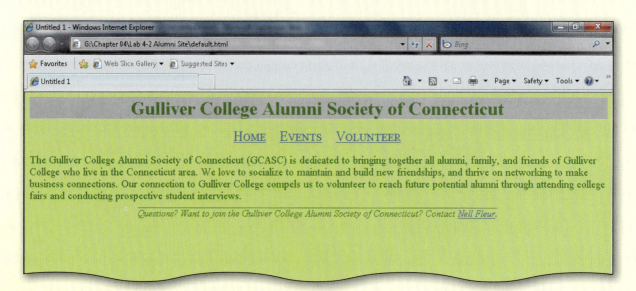

Figure 4–94

Instructions: Start Expression Web. Open the Web site, Lab 4-2 Alumni, from the Data Files for Students. See the inside back cover of this book for instructions for downloading the Data Files for Students, or see your instructor for information about accessing the required files.

Perform the following tasks:

1. Open the style sheet. Click after the comment, press ENTER to start a new line, then type and use the shortcut menu to specify the following style rules for the body: font-family: Times New Roman, Times, serif; color: green; background-color: #CCFF66; font-size: large. (*Hint:* The hex color value must be typed including the semicolon that follows.)

2. Save the style sheet, then open the default.html page and attach the alumni_styles.css style sheet.

3. Modify the style rules for the masthead using the Modify Style dialog box. Specify the following formatting: background-color: silver; font-size: xx-large; font-weight: bold; text-align: center.

4. Modify the style rules for the top_nav div using the CSS Properties panel. Specify the following formatting: margin-top: 16px; margin-bottom: 16px; text-align: center; font-size: x-large; font-variant: small-caps.

5. Use whatever method you prefer to modify the style rules for the footer. Specify the following formatting: margin-top: 10px; text-decoration: overline; font-size: medium; font-style: italic; text-align: center.

6. Save all pages at once.

7. Preview the default.html page in a browser and use the navigation bar to view all pages.

8. Change the site properties as specified by your instructor, then close the site.

9. Using Windows Explorer, rename the site folder Lab 4-2 Alumni Site, then submit the site in the format specified by your instructor.

In the Lab

Lab 3: Creating a Site Using a CSS Layout

Problem: Your client, a preschool, wants to create a home page that it can use to attract clients, and to which it will later add other pages. Create a Web site and use CSS to lay out and format the default.html page shown in Figure 4–95.

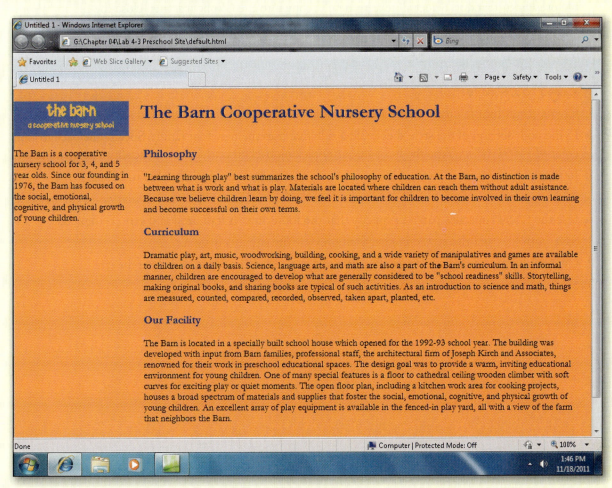

Figure 4–95

Continued >

In the Lab *continued*

Instructions:

1. Start Expression Web.

2. Create a new empty Web site called Lab 4-3 Preschool Site.

3. Add a new page based on the Header, logo, 2 columns, footer CSS layout.

4. Save the page as default.html and the associated style sheet as preschool_styles.css.

5. In the logo div, insert the image preschool_logo.gif from the Lab 4-3 Preschool Files folder in your data files. Resize the logo to 200 pixels wide, then resample it. (*Hint:* Right-click the image, click Picture Properties, click the Appearance tab, enter 200 in the Width box, verify that the 'Keep aspect ratio' check box is checked, click OK, right-click the image, then click Resample.)

6. Create a new style named .image in the preschool_styles.css style sheet. Add a 20px bottom margin to the style and apply it to the preschool_logo.gif image.

7. In the header div, type `The Barn Cooperative Nursery School`, then apply Heading 1 `<h1>` to the div.

8. In the left_col div, type `The Barn is a cooperative nursery school for 3, 4, and 5 year olds. Since our founding in 1976, the Barn has focused on the social, emotional, cognitive, and physical growth of young children.`

9. Start Microsoft Word, navigate to the Lab 4-3 Preschool Files folder in your data files, then open the file preschool_text.doc. Select all text in the file, copy it to the Clipboard, then close the file and Word.

10. In the page_content div (the right column), paste the text without line breaks.

11. Apply Heading 3 `<h3>` to the lines Philosophy, Curriculum, and Our Facility.

12. In the footer div, type `43 Maple Street, Snow Hill, IL 61998`, press ENTER, then type `(224) 555-4098`.

13. Create a new font family with the fonts Garamond, Century Schoolbook, and serif.

14. In the body section of the style sheet, add a rule that uses the new font family. Specify the background color #FF9933. (*Hint:* Type the hex value after picking background-color on the shortcut menu.)

15. In the #page_content section of the style sheet, change the margin-left value to 225px.

16. Add two new styles for h1 and h3 that use the blue font color. Add a 20px left margin to the h1 style.

17. Use the CSS Properties panel to specify that the footer text is italicized and center-aligned.

18. Save both files and the edited image, then preview the site in a browser.

19. Change the site properties as specified by your instructor, then save and close the site.

20. Submit the site in the format specified by your instructor.

Cases and Places

Apply your creative thinking and problem-solving skills to design and implement a solution.

• Easier   •• More Difficult

• 1: Creating a New Page Using CSS Layouts

Create a new blank Web site about a favorite vacation and add a page using the CSS layout of your choice. Enter content in all of the divs. Modify the style sheet to specify formatting for the page. Add rules for the page background, font family, and text color. Use panels and dialog boxes to modify the styles for two content areas, such as the footer or masthead. Close the site without saving any changes, then quit Expression Web.

• 2: Updating a Site Using CSS

Create a new site using a dynamic Web template. Use a small business such as a video store or fitness center as the site's focus. Preview the site in your browser and choose at least four style rules that you would like to modify. Open the CSS (if there is more than one style sheet, choose one) in Code view and change two style rules. Save the style sheet as Cases and Places 4-2.css, close the style sheet, and view the changes. Use the CSS Properties panel to change one style rule and use the Modify Style dialog box to change another. Keep modifying styles until you are satisfied with your changes. Save the modified style sheet.

•• 3: Removing Conflicting CSS Rules

Open any multi-page Web site you created in Chapter 2. Create a new style sheet and add three style rules to it. Attach it to all files in the site at once. Make note of areas where inline styles are taking priority over the style sheet. See if you can remove any conflicting inline styles by deleting them in the Apply Styles panel. Rename and save the pages and style sheets, then close the site.

•• 4: Creating a Personal Home Page

Make It Personal

You want to create a one-page site that includes information about your favorite hobby. Create a new blank site and add a page using one of the two-column CSS layouts. Enter information on the default. html page, and include at least one photo and two heading styles (h1, h2, etc.). Assign style rules using the style sheet that came with the CSS layout. Create a new style sheet and add a title, specifications for the page background, and font-family. Create one rule that changes the font color of all of the heading styles you have used on your default page, and another that defines borders and margins for the image. Apply the new image style and attach the new style sheet to the default.html page. Save the pages and style sheets, then close the site.

•• 5: Enhancing Text Using Styles

Working Together

A tutor wants to create a site for his business with three pages: home, references, and résumé. Working as a team with several of your classmates, plan and create the Web site. Each team member should contribute to creating text for the three pages in Word. As a group, decide on a CSS layout for each page in your site (they can all be the same or all be different) and create the site folder and the pages. Create the navigation bar by inserting hyperlinks in the pages. On each of the three pages, edit the placeholder text and insert the Word files you have created. Use the style sheets to define the page elements. If your site has multiple style sheets, practice copying style rules between the pages, attaching a style sheet to another page, and using other methods to ensure consistency among page elements in the site. Preview the site, test the navigation bar, and make sure that your site is readable and attractive. Save and close the pages and style sheet, then close the site.

5 | Working with Data Tables and Inline Frames

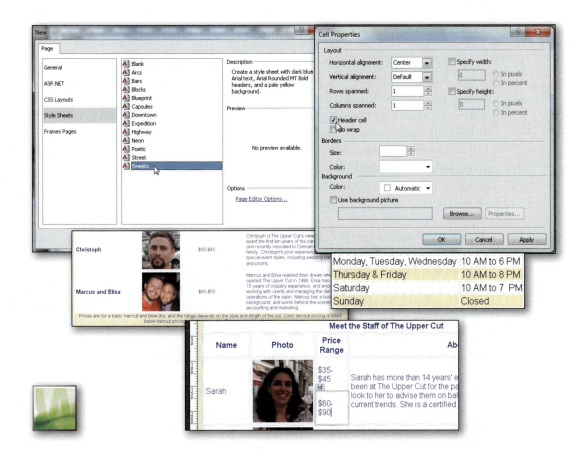

Objectives

You will have mastered the material in this chapter when you can:

- Use a preformatted style sheet
- Insert a data table
- Change table and cell properties
- Add text and images
- Add rows and columns
- Merge and split table cells

- Format a table using CSS
- Convert text to a table
- Use table AutoFormat
- Distribute rows and columns
- Create an inline frame
- Target links in an inline frame

5 | Working with Data Tables and Inline Frames

Introduction

A **data table** is used to display data in a combination of horizontal **rows** and vertical **columns**. The intersection of a row and a column is called a **cell**. Cells organize the table data, such as text, values, or images. By aligning information in rows and columns and using row and column headers to identify categories of information, information can be presented in an orderly, organized way.

Table properties can be defined by specifying the width of the table as a fixed pixel width or as a percentage of a page, or by allowing the width to be manually adjusted or fit to the text. You can modify the table structure by changing the number of columns or rows. You can format data tables using styles or Expression Web tools such as AutoFormat to add borders or background colors.

An **inline frame**, or **I-frame**, is a fixed-size window that displays another HTML page. When the embedded page contains more information than can be shown in the I-frame, scroll boxes appear to allow the visitor to view more of the embedded page.

Project — Hair Salon

Marcus and Elisa Goldman are the owners of The Upper Cut Salon. They want to create a home page for their company that includes a list of their services and prices. They have asked you to create the home page with whatever Web design tools you recommend. Based on the needs of the site, your plan is to create the home page and attach a preformatted style sheet to it. You will create a table on a separate HTML page, enter data and images, format the table, then add the table as an inline frame to their home page. You will also create a table from text on the home page and update it using AutoFormat.

The project in this chapter shows you how to use a preformatted style sheet, insert a table, add data, modify table structure, and format tables to create the pages shown in Figure 5–1. You will also learn how to convert text to a table, use AutoFormat to apply table formatting, and embed an HTML page that contains the table as an inline frame in the home page.

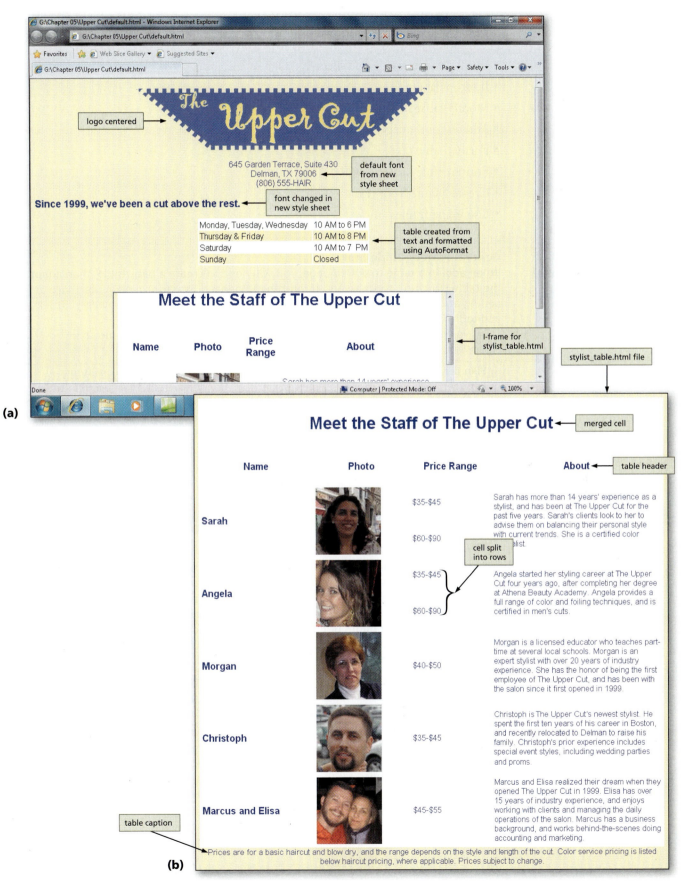

Figure 5–1

Overview

As you read this chapter, you will learn how to create the Web page shown in Figure 5–1 by performing these general tasks:

- Use a preformatted style sheet
- Insert a data table
- Modify table structure
- Add text and images
- Format table text
- Format table backgrounds
- Create a table from text
- Use inline frames

Plan Ahead

General Project Guidelines

When adding a table to a Web page, you will need to create a basic table, then adapt the table structure, content, and formatting as needed by performing actions such as adding and deleting rows and columns, splitting and merging cells, and applying text and table formatting.

As you plan to enhance a Web page by adding a table, such as the one shown in Figure 5–1, you should follow these general guidelines:

1. **Plan the basic table structure.** Use a style sheet to provide formatting consistency between the table content and the rest of the page. When creating a new data table, you should have some idea of the number of rows and columns that you will need before you start, by planning the content that will be displayed in the table. If necessary, sketch a plan for the table on paper, or make a list of the rows and columns you might need.

2. **Add and arrange table content.** Once your table is created, add headings as needed to help you identify where to enter data. Table cells usually contain text (words or numbers), but including images in a table can provide visual data, or make your table more attractive. Once the table's content has been entered, delete rows and columns that you do not need, or add cells for more data. Arranging the table data by combining cells that contain like data, or separating one cell into two to provide additional information within a row or column, helps organize the table.

3. **Design the table.** Determine the degree to which your table should stand out from the rest of the page. Depending on the data in your table and the information on the rest of the page, you may want your table to be a subtle tool to organize data, or it could be a bold page element that will catch a visitor's eye. Choosing the appropriate table background and border options or using AutoFormat will help your table meet the design needs. Using styles to format your table helps maintain consistency with other site pages and makes the table format easier to update.

4. **Organize existing content into the table.** Text that exists in your site can be converted from regular text into a table. The benefit of organizing data into a table is that you can align rows and columns so that the text is easier to read.

5. **Add an inline frame to display a page.** Any HTML page can be embedded into an inline frame on a Web page to provide visitors with a view of the embedded page while controlling the viewing size and not requiring an additional link. For a site that is only one page, you can keep more of the main page visible within the browser window by providing a small, scrollable window that displays additional information.

To Start Expression Web and Reset Workspace Layout

If you are using a computer to step through the project in this chapter, and you want your screens to match the figures in this book, you should change your computer's resolution to 1024 × 768. For information about how to change a computer's resolution, read Appendix G.

The following steps, which assume Windows 7 is running, start Expression Web based on a typical installation, and reset the panels in the workspace to the default layout. You may need to ask your instructor how to start Expression Web for your computer.

Note: If you are using Windows XP, see Appendix E for alternate steps.
If you are using Windows Vista, see Appendix F for alternate steps.

1 Click the Start button on the Windows 7 taskbar to display the Start menu.

2 Click All Programs at the bottom of the left pane on the Start menu to display the All Programs list.

3 Click Microsoft Expression on the All Programs list to display the Microsoft Expression list.

4 Click Microsoft Expression Web 3 to start Expression Web.

5 Click Panels on the menu bar, then click Reset Workspace Layout.

6 Click View on the menu bar, point to Ruler and Grid, then click Show Ruler to turn on the rulers if necessary.

To Create a New Web Site and Web Page

The following steps create the Upper Cut Web site folder and the default.html page.

1
- Click New Site on the Site menu to open the New dialog box (Figure 5–2).

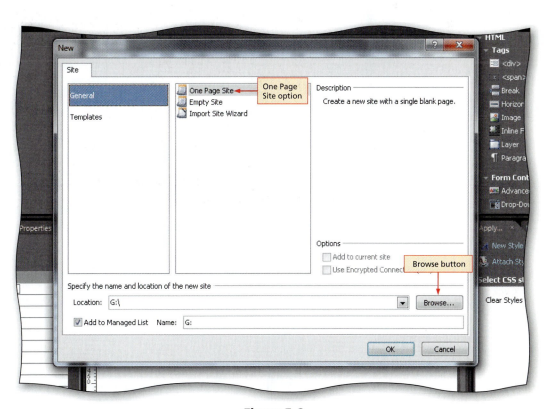

Figure 5–2

2

- Click One Page Site, then click the Browse button to open the New Site Location dialog box.

- Navigate to and open the folder in which you keep your data files, then click Open.

- Type Upper Cut at the end of the folder path in the Location text box, then click the OK button to open the site in Expression Web (Figure 5–3).

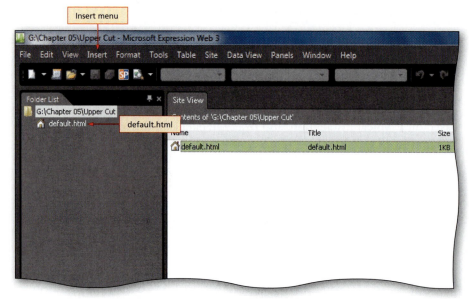

Figure 5–3

3

- Double-click the default.html page in the Folder List to open it.

- Point to Picture on the Insert menu, then click From File to open the Picture dialog box.

- Navigate to the location of your data files, and double-click the uppercut_images folder to open it.

- Click uppercut_logo to select it (Figure 5–4).

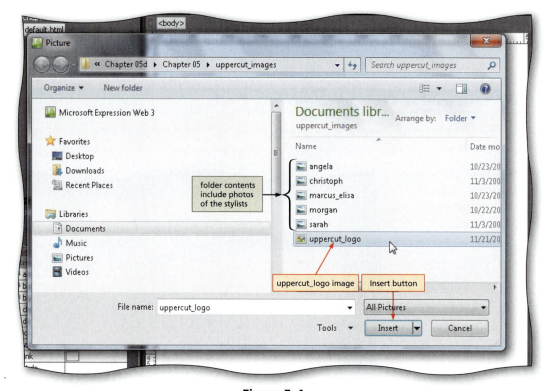

Figure 5–4

4

- Click the Insert button to open the Accessibility Properties dialog box.

- Type The Upper Cut logo in the Alternate text text box (Figure 5–5).

Figure 5–5

5

- Click the OK button to insert the logo at the top of the home page.

- Click the <p> tag on the Quick Tag Selector to select the paragraph containing the image, then click the Center button on the Common toolbar to center the image (Figure 5–6).

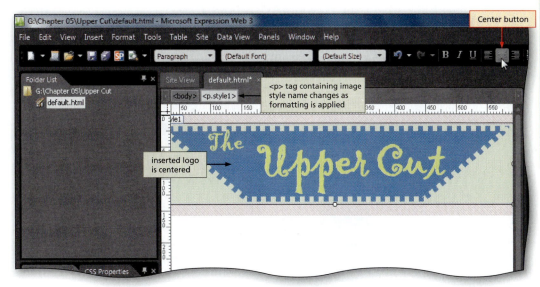

Figure 5–6

6

- Click below the logo to deselect it.

- Double-click Paragraph in the Toolbox to insert a new paragraph.

- Type 645 Garden Terrace, Suite 430 as the first line of the address, then press SHIFT+ENTER to start a new line in the paragraph.

- Type Delman, TX 79006, then press SHIFT+ENTER to start a new line in the paragraph.

- Type (806) 555-HAIR.

- Click the <p> tag on the Quick Tag Selector to select the paragraph, then click the Center button on the Common toolbar to center the paragraph (Figure 5–7).

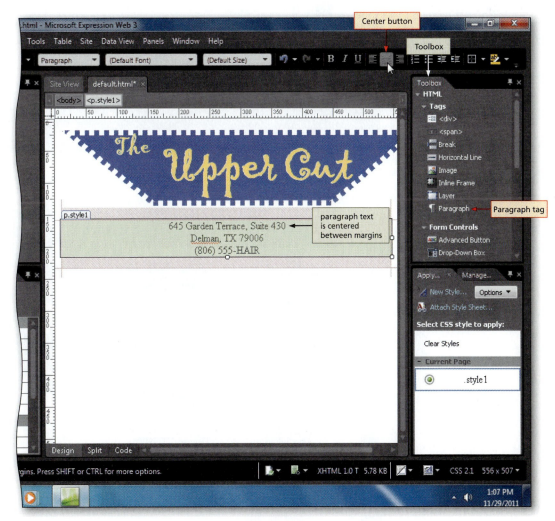

Figure 5–7

7

- Click below the paragraph to position the insertion point.

- Double-click Paragraph in the Toolbox to insert a new paragraph.

- Type Since 1999, we've been a cut above the rest..

- Click the <p> tag on the Quick Tag Selector to select the paragraph.

- Click the Style box arrow on the Common toolbar to display the Style menu, then point to Heading 3 <h3> (Figure 5–8).

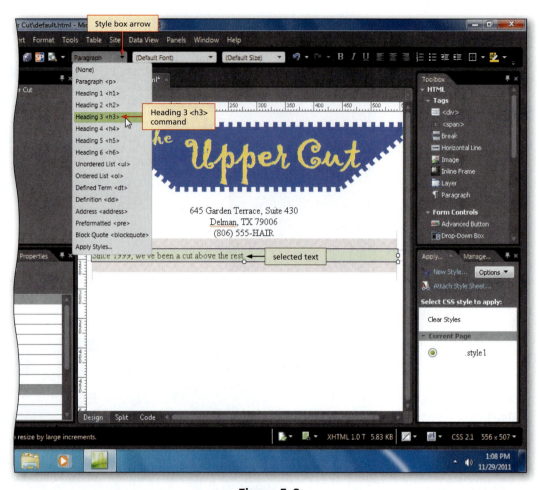

Figure 5–8

8

- Click Heading 3 <h3> to apply it to the text (Figure 5–9).

Figure 5–9

9
- Press CTRL+S to save the default.html page, and click the OK button in the Save Embedded Files dialog box to save the logo to the site (Figure 5–10).

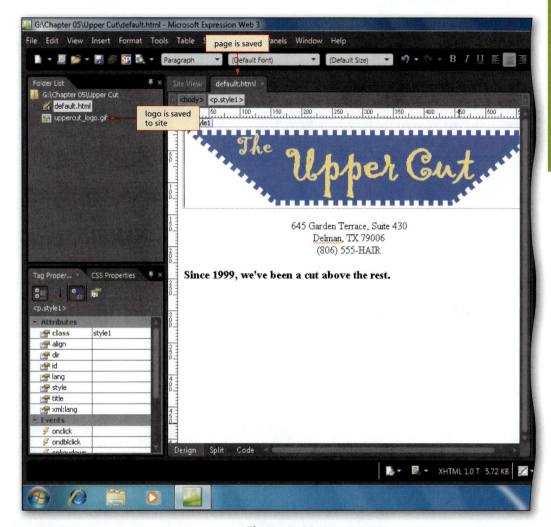

Figure 5–10

Other Ways

1. Point to HTML on the Insert menu, then click Paragraph to insert a new tag

Using a Preformatted Style Sheet

Just as you can create a new Web page using a CSS layout or a new Web site using a dynamic Web template, you can create a new style sheet using a preformatted option provided by Expression Web. Using a preformatted style sheet saves you time and ensures that the code is entered correctly. Like any completed style sheet, a preformatted style sheet contains code that you can edit and modify to suit your needs.

Plan the basic table structure.
Plan the formatting for all pages in the site, including the page that you will embed as an I-frame. Use a preformatted style sheet as a basis, then modify it as necessary. Determine the approximate number of columns and rows that you will need to display the data, including any necessary row and column headers. If your table includes a title, consider whether to add it as a line of text above the table, or as a merged cell that spans the width of the table. A caption above or below your table describes the table contents or its purpose. You should specify table and cell properties, such as text alignment, alignment of the table relative to the page margins, and spacing between cells.

Plan Ahead

BTW
Nested Table
A nested table is a table inside another table.

To Create a New Style Sheet

The following steps create the uppercut_styles.css file using a preformatted style sheet. You want all of the fonts to be the same throughout the page, so you will delete the code that specifies a different font type and color for the heading styles. Then you will attach the style sheet to the default.html page.

- Point to New on the File menu, then click Page to open the New dialog box.

- Click Style Sheets in the left pane to display the style sheet options.

- Click the Sweets style sheet option to select it (Figure 5–11).

🔍 Experiment

- Click different options in the Style Sheets list to view descriptions. Select the Sweets style sheet.

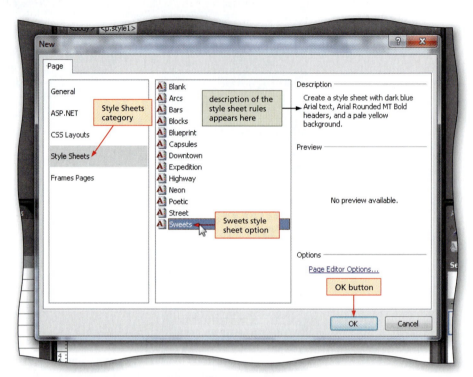

Figure 5–11

- Click the OK button to create the new style sheet (Figure 5–12).

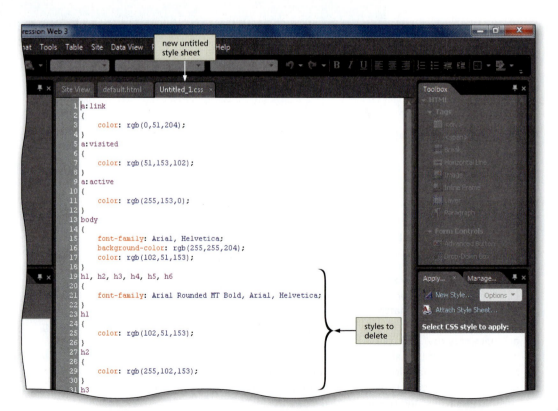

Figure 5–12

3

- Select the code and brackets in lines 19 through 46 that formats the headings in a different font and also in different colors (Figure 5–13).

- Press DELETE to delete the code.

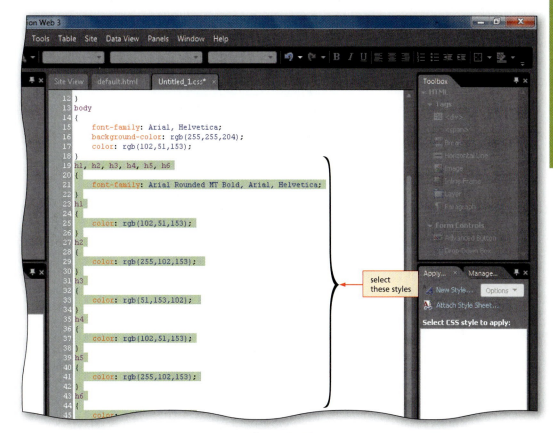

Figure 5–13

4

- On line 17, select rgb(102,51,153).

- Press BACKSPACE twice, press the SPACEBAR to activate the shortcut menu, then point to blue (Figure 5–14).

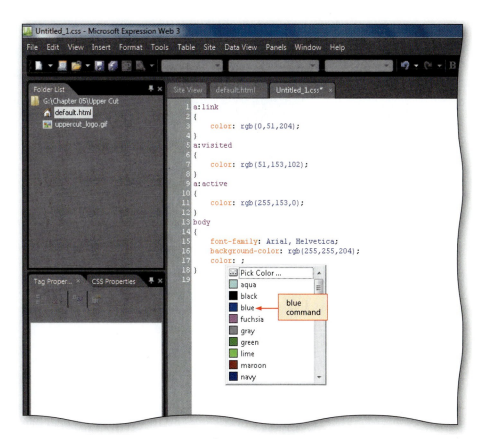

Figure 5–14

• Double-click blue to change the body font to blue (Figure 5–15).

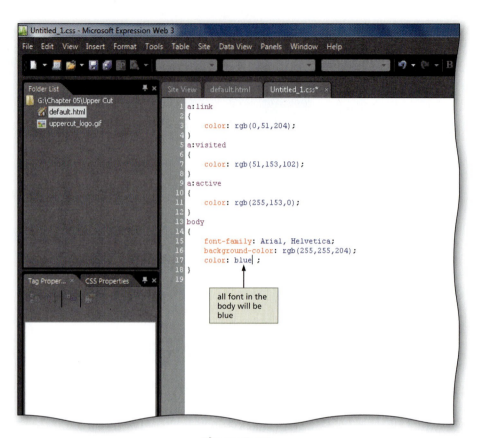

Figure 5–15

• Press CTRL+S to open the Save As dialog box.

• Type uppercut_styles.css in the File name text box (Figure 5–16).

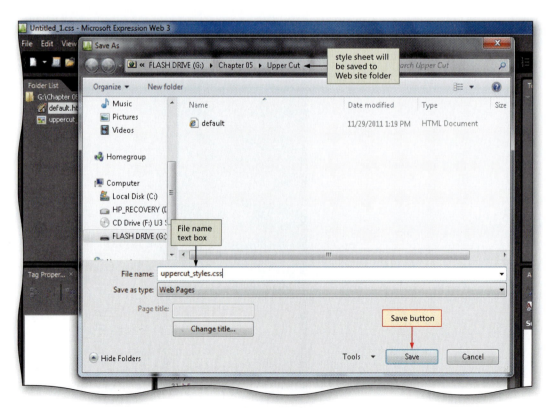

Figure 5–16

7

- Click the Save button to save the style sheet.

- Close the style sheet.

- Click the Attach Style Sheet link in the Apply Styles panel to open the Attach Style Sheet dialog box (Figure 5–17).

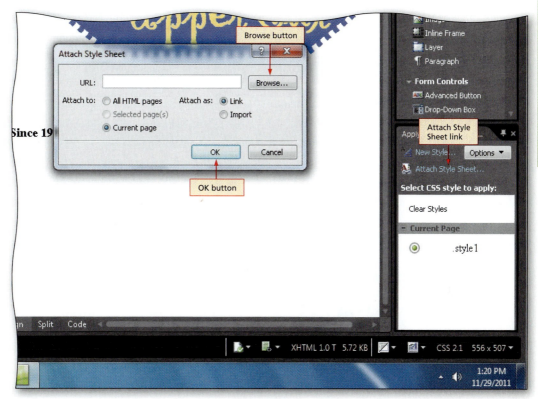

Figure 5–17

8

- Click the Browse button to open the Select Style Sheet dialog box.

- Click uppercut_styles to select it (Figure 5–18).

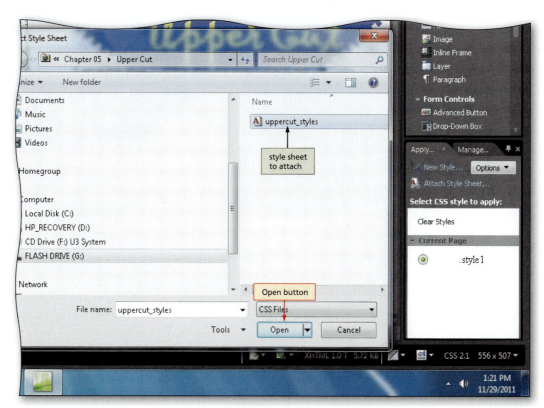

Figure 5–18

9

- Click the Open button to close the Select Style Sheet dialog box.

- Click the OK button to close the Attach Style Sheet dialog box and attach the style sheet to the page (Figure 5–19).

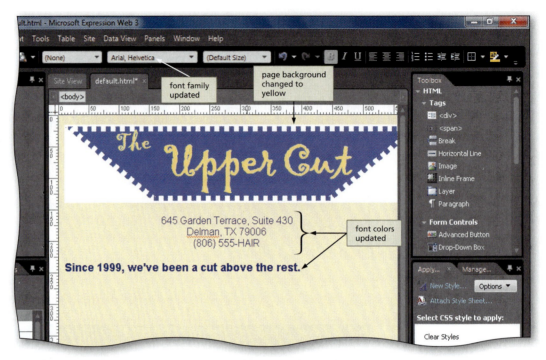

Figure 5–19

10

- Right-click the toolbar to display the shortcut menu, then click Pictures to display the Pictures toolbar.

- Click the logo to select it.

- Click the Set Transparent Color button on the Pictures toolbar to change the pointer to the transparency pointer.

- Click an area of the white color around the logo to make it transparent (Figure 5–20).

Figure 5–20

- Save the default.html page and click OK to save embedded files.

Other Ways

1. Click the New Document button arrow on the Common toolbar, then click Page to open the New dialog box

2. Point to CSS Styles on the Format menu, then click Attach Style Sheet to open the Attach Style Sheet dialog box

To Create a New Page and Attach a Style Sheet

You must create a new page for the table so that you can embed it as an inline frame on the home page. The page background, font family, and other styles for the page containing the table should be consistent with other pages in the site, so you will attach the style sheet from the default.html page to the new page. The following steps create a new blank page and attach the uppercut_styles CSS.

1

- Click the New Document button on the Common toolbar to insert a new blank page.

- Click the Attach Style Sheet link in the Apply Styles panel to open the Attach Style Sheet dialog box (Figure 5–21).

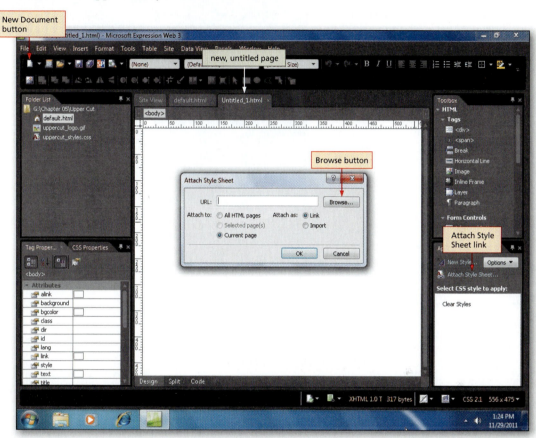

Figure 5–21

2

- Click the Browse button to open the Select Style Sheet dialog box.

- Click uppercut_styles to select it.

- Click the Open button to close the Select Style Sheet dialog box (Figure 5–22).

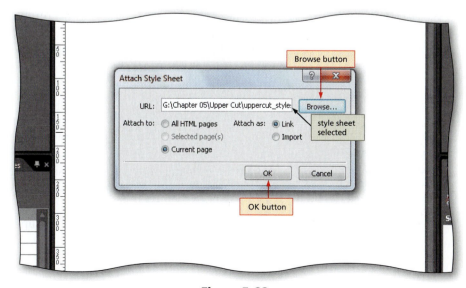

Figure 5–22

3

- Click the OK button to close the Attach Style Sheet dialog box.

- Press CTRL+S to open the Save As dialog box.

- Type `stylist_table.html` in the File name text box, then click the Save button to save the new page (Figure 5–23).

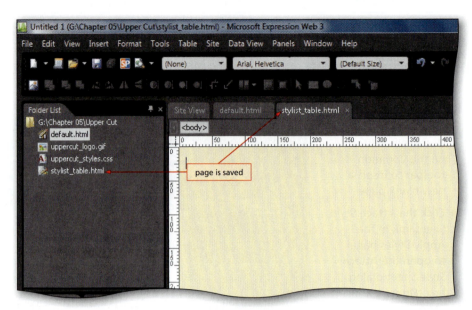

Figure 5–23

Other Ways

1. Press CTRL+N to open a new blank page

Creating Data Tables

Table Background Image
Another way to make your table stand out is to add a background image that appears behind the table. Only use this option when necessary because it increases the file size (causing slower download time in a browser), and can distract from the table data.

Saving Default Table Settings
In the Table Properties dialog box, click the 'Set as default for new tables' check box to save your settings for future tables in your site to ensure consistency and save you time.

A table used to present data is called a **data table**, or just a table. Data is entered into cells, and cells are arranged in horizontal rows and vertical columns. When creating a table, you begin by specifying numbers of rows and columns, and then you modify the table properties to customize its appearance.

Tables are often used on Web pages and other documents to list items and characteristics. For example, a list of products offered at a store can show each product on its own new row, with columns of characteristics, such as description, price, item number, and so on. Column headers for each characteristic enable the visitor to scan through the list of items and determine the relevant information about each.

You could attempt to present information in columns and rows by using the TAB key to insert space between words to simulate columns and the ENTER key to start new lines to simulate rows, but this method will cause your text to misalign when presented at different screen resolutions and is not a good practice. Creating a table enables you to use CSS to ensure that your data will be accessible, consistently presented, and easy to format and reorganize. Tables use HTML tags to define captions (<tc>), rows (<tr>), headers (<th>), cell data (<td>), and the entire table (<table>).

A **caption** is a line of text used to describe the table to visitors using screen readers or other adaptive devices, or to provide additional information about the table. A caption typically appears above or below the table. Although CSS has the option to create a caption on the side of the table, this is not widely supported by browsers, so Expression Web does not offer this capability.

Working with Data Tables

Cell divisions in a table are shown as dotted lines, which are a type of visual aid called **tracer lines**. By default, there are no gridlines that separate table row and column borders, so it is important to have Visual Aids turned on when working with a table so that you can see where cells are divided.

To Insert a Data Table

All of the information on the new page will be included as part of the table. The salon has three stylists, each of whom will have his or her own row; you will need one row for owners Marcus and Elisa; and you will need to include a row that contains column headers — so you will include a total of five rows. Each stylist will have a column for his or her name, a picture, and a description of the stylist's background and services, so you will need three columns — a total of 15 cells. You will also add a table caption to appear at the bottom of the table. The following steps insert a new blank table using the Insert Table dialog box and add a table caption.

1

- Right-click the toolbar to display the shortcut menu, then click Pictures to close the Pictures toolbar.

- Click Insert Table on the Table menu to open the Insert Table dialog box.

- Type 5 in the Rows box to specify a five-row table, then press TAB to move to the Columns box.

- Type 3 in the Columns box to specify a three-column table (Figure 5–24).

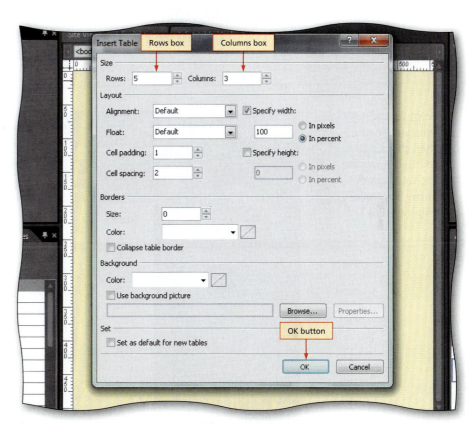

Figure 5–24

2

- Click the OK button to close the Insert Table dialog box and insert the new table (Figure 5–25).

Why can't I see the borders of the table on my screen?

Visual Aids must be turned on to see the table borders. Point to Visual Aids on the View menu and click Show to turn on Visual Aids.

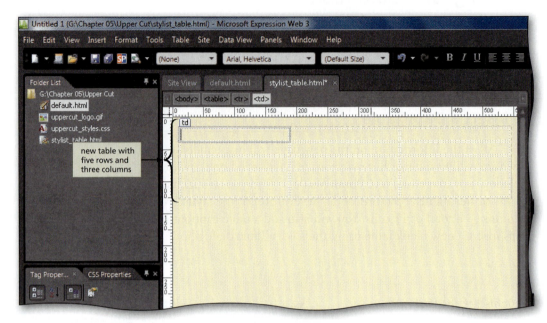

Figure 5–25

3

- Point to Insert on the Table menu, then click Caption to insert a tag for the table caption above the table (Figure 5–26).

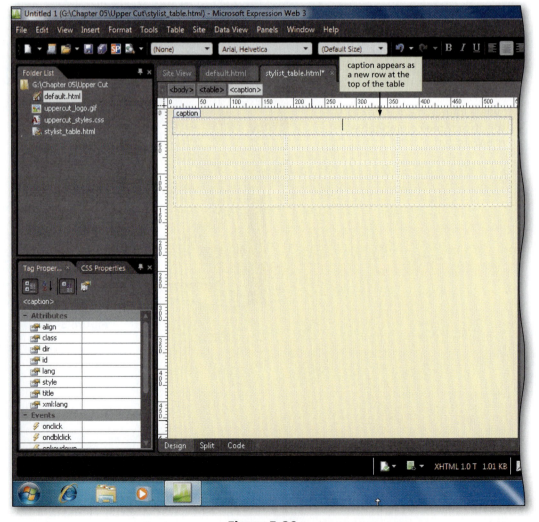

Figure 5–26

• Right-click the caption row to open the shortcut menu, then click Caption Properties to open the Caption Properties dialog box (Figure 5–27).

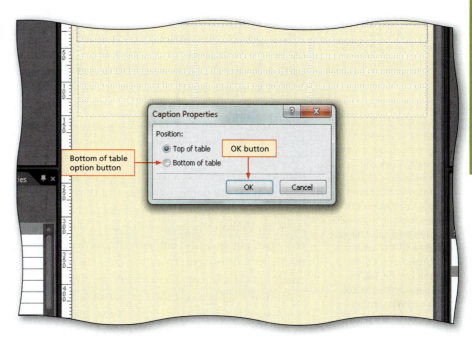

Figure 5–27

5

• Click the 'Bottom of table' option button to select it.

• Click the OK button to close the Caption Properties dialog box and position the caption at the bottom of the table (Figure 5–28).

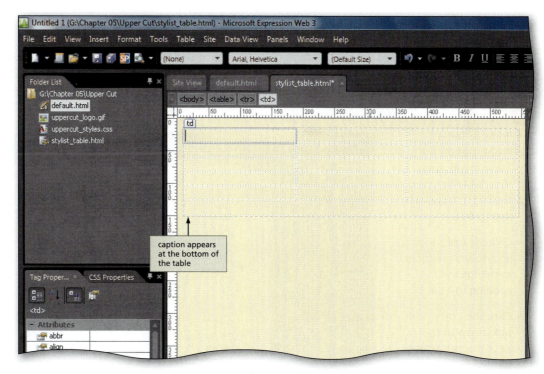

Figure 5–28

Other Ways

1. Point to Table Properties on the Table menu, then click Caption to open the Caption Properties dialog box

Table and Cell Properties

Table properties define the alignment, borders, and background of the table, and also define default cell settings, such as padding and text alignment. Table properties apply to all cells in a table. You can change the same settings (alignment, background, and so on) for a certain

Web Accessibility
See Appendix B for more information about accessibility and assistive technology.

BTW

Adjusting Cell Margins
To adjust the column width or row height, drag the column divider manually. Click the Distribute Rows Evenly or Distribute Columns Evenly buttons on the Tables toolbar to make all rows and columns the same height or width. The AutoFit to Contents button on the Tables toolbar adjusts the column width based on the cell with the most content in that column.

amount of cells by changing their cell properties. Changing the cell properties modifies the settings for the cell containing the insertion point, or for any selected cells, rows, or columns.

To select an entire row or column, position the I-beam pointer to the left of the row or the top of the column to select; then when the pointer changes to the row selector, a small black arrow, click to select the row or column.

Defining a **header** row assigns the <th> HTML tag for that row and applies bold formatting to the text in that row. Headers are often distinguished from the body of the table with different text formatting, such as a heading style or bold, or by applying a different background color. When a table is being read by a screen reader for a visitor with visual impairment, the screen reader will read the header categories when reading the data for each row. For example, in a table that lists the members of John's basketball team and includes the name, number, and position of each player, the screen reader would read Name: John; Number: 33; Position: Center.

By default, the table will span 100% of the page width. You can create a data table that does not span the entire width of the page by reducing the width percentage to less than 100% or by specifying the data table's width in pixels instead of a percentage. A data table that does not span the entire width of the page can be aligned at the left or right margin of the page or centered between the margins. By default, the height of a table is not specified when you create the table. Because the height for each row might need to expand to fit the cell contents, it is best to leave the height of the table unspecified in order to avoid truncating table data.

To Change Table and Cell Properties

The following steps use the Table Properties dialog box to add padding to increase the white space between the cell contents and cell margins. You will also add a table background color, format the cell properties of the top row to change the text alignment to center, and specify the table header.

1

• Point to Table Properties on the Table menu, then click Table to open the Table Properties dialog box.

• Click the Cell padding up arrow three times to change the padding to 4 pixels.

• Click the Color box arrow in the Background section to display the color palette (Figure 5–29).

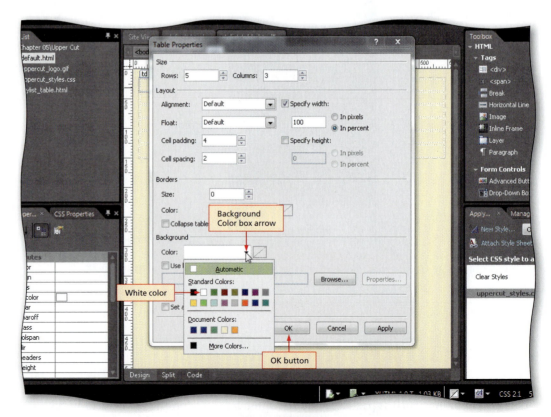

Figure 5–29

2

- Click White on the color palette to change the table background to white.

- Click the OK button to close the Table Properties dialog box (Figure 5–30).

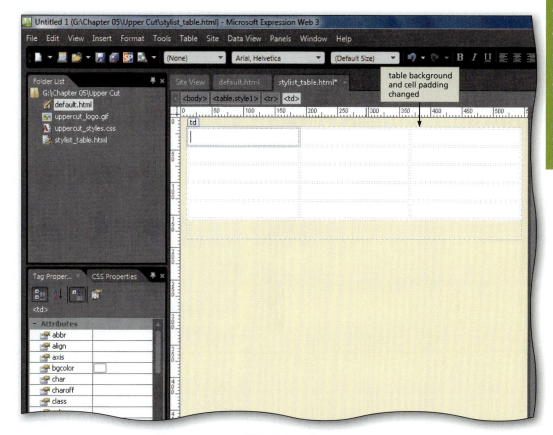

Figure 5–30

3

- Position the pointer over the left side of the top row until the pointer becomes the row selector, a black, right-pointing arrow.

- Click to select the top row of the table (Figure 5–31).

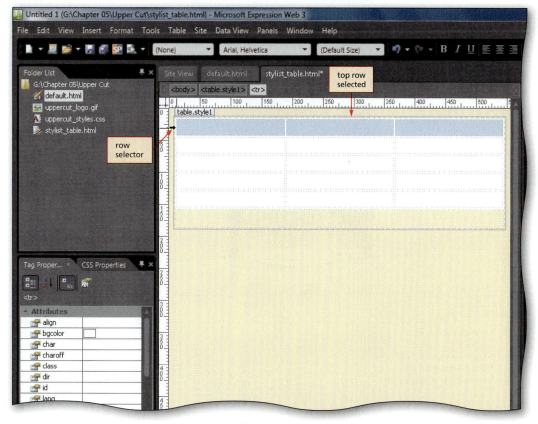

Figure 5–31

4

- Point to Table Properties on the Table menu, then click Cell to open the Cell Properties dialog box.

- Click the Horizontal alignment box arrow, then click Center to center-align the text in the top row of the table.

- If necessary, click the Header cell check box to select it and define the top row of the table as the header (Figure 5–32).

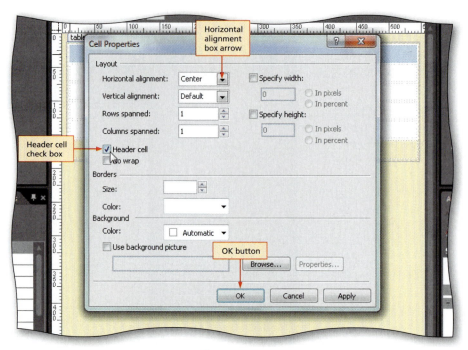

Figure 5–32

5

- Click the OK button to close the Cell Properties dialog box (Figure 5–33).

Experiment

- Open the Table Properties dialog box again and select different options, such as changing the table width or background. Close the dialog box, view your changes, then press CTRL+Z to undo them.

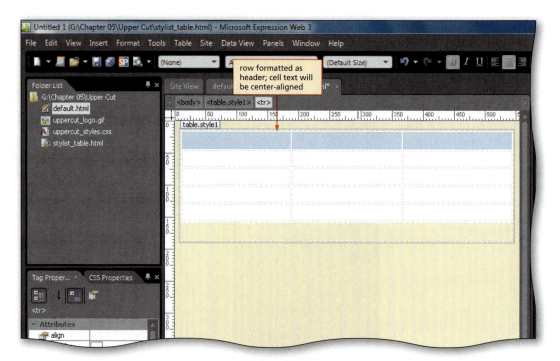

Figure 5–33

Other Ways

1. Right-click an area of the table, then click Table Properties or Cell Properties to open the Table or Cell Properties dialog box

Add and arrange table content.

Including a table header simplifies data entry by clearly indicating where information should appear. Once the content has been added to the table, you should evaluate the table to see whether additional rows or columns are needed, and whether any cells should be combined or divided. Consulting with a colleague or your client is a good way to ensure that your table reads well to others and that no additional content is needed. Splitting and merging cells gives you flexibility when presenting data — you can combine cells to show relationships between data or to create a table header, or you can separate cells to add additional information.

Plan Ahead

BTW

Controlling Column Width

To control a column's width when typing the header data, position cell content onto two lines by pressing SHIFT+ENTER to insert a line break. Do not insert line breaks in non-header cells, as this will cause your table data to flow awkwardly when viewed at different screen resolutions.

Entering Text into Cells

In a blank data table, all columns are the same width and all rows are the same height. As you enter data, the width of the current column expands and the other columns adjust.

Click the cell in which you want to enter content, then start typing. To navigate in a table, you can use the pointer to click a cell or use the keyboard shortcuts outlined in Table 5–1 to move the insertion point around the table.

Table 5–1 Table Navigation Keyboard Shortcuts

Press	To go to
TAB	The next cell in the row, or when at the end of a row, to the first cell in the next row.
SHIFT+TAB	The previous cell in the row, or when at the beginning of a row, to the last cell in the previous row.
DOWN ARROW	The cell in the row below.
UP ARROW	The cell in the row above.
RIGHT ARROW	The next empty cell in the table, if there is no content in the cell. If there is content in the cell, the insertion point moves forward through the content one character at a time.
LEFT ARROW	The previous empty cell in the table, if there is no content in the cell. If there is content in the cell, the insertion point moves backward through the content one character at a time.

To Add Text to a Table

The following steps enter data in the header row, caption, and other cells in the table. You will leave the Photo column blank for now.

- Click the upper-left cell in the table to position the insertion point in the header row.

- Type Name, then press TAB to move to the next cell (Figure 5–34).

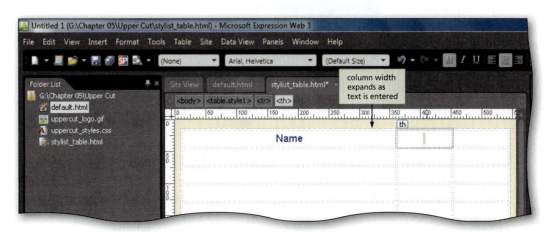

Figure 5–34

2

• Type Photo, then press TAB to move to the next cell.

• Type About, then press TAB to move to the first cell in the next row (Figure 5–35).

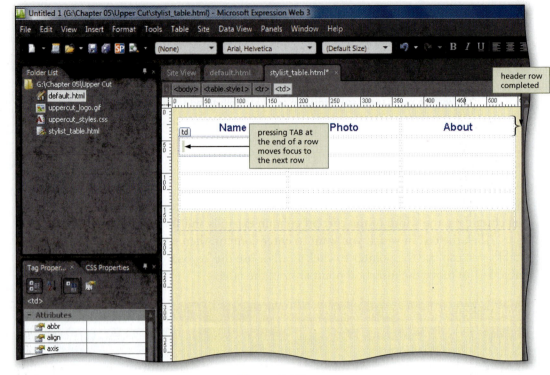

Figure 5–35

3

• Type Sarah, then press TAB twice to move to the About column.

• Type Sarah has more than 14 years' experience as a stylist, and has been at The Upper Cut for the past five years. Sarah's clients look to her to advise them on balancing their personal style with current trends. She is a certified color specialist., then press TAB to move to the first cell in the next row (Figure 5–36).

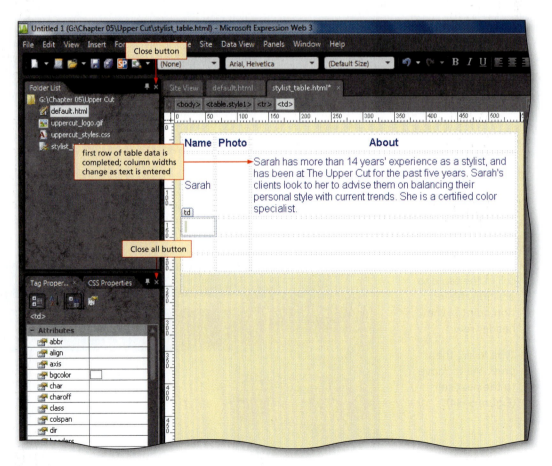

Figure 5–36

4

- Click the Close button on the Folder List and click the Close all button on the Tag Properties panel to provide more space in the editing window.

- If necessary, click in the first cell of the third row, type `Angela`, then press TAB twice to move to the About column.

- Type `Angela started her styling career at The Upper Cut four years ago, after completing her degree at Athena Beauty Academy. Angela provides a full range of color and foiling techniques, and is certified in men's cuts.`, then press TAB to move to the first cell in the next row.

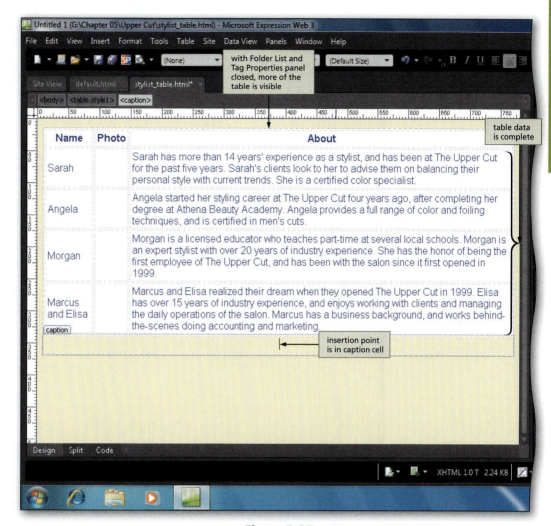

Figure 5–37

- Type `Morgan`, then press TAB twice to move to the About column.

- Type `Morgan is a licensed educator who teaches part-time at several local schools. Morgan is an expert stylist with over 20 years of industry experience. She has the honor of being the first employee of The Upper Cut, and has been with the salon since it opened in 1999.`, then press TAB to move to the first cell in the next row.

- Type `Marcus and Elisa`, then press TAB twice to move to the About column.

- Type `Marcus and Elisa realized their dream when they opened The Upper Cut in 1999. Elisa has over 15 years of industry experience, and enjoys working with clients and managing the daily operations of the salon. Marcus has a business background, and works behind-the-scenes doing accounting and marketing.`

- Click in the caption cell to position the insertion point (Figure 5–37).

5

- Type Prices are for a basic haircut and blow dry, and the range depends on the style and length of cut. Color service pricing is listed below haircut prices, where applicable. Prices subject to change. as the caption text (Figure 5–38).

- Press CTRL+S to save the page.

caption text is center-aligned

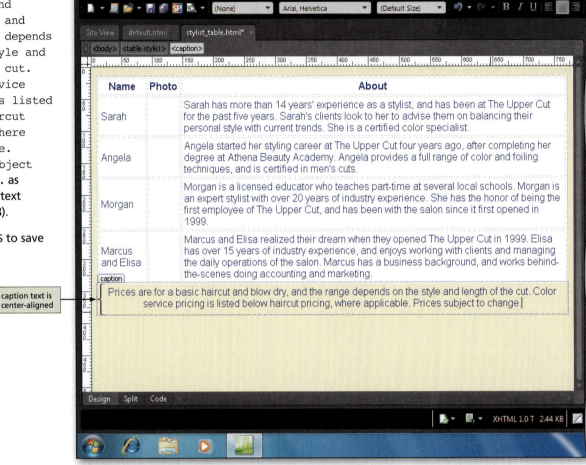

Figure 5–38

BTW

Inserting Images
Use images to illustrate text, or to define a company by including a logo. Consider the quality and file size of the image, make sure that you have the proper permissions, and modify the images by resizing, cropping, or using other techniques to enhance them.

Adding Images into Cells

Images will increase the file size of the page containing the table, so you should take into consideration some of the decisions and actions discussed in Chapter 2. Use images that display with the correct quality, but with a file size that does not considerably slow down the page when downloading in a browser. Only include images to enhance and illustrate table data, and make sure that the image is resized to fit the desired space.

To Add Images to a Table

The following steps add images to the Photo column for Sarah, Angela, Morgan, and Marcus and Elisa.

- Click the cell to the right of the word, Sarah, to position the insertion point.

- Point to Picture on the Insert menu, then click From File to open the Picture dialog box.

- Click the sarah file to select it (Figure 5–39).

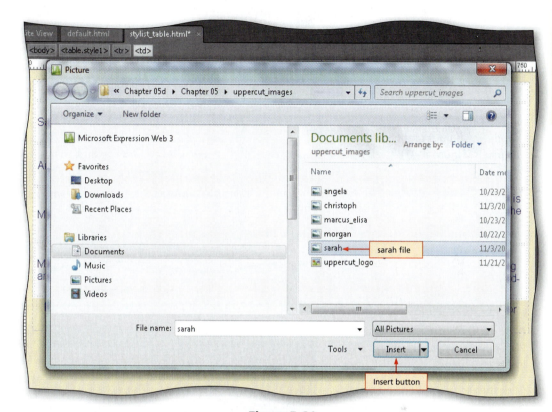

Figure 5–39

- Click the Insert button to open the Accessibility Properties dialog box.

- Type `Sarah's photo` in the Alternate text text box, then click the OK button to insert the image (Figure 5–40).

Figure 5–40

- Right-click the image to open the shortcut menu, then click Picture Properties to open the Picture Properties dialog box.

- Click the Appearance tab to display the sizing options.

- Verify that the 'Keep aspect ratio' check box is checked, then type 125 in the width box to change the height and width to 125 pixels (Figure 5–41).

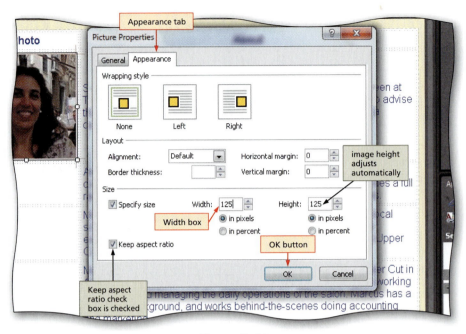

Figure 5–41

- Click the OK button to close the Picture Properties dialog box and insert the image.

- Click the Picture Actions button to display the menu (Figure 5–42).

- Click the Resample Picture To Match Size option button to resample the image.

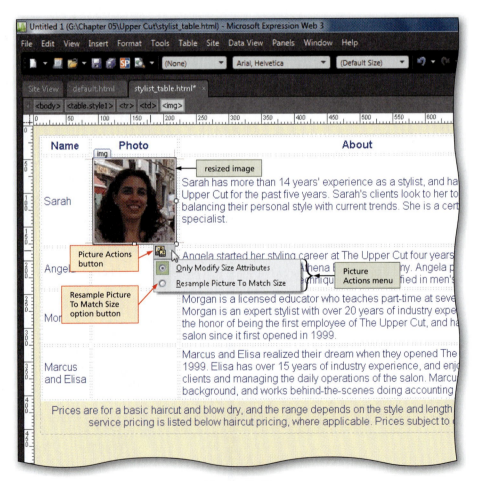

Figure 5–42

5

- Repeat Steps 1 through 4 to insert and resample the angela.jpg, morgan.jpg, and marcus_elisa.jpg images (Figure 5–43).

- Save the page and all embedded images.

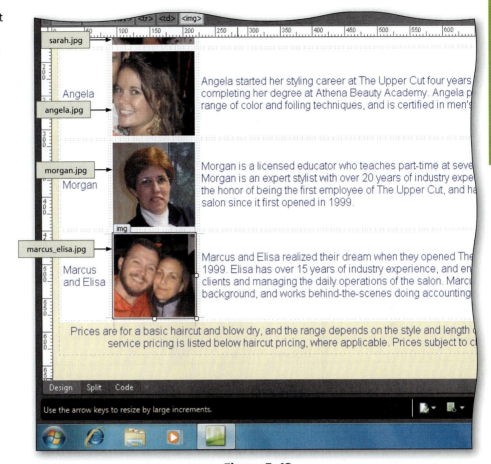

Figure 5–43

Other Ways

1. Click the Insert Picture from File button on the Common toolbar to open the Picture dialog box

Adding Rows and Columns

After creating a table, you might need to add rows and columns to it. To add a row when entering content, you can simply press TAB after entering data in the last cell in the table, and a new row is automatically added to the end of a table. You can also insert rows above or below any row in the table, or insert columns to the left or right of any column in the table.

The Tables Toolbar

The commands for adding rows and columns are available on the Table menu, as well as on a task-specific Tables toolbar. Like the Pictures toolbar that you used in previous chapters to modify images, the Tables toolbar provides access to the necessary tools to make modifications to your table. Using buttons on the Tables toolbar, you can insert and delete rows and columns, merge and split cells, and specify table and cell properties, such as text alignment and background color.

To Add Rows and Columns

The following steps display the Tables toolbar, add a column for the price range for each stylist, add a new row for a stylist who has just joined The Upper Cut staff, and then enter his data.

- Right-click a blank area above the Common toolbar to open a shortcut menu, then click Tables to display the Tables toolbar (Figure 5–44).

Q&A

My Tables toolbar is not docked.

Position the insertion point over the toolbar's title bar, click, then drag the toolbar up below the Common toolbar until it docks.

Figure 5–44

2

- Click any cell in the About column to position the insertion point.

- Click the Column to the Left button on the Tables toolbar to add a new column (Figure 5–45).

Figure 5–45

3

- Click the top cell in the new column to position the insertion point in the column header.

- Type `Price Range` to add a header to the new column (Figure 5–46).

Figure 5–46

4

- Click any cell in the Morgan row to position the insertion point.

- Click the Row Below button on the Tables toolbar to add a new row (Figure 5–47).

Experiment

- Add another row or column, select it, then click the Delete Cells button on the Tables toolbar to practice deleting rows or columns.

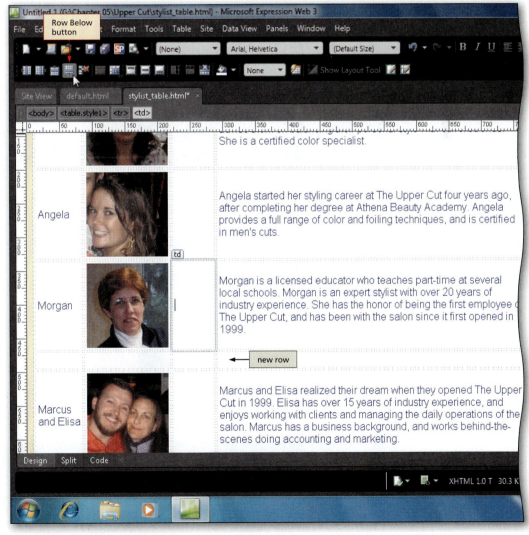

Figure 5–47

5

- Click the first cell in the new row to position the insertion point.

- Type Christoph, then press TAB to move to the next cell.

- Point to Picture on the Insert menu, then click From File to open the Picture dialog box.

- Click the christoph image to select it.

- Click the Insert button to open the Accessibility Properties dialog box.

- Type Christoph's photo, then click the OK button to close the Accessibility Properties dialog box and insert the image.

- Right-click the image to open the shortcut menu, then click Picture Properties to open the Picture Properties dialog box.

- Click the Appearance tab, then type 125 in the Width box to change the height and width to 125 pixels (Figure 5–48).

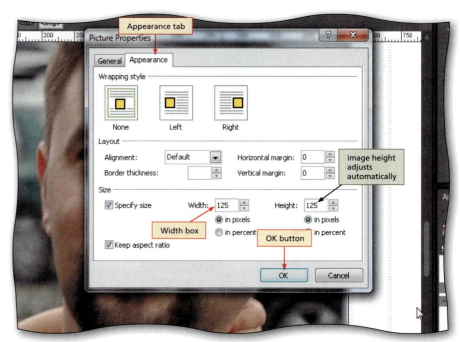

Figure 5–48

6

- Click the OK button to close the dialog box and insert the image.

- Click the Picture Actions button to display the menu.

- Click the Resample Picture To Match Size option button to resample the image (Figure 5–49).

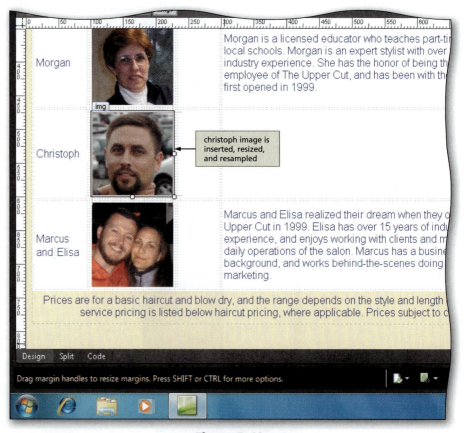

Figure 5–49

- If necessary, press RIGHT ARROW to deselect the image but keep the insertion point in the cell.

- Press TAB twice to position the insertion point in the About column.

- Type Christoph is The Upper Cut's newest stylist. He spent the first ten years of his career in Boston, and recently relocated to Delman to raise his family. Christoph's prior experience includes special event styles, including wedding parties and proms. to complete the new row content (Figure 5–50).

- Save the stylist_table.html page and embedded files.

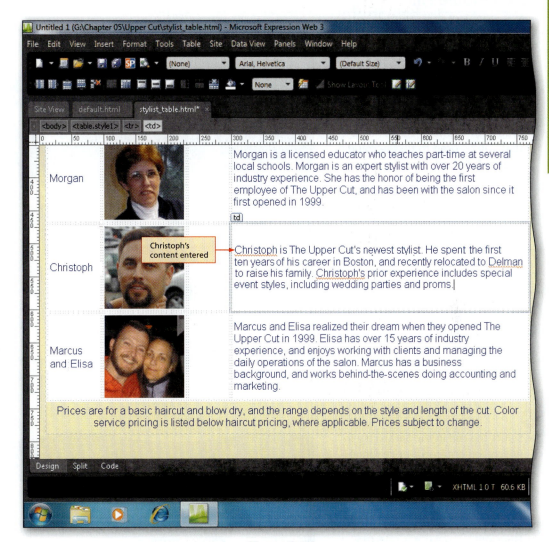

Figure 5–50

Other Ways

1. Point to Insert on the Table menu, then click an option to add or delete rows or columns

Table Fill

Using the **Table Fill** command, you can complete a column or row of data with the same data content to save time when entering table data. Table Fill is a useful feature when most or all of the data in a row or column is the same. For example, at the salon, many of the stylists have the same rates for services. For the cells with content that differs from the filled data, select the cells and replace the data with the correct data.

To Use Table Fill

The following steps use Table Fill to fill the price range column. You will then edit two entries in the column.

 1

- Click the third cell in the Sarah row to position the insertion point in the new Price Range column.

- Type $35–$45 to enter the data that will be used to fill the column (Figure 5–51).

Figure 5–51

2

- Select the cell in the Sarah row in which you entered a price range and drag down to select the rows below it to specify the fill value and range (Figure 5–52).

Q&A

I can't see the cell in the last row. How will I know if it is selected?

When selecting the column, drag down below the document window over the status bar. The last cell in the column should be selected even though it isn't visible.

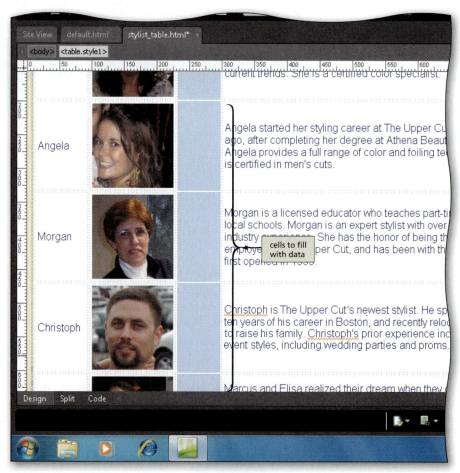

Figure 5–52

3

- Point to Fill on the Table menu (Figure 5–53).

Figure 5–53

4

- Click Down to fill the value in the column (Figure 5–54).

 Experiment

- Add a new row, type text into the first cell, then select the row. Point to Fill on the Table menu, then click Right to practice filling a row. Delete the row.

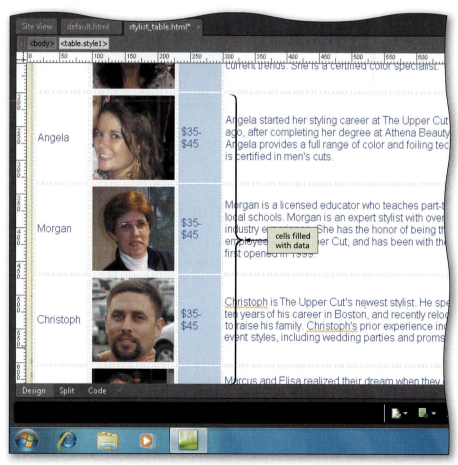

Figure 5–54

5

- Click in the cell containing Morgan's price range.

- Select the current text, then type $40–$50.

- Click in the cell containing Marcus and Elisa's price range.

- If necessary, select the current text, then type $45–$55 (Figure 5–55).

- Save the stylist_table.html page.

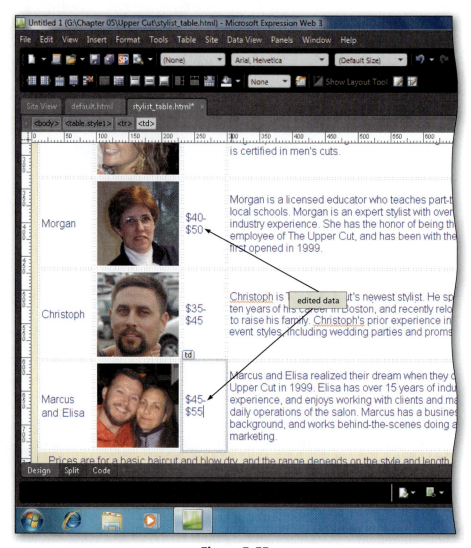

Figure 5–55

BTW

Splitting and Merging Cells

When you merge cells that contain data, the data from both cells is combined in the merged cell. When you split a cell that contains data, the data appears in the left or top cell, depending on whether you split it into rows or columns.

Merging and Splitting Cells

Combining two or more adjacent cells is called **merging**. **Splitting** a cell creates two or more rows or columns within a cell. Merging and splitting cells is done to combine or separate content in order to clarify table data.

Merging a row at the top of the table is often done to create a **title row** for the table; the title row has the same properties as the rest of the table. A title row differs from a caption. A caption is a description of the table contents or purpose, whereas a title row is used to name the rows in the table.

To Merge Table Cells

The following steps add a new row for the table title, then merge the cells in the new row.

1

- Click anywhere in the table header row to position the insertion point.

- Click the Row Above button on the Tables toolbar to insert a new row (Figure 5–56).

Figure 5–56

2

- Position the pointer over the left side of the new row to change the pointer to the row selector.

- Click to select the top row of the table.

- Click the Merge Cells button on the Tables toolbar to merge all the header cells into one cell (Figure 5–57).

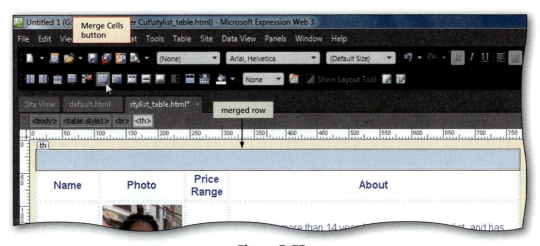

Figure 5–57

3

- Click in the merged cell to position the insertion point.

- Type Meet the Staff of The Upper Cut to enter the table title (Figure 5–58).

- Save the page.

Q&A

Why is the text centered in the cell?

Because the merged cells were inserted above the table header row, they are formatted as a header; in this case, with centered text.

Figure 5–58

To Split Table Cells

As noted in the text you typed in the table caption, some stylists have a separate price range for their haircut and coloring services. The following steps split the price range cells for Sarah and Angela into rows and enter price ranges for coloring services.

- Click in the Price Range cell in Sarah's row to position the insertion point.

- Click the Split Cells button on the Tables toolbar to open the Split Cells dialog box.

- Click the 'Split into rows' option button to select it (Figure 5–59).

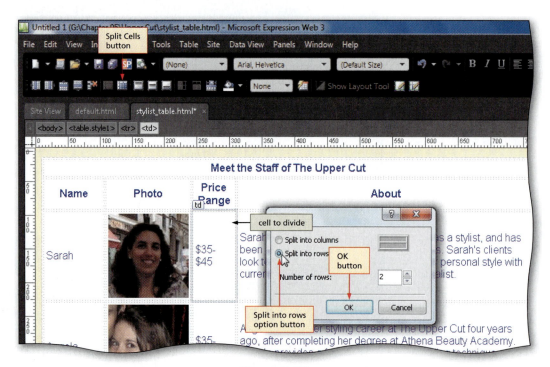

Figure 5–59

- Click the OK button to split the cells (Figure 5–60).

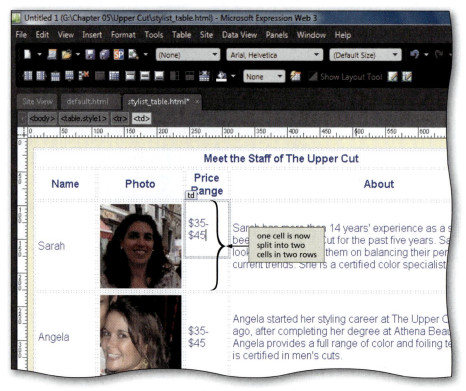

Figure 5–60

3

- Click the second row of the split cell to position the insertion point.

- Type $60–$90 to enter the cell content (Figure 5–61).

Figure 5–61

4

- Repeat Steps 1 through 3 to split Angela's price range cell into two rows and enter $60–$90 as the content for the second row of the split cell (Figure 5–62).

- Save the page.

 Experiment

- Select any cell in the table, then click the Split Cells button. Click the 'Split into columns' option button, type 3 in the 'Number of columns' box, then click the OK button to close the dialog box and see the cell split into three columns. Press CTRL+Z to undo the split.

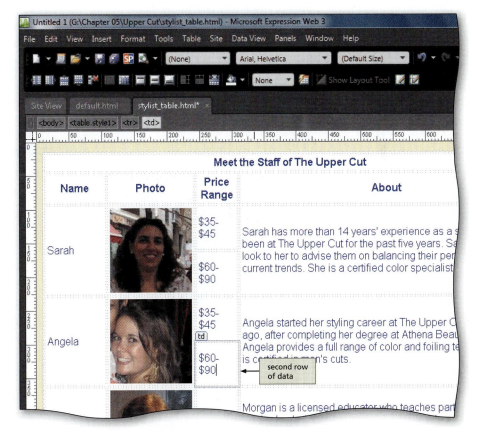

Figure 5–62

Formatting Table Text

CSS text styles, such as headings, can be used to format table text so that it uses the styles defined in the attached style sheet. Using an AutoFormat allows you to apply several formatting choices at once, including font color and contrasting background colors for rows and columns (called **striping**).

<table>
<tr><td>**Plan Ahead**</td><td>**Design the table.**
Determine the style of the table and how much emphasis it should have on the page: a strong emphasis, as in a different background color or with bold font color choices, or more subtle, to blend in with the existing page content. Using styles to format the table ensures consistency and enables you to update your table as changes are made to styles that affect the rest of the page or pages in your site. When choosing an AutoFormat, make sure that the look of the table matches your design plan.</td></tr>
</table>

To Apply Styles to Table Text

The following steps assign text styles to distinguish the row and column headers.

1
- Click anywhere in the merged cell at the top of the table to position the insertion point.

- Click the <th> tag on the Quick Tag Selector to select the tag.

- Click the Style box arrow on the Common toolbar, then point to Heading 1 <h1> (Figure 5–63).

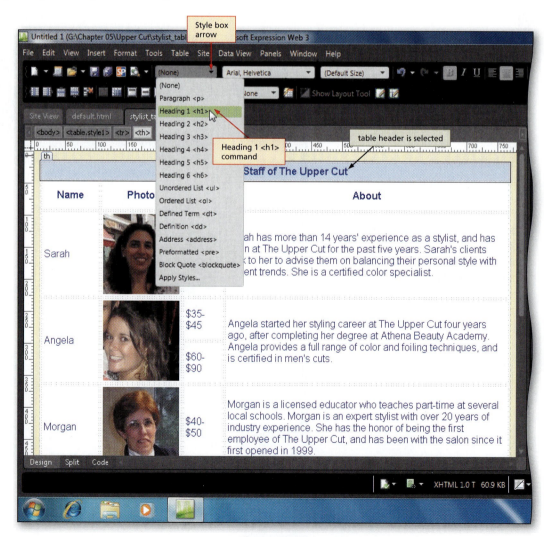

Figure 5–63

- Click Heading 1 <h1> to apply the style to the title row.

- Position the pointer to the left of row 2 to change the pointer to the row selector.

- Click to select row 2.

- Click the Style box arrow on the Common toolbar, then point to Heading 3 <h3> (Figure 5–64).

Figure 5–64

- Click Heading 3 <h3> to apply the style to the header row.

- Select the five cells containing the stylists' names.

- Click the Style box arrow on the Common toolbar, then click Heading 3 <h3> to apply the style to the selected cells (Figure 5–65).

- Save and close the stylist_table.html page.

Figure 5–65

Converting Text to a Table

You may encounter a situation when you realize that text you entered on a page would be better formatted as a table. When entering large amounts of text in a document, you should consider this before you start typing; but for small amounts of text, it is fine to convert text to a table after it is typed. In order to convert text into a table, it needs to be properly **delineated**, or separated into groupings using commas, spaces, or tabs. When entering text, do not attempt to align it by adding extra spaces or tabs. Doing so will create cells for each extra delineation, causing your table to be misaligned.

Plan Ahead

Organize existing content into the table.
Converting text to a table allows text to be aligned in columns and rows and formatted consistently. Text in tables appears in rows and columns, and you can add headers to describe the table data.

To Convert Text to a Table

The following steps return to the default.html page, enter text in a new paragraph tag, and convert it to a table.

- Verify that default .html is open in Expression Web, then click below the line with the words, Since 1999, to position the insertion point.

- Double-click Paragraph in the Toolbox to insert a new paragraph.

- Type Monday, Tuesday, Wednesday, then press TAB to insert space as the column delineator.

- Type 10 AM to 6 PM, then press ENTER to complete the first line of the table text (Figure 5–66).

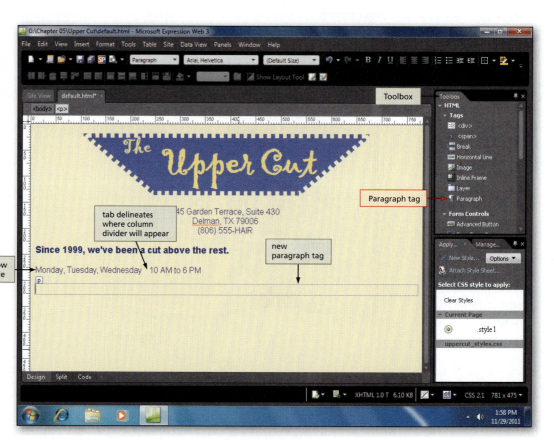

Figure 5–66

2

- Type `Thursday & Friday`, then press TAB to insert space.

- Type `10 AM to 8 PM`, then press ENTER to complete the second line of the table text.

- Type `Saturday`, then press TAB to insert space.

- Type `10 AM to 7 PM`, then press ENTER to complete the third line of the table text.

- Type `Sunday`, then press TAB to insert space.

- Type `Closed`, then press ENTER to complete the table text (Figure 5–67).

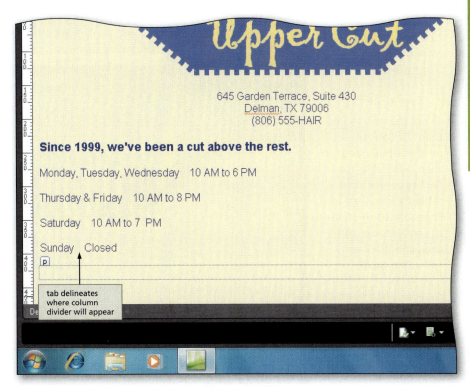

tab delineates where column divider will appear

Figure 5–67

3

- Select the four new lines of text.

- Point to Convert on the Table menu, then click Text To Table to open the Convert Text To Table dialog box.

- Click the Tabs option button to select it (Figure 5–68).

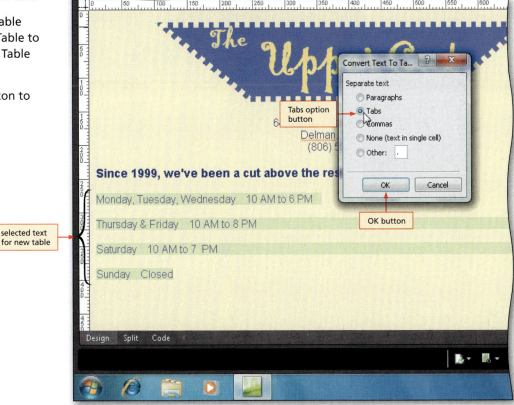

Tabs option button

selected text for new table

OK button

Figure 5–68

4

- Click the OK button to create a table from the text (Figure 5–69).

Experiment

- Select the new table, point to Convert on the Table menu, then click Table To Text to convert the table back to text. Press CTRL+Z to undo the conversion, and then click the last cell in the table.

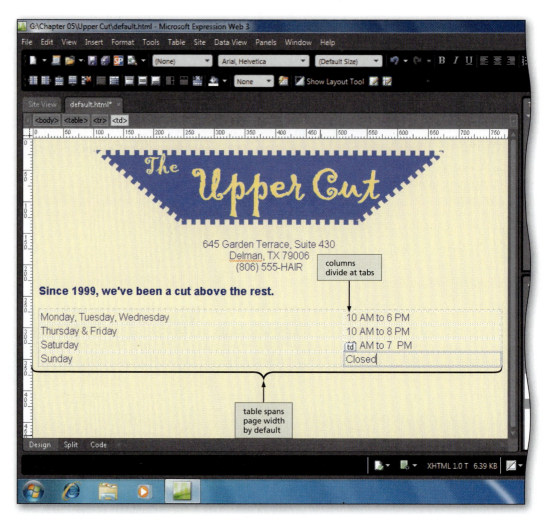

Figure 5–69

To Distribute Rows and Columns

The following steps deselect the Specify width table property; doing so automatically **distributes** the columns, or resizes the width of each column to fit to the width of its content. You will then center the table on the page.

- Right-click the table to open the shortcut menu, then click Table Properties to open the Table Properties dialog box.

- Click the Specify width check box to deselect it (Figure 5–70).

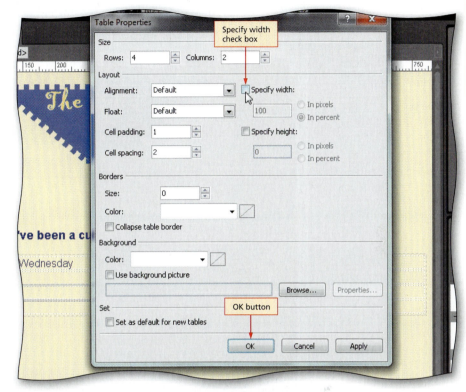

Figure 5–70

- Click the OK button to close the Table Properties dialog box and change the column width (Figure 5–71).

🔍 Experiment

- Position the pointer between two columns until the pointer turns into a two-sided arrow, then drag left or right to manually adjust the column width. Press CTRL+Z to undo the change.

Figure 5–71

3

- Click the <table> tag on the Quick Tag Selector to select the table.

- Click the Center button on the Common toolbar to center the table (Figure 5–72).

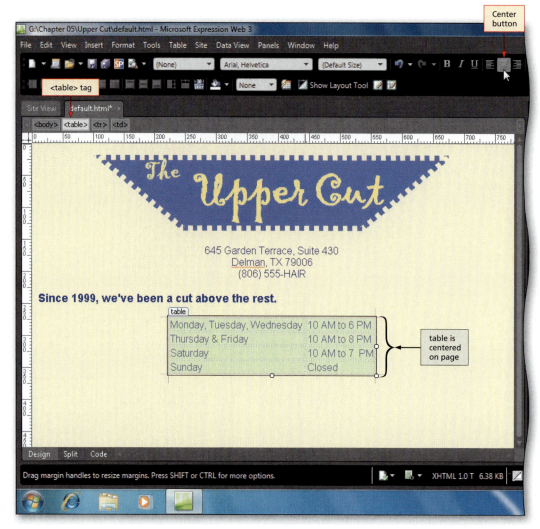

Figure 5–72

BTW

Quick Reference
For a table that lists how to complete the tasks covered in this book using the mouse, shortcut menu, and keyboard, see the Quick Reference Summary at the back of this book, or visit the Expression Web 3 Quick Reference Web page (scsite.com/ew3/qr).

Table AutoFormat

Table AutoFormat is an Expression Web feature that offers predetermined formatting options for tables. AutoFormat lets you specify rows or columns to differentiate as headers, and specify whether to modify features such as the border, shading, or font. AutoFormat is a formatting feature unique to Microsoft applications such as Microsoft Word. In Expression Web AutoFormat is used to format Web pages. As an AutoFormat is applied, Expression Web creates and saves styles as inline styles, not to a style sheet.

To Use Table AutoFormat

To add visual appeal, Marcus and Elisa want to add formatting to the table on the default.html page. The following steps apply an AutoFormat to the new table. Your table does not have header or column row text, so you will not have special formatting applied to the first row or column in the table.

- Click the Table AutoFormat button on the Tables toolbar to open the Table AutoFormat dialog box (Figure 5–73).

Experiment

- Click options in the Formats list to view them in the Preview window.

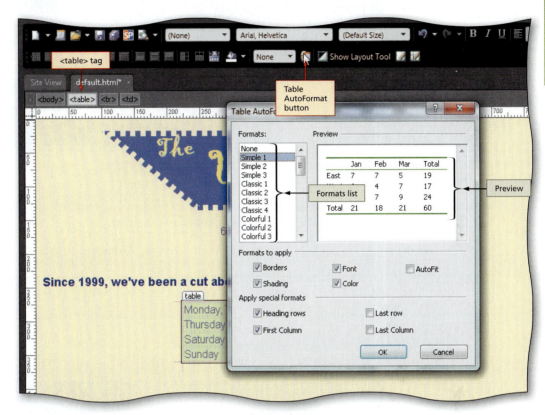

Figure 5–73

2

- Click the Heading rows check box to deselect it.

- Click the First Column check box to deselect it.

- Click the Borders check box to deselect it.

- Scroll down the Formats list, then click the Subtle 1 option to select it (Figure 5–74).

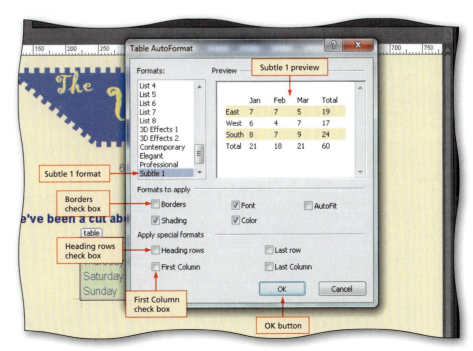

Figure 5–74

3

- Click the OK button to close the Table AutoFormat dialog box and apply the formatting to the table.

- Click outside of the table to deselect it (Figure 5–75).

- Save the page.

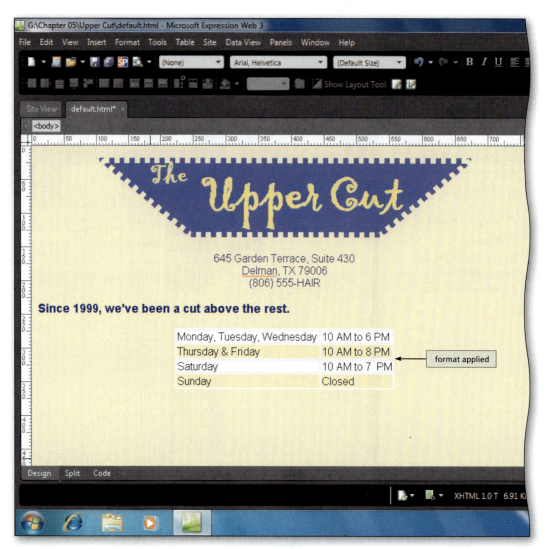

Figure 5–75

BTW

I-Frame Security
I-frames have been used by hackers to implant malicious code onto legitimate Web sites, causing security issues for the site visitors.

About Inline Frames

An inline frame, or an I-frame, is a way to embed one HTML file into another. Specifying the size of the frame that contains the embedded HTML page helps control the page size of the original HTML file when it is viewed in the browser. Recall that every element on a Web page contributes to the page's overall file size. Scroll boxes make it possible to view the content of the embedded HTML file if the frame in which it is embedded is not large enough to view the entire HTML file.

I-frames are helpful to display a table or other pages with large amounts of data that may not be of interest to all visitors. Embedding an advertisement or including information that may be in a sidebar of a printed publication are other uses for I-frames.

One advantage of using an I-frame is that the main page and the embedded file load in a browser separately. The site visitor can perform various actions within the embedded file without affecting the main page. For instance, clicking an item on a navigation bar can cause a new embedded HTML page to load without the browser having to reload the original page.

Add an I-frame to display a page.

An important consideration when adding an I-frame to a Web page is the display size of the main HTML page. Adding a frame for a table allows the visitor to see all or most of the page content without scrolling. For a table that provides additional reference information but is not the main focus of the page, having a small, scrollable window allows visitors to peruse the information in the table if they wish, while keeping their browser window on the original page. Changes to the table do not affect the main page, and vice versa.

**Plan
Ahead**

To Create an I-Frame

The following steps insert and resize the I-frame that will contain the stylist table.

- Click below the table, then press ENTER to position the insertion point where the I-frame will appear (Figure 5–76).

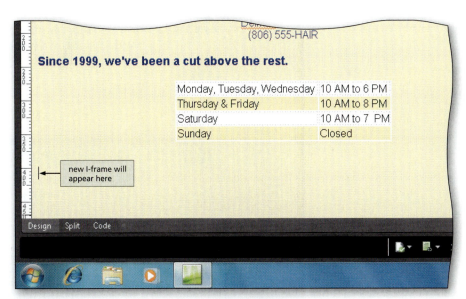

Figure 5–76

- If necessary, double-click Paragraph in the Toolbox to insert a new paragraph tag.

- Point to HTML on the Insert menu, then click Inline Frame to insert a new I-frame (Figure 5–77).

Q&A

Why is my I-frame in a different location?

If there are extra <p> tags between the table and the I-frame, delete them so that your I-frame placement matches Figure 5–79.

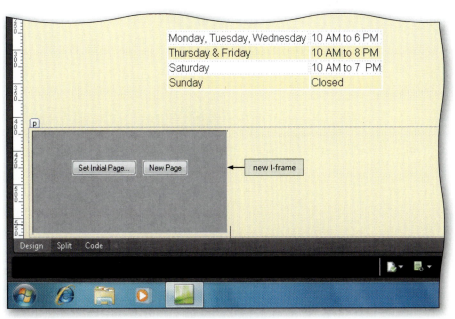

Figure 5–77

3

• Click the right edge of the frame, then click the sizing handle and drag to the right until the right edge is at 700 on the horizontal ruler and the status bar reads, width: 680px (Figure 5–78).

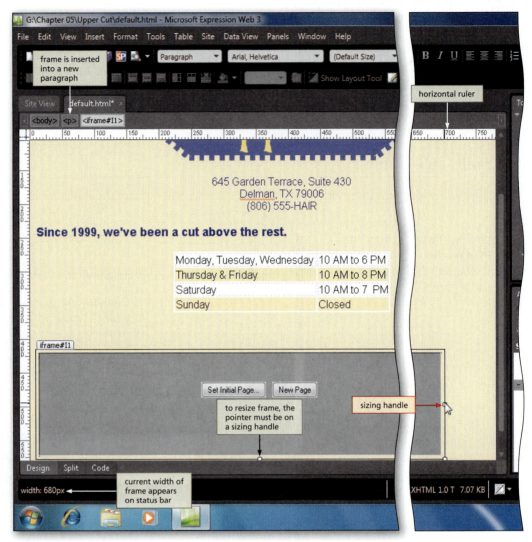

Figure 5–78

4

- Click the Center button on the Common toolbar to center the frame between the page margins.

- Click the bottom sizing handle on the frame, then drag down until the bottom edge is at 750 pixels on the vertical ruler and the status bar reads, height: 325px (Figure 5–79).

- Save the page.

Q&A

Can I increase the height of the I-frame if 750 is not visible on the vertical ruler?

Yes, drag the bottom sizing handle down and the window will scroll as you drag until 750 comes into view on the vertical ruler.

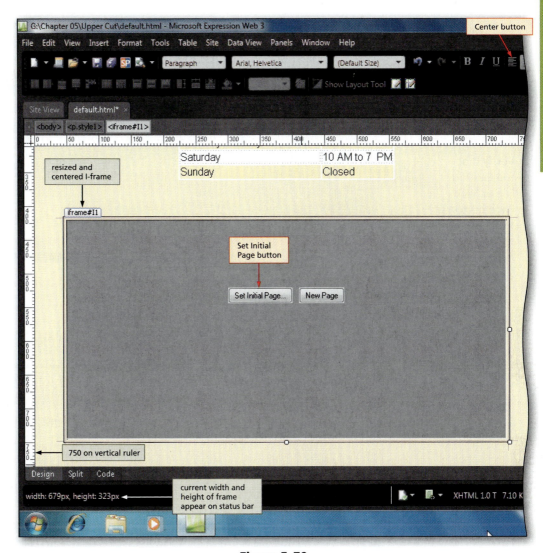

Figure 5–79

Other Ways
1. Double-click the Inline Frame tag in the Toolbox to insert an I-frame

To Target Links in an I-Frame

The following steps embed the stylist_table.html file into the I-frame.

- Click the Set Initial Page button in the Frame to open the Insert Hyperlink dialog box.

- Verify that the Existing File or Web Page button is selected, then click stylist_table to select it as the frame link (Figure 5–80).

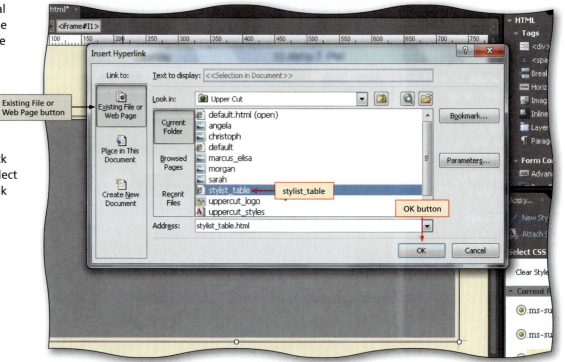

Figure 5–80

- Click the OK button to close the Insert Hyperlink dialog box and insert a link to the table (Figure 5–81).

- Save the page.

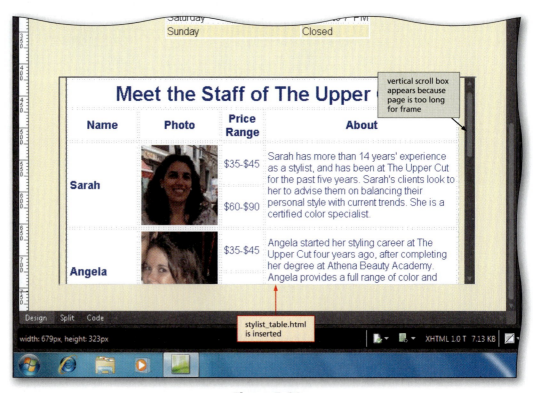

Figure 5–81

3

- Click the 'Preview in browser' button arrow on the Common toolbar, then click Windows Internet Explorer 8.0 to open the page in the browser (Figure 5–82).

 Q&A Why does my table caption appear at the top of the table?

Expression Web uses the valign attribute with the caption tag to align a table caption. This attribute is incompatible with some browsers. To align the caption correctly, open the stylist_table.html page in Code view, change valign on line 105 to align, save the page, then refresh your browser.

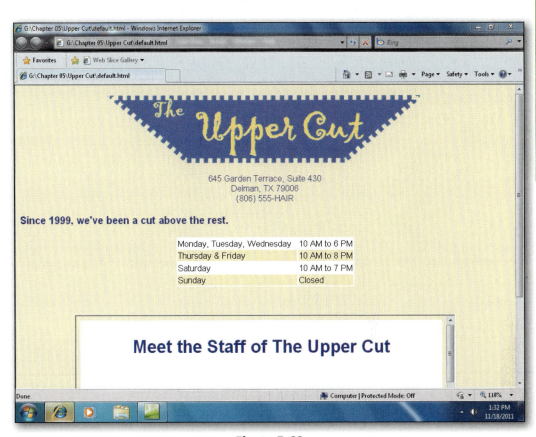

Figure 5–82

4

- Scroll through the embedded page to view the table contents (Figure 5–83).

- Click the Close button on the browser title bar to close the browser window.

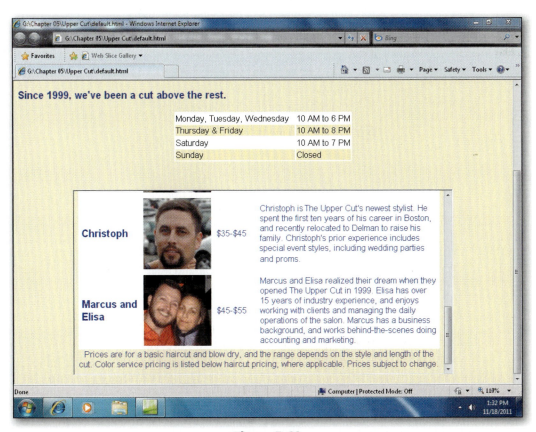

Figure 5–83

Using Frames and Tables to Lay Out a Web Page

Framesets and HTML tables are two methods that have historically been used to lay out Web pages. A **frameset** is a single Web page constructed from multiple HTML files (the "frames"), while an HTML **layout table** controls the positioning of elements within a page by the table properties. With the development of CSS and other style sheet languages that position page elements using styles, however, frames and tables are now considered outdated, non-standards-compliant techniques. Layout frames and layout tables can cause issues with browsers, bookmarks, search engines, and printing. You may encounter existing Web pages designed using layout frames or tables, which is why these approaches are mentioned here.

Framesets define page areas by including each area (footer, content, navigation, and so on) as a separate HTML file. Frames allow certain page elements, such as the masthead and navigation area, to remain consistent and only load once in the browser, while the main page content changes from page to page. Frames also can be used to separate page content to make a page easier to update. If you only wanted to change the navigation bar, you would simply replace that HTML file, and the rest of the page would be unchanged.

To create a frames page in Expression Web, choose one of the Frames Pages options in the New dialog box. For each frame, click the Set Initial Page button, then select the page to display within that frame. You can customize the frames page by resizing, splitting, and deleting frames, or changing the page that displays.

Layout tables are another method that can be used to lay out Web pages. Unlike framesets, which treat each page element as a separate file, tables include each page component within a row, column, or cell. Layout tables must be copied from page to page to maintain consistency of common elements such as navigation, which makes updating these items problematic.

To create a page using a layout table in Expression Web, click Layout Tables from the Table menu to display the Layout Tables panel. Click an option in the Table layout section of the panel to get started, then add, delete, resize, split, and merge cells to create the page layout you want, then enter the page content.

To Close a Site and Quit Expression Web

1 On the Site menu, click Close.

2 On the File menu, click Exit.

Chapter Summary

In this chapter, you have learned to create and modify a new style sheet using a preformatted style sheet provided by Expression Web. You created a data table, entered text and added images, defined cell and table properties, added styles, and split and merged cells. You created a table from delineated text, then applied an AutoFormat. Lastly, you created an I-frame, resized it, and added a link to an HTML page.

The items listed below include all the new Expression Web skills you have learned in this chapter.

1. Create a New Web Site and Web Page (EW 305)
2. Create a New Style Sheet (EW 310)
3. Create a New Page and Attach a Style Sheet (EW 315)
4. Insert a Data Table (EW 317)
5. Change Table and Cell Properties (EW 320)
6. Add Text to a Table (EW 323)
7. Add Images to a Table (EW 327)
8. Add Rows and Columns (EW 330)
9. Use Table Fill (EW 334)
10. Merge Table Cells (EW 337)
11. Split Table Cells (EW 338)

12. Apply Styles to Table Text (EW 340)
13. Convert Text to a Table (EW 342)
14. Distribute Rows and Columns (EW 345)
15. Use Table AutoFormat (EW 347)
16. Create an I-Frame (EW 349)
17. Target Links in an I-Frame (EW 352)

 For current SAM information, including versions and content details, visit SAM Central (http://samcentral.course.com). If you have a SAM user profile, you may have access to hands-on instruction, practice, and assessment of the skills covered in this chapter. Since various versions of SAM are supported throughout the life of this text, check with your instructor for the correct instructions and URL/Web site for accessing assignments.

Learn It Online

Test your knowledge of chapter content and key terms.

Instructions: To complete the Learn It Online exercises, start your browser, click the Address bar, and then enter the Web address `scsite.com/ew3/learn`. When the Expression Web Learn It Online page is displayed, click the link for the exercise you want to complete and then read the instructions.

Chapter Reinforcement TF, MC, and SA
A series of true/false, multiple choice, and short answer questions that test your knowledge of the chapter content.

Flash Cards
An interactive learning environment where you identify chapter key terms associated with displayed definitions.

Practice Test
A series of multiple choice questions that test your knowledge of chapter content and key terms.

Who Wants To Be a Computer Genius?
An interactive game that challenges your knowledge of chapter content in the style of a television quiz show.

Wheel of Terms
An interactive game that challenges your knowledge of chapter key terms in the style of the television show *Wheel of Fortune*.

Crossword Puzzle Challenge
A crossword puzzle that challenges your knowledge of key terms presented in the chapter.

Apply Your Knowledge

Reinforce the skills and apply the concepts you learned in this chapter.

Creating a Data Table
Instructions: Start Expression Web. Create a new Web site, add a new page, and create and attach a new style sheet to each page. Create a data table and enter data and change the properties, then insert a new page into an I-frame so that the page looks like Figure 5–84.

Continued >

Apply Your Knowledge *continued*

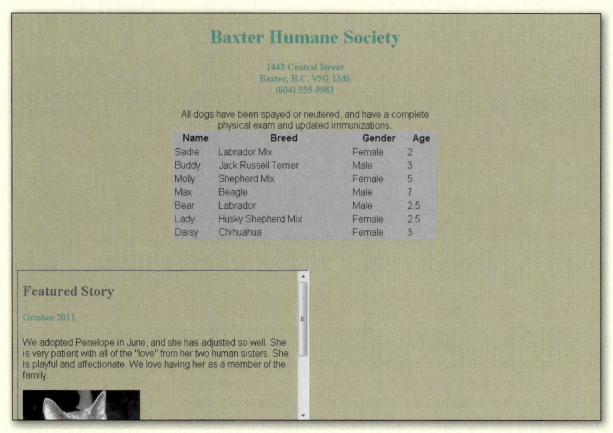

Figure 5–84

Perform the following tasks:

1. Click New Site on the Site menu, then click One Page Web Site in the General category.

2. Click Browse, then navigate to the drive and folder where you save your data files, type `Apply 5-1 Baxter` at the end of the file path in the Location text box, then click OK.

3. Point to New on the File menu, then click Page. Click Style Sheets, click the Bars style sheet type, then click the OK button.

4. Save the new style sheet as `baxter_styles.css`.

5. Open the default.html page, then attach baxter_styles.css.

6. Insert a paragraph tag for the page header, type `Baxter Humane Society`, then format the paragraph with the Heading 1 <h1> style and center it.

7. Click below the header, select the Heading 4 <h4> style and center the heading, then type the following, pressing SHIFT+ENTER at the end of lines one and two:

   ```
   1443 Central Street

   Baxter, B.C. V5G 1M6

   (604) 555-9983
   ```

8. Click below the phone number, then insert a new table with seven rows and four columns. Type the following headers and data into the table:

Name	Breed	Gender	Age
Sadie	Labrador Mix	Female	2
Buddy	Jack Russell Terrier	Male	3
Molly	Shepherd Mix	Female	5
Max	Beagle	Male	7
Lady	Husky Shepherd Mix	Female	2.5
Daisy	Chihuahua	Female	3

9. Right-click the table, then click Table Properties to open the Table Properties dialog box.

10. Verify that the Specify width check box is checked, type 450 in the Specify width box, click the In pixels option button if necessary, center-align the table, apply a silver table background, then click the OK button to close the dialog box.

11. Select the top table row, right-click the row, then click Cell Properties to open the Cell Properties dialog box.

12. Click the Header cell check box, then click the OK button to close the dialog box.

13. Insert a new row above the row with Lady's data. (*Hint:* Use the Tables toolbar.)

14. Type the following in the new row:

Bear	Labrador	Male	2.5

15. Right-click the table, point to Insert, then click Caption. Right-click the caption, then click Caption Properties to open the Caption Properties dialog box.

16. Click the 'Bottom of table' option button, then click the OK button. Type the caption, All dogs have been spayed or neutered, and have a complete physical exam and updated immunizations.

17. Press CTRL+N to create a new blank page, then save it as october_feature.html.

18. Attach the baxter_styles.css style sheet to the new page.

19. Insert a paragraph tag for the page header, type Featured Story, then format the paragraph with Heading 2 <h2>.

20. Click below the Featured Story header, insert a paragraph tag for the page subheading, type October 2011, then format the paragraph with Heading 4 <h4>.

21. Insert a new paragraph tag and type the following: We adopted Penelope in June, and she has adjusted so well. She is very patient with all of the "love" from her two human sisters. She is playful and affectionate. We love having her as a member of the family.

22. Press ENTER, click the Insert Picture from File button on the Common toolbar, navigate to your data files folder, double-click the humane_image folder to open it, click the penelope image, then click the Insert button to open the Accessibility Properties dialog box.

23. Type Gray cat in the Alternate text text box, then click the OK button.

24. Double-click the image to open the Picture Properties dialog box, click the Appearance tab, type 200 in the Width text box, then click the OK button.

25. Click the Picture Actions button, then click the Resample Picture To Match Size option button.

26. Save the page and the embedded image, then close the page.

27. Return to the default.html page, click below the table, press SHIFT+ENTER twice, then double-click Inline Frame in the Toolbox to insert a new I-frame.

Continued >

Apply Your Knowledge *continued*

28. Select the I-frame, then drag the right and bottom sizing handles to resize the frame to 500 pixels wide and 250 pixels high.

29. Click the Set Initial Page button, click the october_feature file, then click the OK button.

30. Save the default.html page.

31. Preview the site and test the I-frame and image.

32. Change the site properties, as specified by your instructor. Save all pages, then close the site.

33. Submit the revised site in the format specified by your instructor.

Extend Your Knowledge

Extend the skills you learned in this chapter and experiment with new skills. You may need to use Help to complete the assignment.

Converting Text to a Table

Instructions: Start Expression Web. You will open a Web site and insert a text file with delineated data, then convert the data to a table. Change the table properties to add a background image, and manually adjust the column width. Add a new I-frame to make the default.html page match the one shown in Figure 5–85.

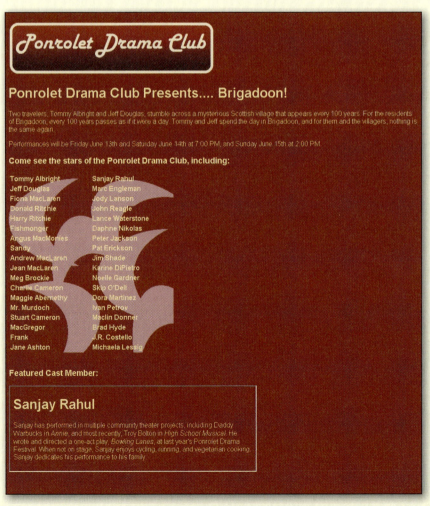

Figure 5–85

Perform the following tasks:

1. Click Site on the menu bar, then click Open Site.

2. Click the Browse button and navigate to your data files folder, click the Extend 5-1 Drama folder to select it, click the Open button, then click the second Open button.

3. Open the default.html page, then position the insertion point in the paragraph tag below the line, Come see the stars…

4. Open Microsoft Word and open the file brigadoon_cast.doc from the drama_files folder in your data files folder.

5. Select the text, copy it to the Clipboard, then quit Microsoft Word.

6. Click Paste Text on the Edit menu, click the 'Normal paragraphs with line breaks' option, then click the OK button.

7. Select the pasted text.

8. Point to Convert on the Table menu, then click Text to Table.

9. Click the Commas option button, then click the OK button.

10. Open the Table Properties dialog box, then specify that the table width is 400 pixels.

11. Add a background image, using the file background_image.gif from the drama_files folder, then close the Table Properties dialog box. (*Hint:* Click the 'Use background picture' check box, then browse to the background image.)

12. Drag the divider between the two columns until the first column is 196 pixels wide. (*Hint:* View the ScreenTip to note the width as you drag.)

13. Select the table, then click the Bold button.

14. Select the right column, then click the AutoFit to Contents button on the Tables toolbar.

15. Click in the last cell in the table, after the name, then press TAB to insert a new row.

16. Type Jane Ashton, press TAB, then type Michaela Lessig. Apply bold to these two new cells, if necessary.

17. If necessary, insert a new paragraph tag below the table, type Featured Cast Member:, then format the paragraph as Heading 3 <h3>.

18. Click below the heading, then insert a new I-frame. Resize the frame to 600 pixels wide and 200 pixels high.

19. Set the initial page to the sanjay_feature.html page from the Extend 5-1 Drama folder.

20. Save the default.html page and the embedded image. Preview the page, scroll to view the entire page contents, then close the browser window.

21. Change the site properties as specified by your instructor. In Windows Explorer, rename the site folder Extend 5-1 Drama Site. Submit the revised site in the format specified by your instructor.

Make It Right

Analyze a site and correct all errors and/or improve the design.

Creating and Fixing a Data Table

Instructions: Start Expression Web. Open the Web site, Make It Right 5-1 Fitness, from the Data Files for Students. See the inside back cover of this book for instructions for downloading the Data Files for Students, or see your instructor for information about accessing the required files.

Continued >

Make It Right *continued*

Figure 5–86

Open the default.html page. Find the five issues in the text that will cause problems when the text is converted into rows and columns. Make the necessary changes to the file. (*Hint:* The issues will lead to an extra row and column being added to the table. If the table doesn't look right when you create it, undo then try again.) Select the lines of delineated text (from Class to Friday 6:00 pm). Create a new data table on the default.html page by converting the lines of delineated text into a table, separating text at commas. Add a new row between the second and third rows, and enter the following data: Boot Camp, press tab, Sam, press tab, Monday, press tab, 12:00 PM. Define the top row as a table header and center-align the text. Add a caption to the top of the table, and type All classes are 50 minutes long. Instructors can change without notice. Apply the List 1 Table AutoFormat to the table and set the first column so it is the same as the others. (*Hint:* Deselect the First Column check box in the Table AutoFormat dialog box) to create the page shown in Figure 5–86. Change the site properties as specified by your instructor. Save and close the site. In Windows Explorer, rename the site using the folder name Make It Right 5-1 Fitness Site. Submit the revised site in the format specified by your instructor.

In the Lab

Design and/or format a Web site using the guidelines, concepts, and skills presented in this chapter. Labs are listed in order of increasing difficulty.

Lab 1: Creating a New Table

Problem: You are a photographer and want to update your home page by creating a list of prices for printed photos. Insert a table, specify the table and cell properties, and enter table data to create the page shown in Figure 5–87.

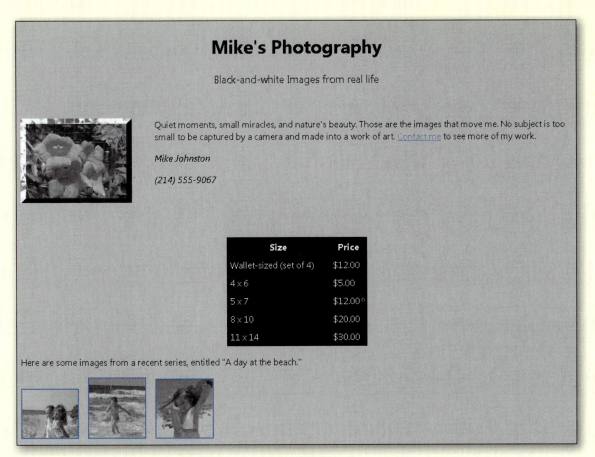

Figure 5–87

Instructions:

1. Start Expression Web.

2. Open the Web site, Lab 5-1 Photo, from your data files folder, and open the default.html page.

3. Scroll down and create a new table with five rows and two columns in the empty paragraph just above the line, Here are some images...

4. Enter the following headers and data into the table, pressing TAB at the end of the last row in the table in order to create a new row for the last row of data:

Size	Price
Wallet-sized (set of 4)	$12.00
4 x 6	$5.00
5 x 7	$12.00
8 x 10	$20.00
11 x 14	$30.00

5. Define the top row as the header.

6. Specify the following table properties: black background, 250 pixels wide, and 4 pixels of cell padding.

7. Change the font color of the table text to white and center the table on the page.

8. Save the changes to the default.html page, preview the site in a browser, then scroll to view the entire page content.

9. Close the site, then submit the site in the format specified by your instructor.

In the Lab

Lab 2: Creating an I-Frame

Problem: You have volunteered to update the Web site for the Connecticut branch of the Gulliver College Alumni Society. Create a new page with a table and insert it as an I-frame onto the default.html page, as shown in Figure 5–88.

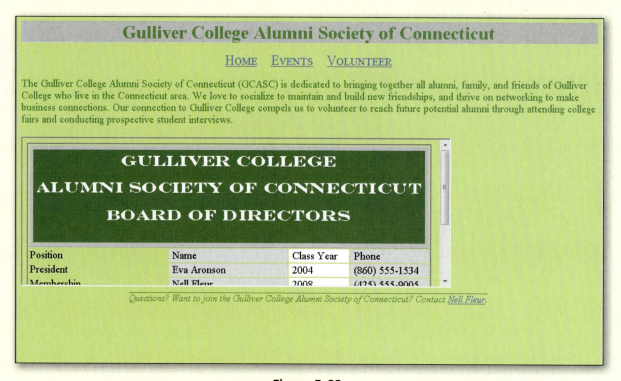

Figure 5–88

Instructions: Start Expression Web. Open the Web site, Lab 5-2 Alumni, from the Data Files for Students. See the inside back cover of this book for instructions for downloading the Data Files for Students, or see your instructor for information about accessing the required files.

Perform the following tasks:

1. Create a new, blank page. Save it as alumni_board.html and attach the alumni_styles.css style sheet.

2. Open Microsoft Word and open the board.doc file from the Lab 5-2 Documents folder. Copy and paste the contents of the Word document into Expression Web as normal paragraphs with line breaks. Close the Word document and quit Microsoft Word.

3. Convert the pasted text into a table.

4. Use the Table Properties dialog box to set the table at a fixed width of 700 pixels.

5. Create a new row above the table and merge the cells into one.

6. Insert the board_logo.gif file from the Lab 5-2 Documents folder into the merged cell. Enter `Gulliver College Alumni Society of Connecticut Board of Directors logo` as the alternate text.

7. Apply the Column 5 Table AutoFormat, keeping the Heading rows and First Column check boxes selected.

8. Modify the .ms-column5-left style that is created from the AutoFormat using the Modify Style dialog box to have normal font-weight instead of bold.

9. Save and close the alumni_board.html page and the embedded file, then open the default.html page.

10. Click after the words, student interviews (be sure to click after the period), then press ENTER twice.

11. Insert a new I-frame using the Toolbox.

12. Drag to resize the I-frame so that it is 750 pixels wide and 250 pixels high.

13. Set the initial page to the alumni_board.html page.

14. Save the default.html page.

15. Preview the page in a browser and scroll through the table.

16. Close the site, in Windows Explorer rename the site folder Lab 5-2 Alumni Site, and submit the site in the format specified by your instructor.

In the Lab

Lab 3: Creating a New Web Page as an I-Frame

Problem: Your client, a tutor, wants to create a home page that he can use to attract clients. Create a one-page Web site and a new style sheet using a preformatted style sheet, and add another page in an I-frame to the home page shown in Figure 5–89.

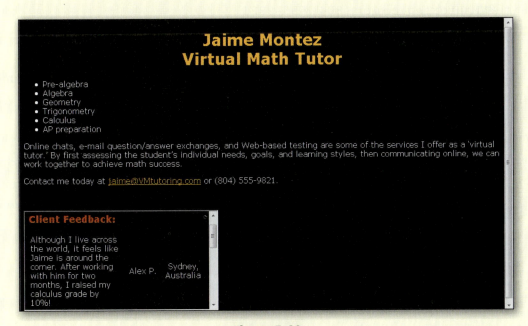

Figure 5–89

Continued >

In the Lab *continued*

Instructions:

1. Start Expression Web.

2. Create a one-page Web site called Lab 5-3 Tutor Site, then open the default.html page.

3. Create a new style sheet based on the Highway style sheet, save it as tutor_styles.css, then attach it to the default.html page.

4. Insert a new blank paragraph.

5. Type Jaime Montez, press SHIFT+ENTER, then type Virtual Math Tutor.

6. Format the paragraph tag as h1, then center it.

7. Click below the heading, then insert a new bulleted list.

8. Type the following as the bulleted list text, pressing ENTER after each line and pressing ENTER twice at the end of the last line:
   - Pre-algebra
   - Algebra
   - Geometry
   - Trigonometry
   - Calculus
   - AP preparation

9. In the new paragraph tag, type the following: Online chats, e-mail question/answer exchanges, and Web-based testing are some of the services I offer as a 'virtual tutor.' By first assessing the student's individual needs, goals, and learning styles, then communicating online, we can work together to achieve math success.

10. Press ENTER to start a new paragraph, then type Contact me today at jaime@VMtutoring.com or (804) 555-9821..

11. Press ENTER twice, then insert a new I-frame.

12. Resize the I-frame to 400 pixels wide and 200 pixels high.

13. Click the New Page button in the I-frame to create a new blank HTML page within the frame.

14. Save the page as client_feedback.html. (*Hint:* If necessary, press CTRL+S to open the Save As dialog box for the new page.)

15. Open the client_feedback.html file, then attach the tutor_styles.css style sheet.

16. Insert a new paragraph tag, type Client Feedback:, then format the text as Heading 3 <h3>.

17. Create a new table with four rows and three columns, then type the following data into the table:

Although I live across the world, it feels like Jaime is around the corner. After working with him for two months, I raised my calculus grade by 10%!	Alex P.	Sydney, Australia
The extra online exams I took helped increase my confidence in test taking, and allowed me to see my progress.	Sarah J.	Ithaca, NY
Our weekly online chats gave me the personal, real-time instruction that I needed to fully understand the concepts being taught in my geometry class.	Wilhelm C.	Enid, OK
I recommend Jaime to all of my AP math students. He will work with them individually to offer extra one-on-one assistance as well as test-taking skills.	Bailey W.	Strayer, WI

18. Save both files, then preview the default.html page in a browser.

19. Change the site properties as specified by your instructor, then close the site.

20. Submit the site in the format specified by your instructor.

Cases and Places

Apply your creative thinking and problem-solving skills to design and implement a solution.

● Easier ●●More Difficult

● 1: Creating a New Table

Create a new blank Web site that contains information about your favorite musician or musical group, and add a page using the CSS layout of your choice. Enter content in all of the divs. Create a new style sheet based on a preformatted style sheet and attach it to the page. Modify at least one of the styles, such as the page background or font family. Create a table listing the musician's albums and songs and format it using headings. Merge the top row of the table to create a table title. Enter a caption at the bottom of the table. Define and enter content for a header row. Delete a row from the middle of the table, and add a row at the end of the table by pressing TAB. Save and close all pages, then quit Expression Web.

● 2: Creating an I-Frame

Create a new one-page Web site dedicated to your favorite professional athlete. Add a new blank HTML page to the site. Create a style sheet using a preformatted option, and attach it to both pages. Enter data into both pages, featuring career highlights on the default.html page. On the second page, include at least one table of statistics to which you add an image, apply an AutoFormat, and merge and split cells. Create an I-frame Create an I-frame on the home page and set the second page as the initial page. Resize the frame so that when the home page is previewed in the browser, the entire home page is visible.

●● 3: Troubleshooting Tables

Create a new blank HTML page for your current class schedule. Enter information that you will convert to a table and delineate the data using commas or tabs. In at least one row, add an extra delineator, and add a blank line in the middle of the table. Convert the text to a table, then move data, and delete rows and columns. Select the table, then convert it back to text. Select the data and convert it back to a table and fix any table errors. Change the table properties and formatting of the table. Save the page, then close it.

●● 4: Creating a Research Home Page

Make It Personal

You want to create a one-page site that includes information from a paper or research project you have done for another class. Create a new one-page site and a style sheet from a preformatted style sheet and attach the style sheet. Enter information on the default.html page, including a table with a caption and header row. Create an I-frame and a page to link to it that includes information relevant to the topic. Save the pages and style sheets, then close the site.

●● 5: Creating a Web Page with an I-Frame

Working Together

A video store wants to display a list of new releases in an I-frame on its home page. Working as a team with several of your classmates, you are to plan and create the home page and table page. Each team member should contribute to supplying titles, ratings, descriptions, or other information for the list. As a group, decide on the information you need for the table, including the number of columns of information and the number of rows you need to list all of the titles you have come up with. Create a site folder with a blank page and attach a style sheet that you create using a preformatted style sheet.

Continued >

Cases and Places *continued*

Make at least one modification to the styles in the style sheet. Enter information on the page, such as a logo or masthead, address, and other relevant information. Create a new blank page and attach the style sheet to it. Create a table using the planned data, and make sure to merge and split some cells. Format the site using table and cell properties, headings, and other formatting techniques. Insert and resize an I-frame on the home page, and link the table page to it. Preview the site, test the navigation bar, and make sure that your site is readable and attractive. Save and close the pages and style sheet, then close the site.

6 Adding Interactivity

Objectives

You will have mastered the material in this chapter when you can:

- Create an interactive button
- Duplicate an interactive button
- Edit an interactive button
- Test an interactive button
- Define how behaviors work
- Use the Behaviors panel

- Add a jump menu behavior
- Add a status message behavior
- Add a swap image behavior
- Modify a behavior
- Test a behavior
- Create an image map

6 | Adding Interactivity

Introduction

Interactivity is the term used to describe the connection that occurs between a Web site and a site visitor through actions such as clicking a button, list item, or part of an image. Interactivity goes beyond simple site navigation through hyperlinks; users can trigger an event, such as opening a new Web page or e-mail, zooming in on an image, or launching a chat window by performing actions such as clicking or hovering the mouse pointer over an element. Interactive tools are commonly used in site navigation, but can also provide additional information to site visitors by changing an image or displaying a message in a new window or in the status bar.

Elements that are interactive have behaviors attached to them. **Behaviors** are the embedded functions that occur as a result of site events, such as a page opening in a browser window, or user interaction, such as clicking or hovering the mouse. Expression Web tools create behaviors using code from a scripting language called **JavaScript**. As with HTML and CSS, you do not need to know JavaScript to create and modify behaviors in Expression Web.

There are many ways to add interactivity to your Web page, including **interactive buttons**, also called **rollover buttons**, that look different when they are inactive, have a mouse pointer hovering over them, and are clicked. **Jump menus** are lists that contain links. **Image maps** are graphics that have links, called **hotspots**, associated with different areas of the graphic.

Project — Farm Stand Web Site

Wisteria Farms, a farm stand and grocery store in Dilton, New Hampshire, currently has a Web site that needs more interactivity. The site has four main pages for the home page, store, events, and directions, but no method for navigating between them. You will create a navigation bar for the main site pages by adding interactive buttons to each page. The owners want it to be easy to view descriptions of the store's main areas. You will create a jump menu on the home page as well as an image map on the store page that allows users to view pages about the different store departments.

The project in this chapter shows you how to use Expression Web to add interactivity to create the site shown in Figure 6–1. You will create a navigation bar using interactive buttons that you will copy to each main page of the site. You will create a jump menu and an image map and place them appropriately to link to each of the store pages. You will create behaviors for an image swap and a status bar message. Although Expression Web provides tools for creating many types of interactivity, you will add only these four types of behaviors so that your site is not overwhelmed by interactivity.

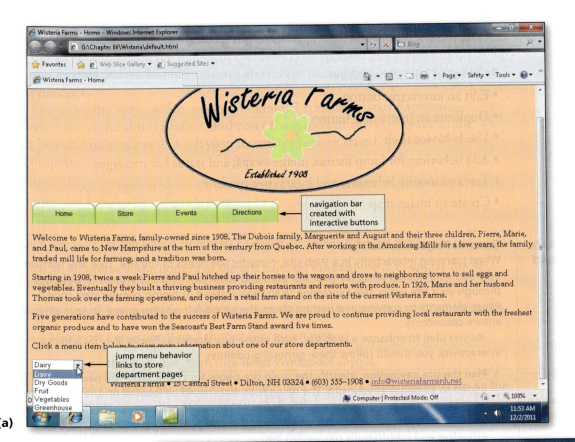

Figure 6–1

• Click the Back button to return to the default.html page.

• Click the Events button to display the events.html page (Figure 6–22).

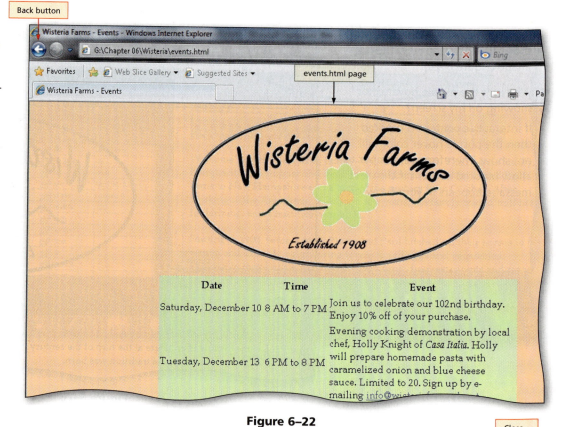

Figure 6–22

• Click the Back button to return to the default.html page.

• Click the Directions button to display the directions.html page (Figure 6–23).

• Click the Close button to close the browser and return to Expression Web.

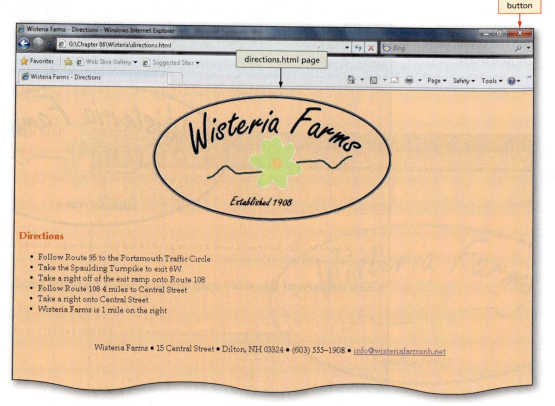

Figure 6–23

To Copy and Paste the Navigation Bar

The following steps open the three other main site pages: store.html, events.html, and directions.html; and copy the navigation bar from the default.html page and paste it into the navigation div for each page to create a consistent and functional navigation bar.

1

- Click the div#top_nav visual aid to select the navigation bar (Figure 6–24).

- Press CTRL+C to copy the navigation bar to the Clipboard.

Q&A Can I just select the buttons?

Make sure to select the entire navigation div when both copying and pasting the navigation bar.

Figure 6–24

2

- Click the store folder plus sign in the Folder List to display the contents of the folder.

- Double-click the store.html page in the Folder List to open it (Figure 6–25).

store folder plus sign changes to minus sign when folder contents are expanded

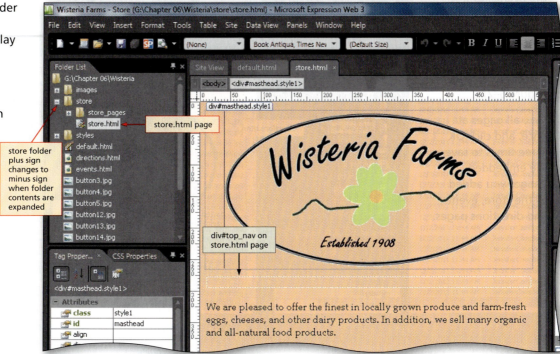

Figure 6–25

7

• Position the mouse pointer over the image to swap it (Figure 6–55).

• Click the Expression Web program button on the Windows 7 taskbar to return to Expression Web and leave the browser window open.

Q&A

Why does the image text say to click it, but the image changes when I position the mouse over it?

The default event for a swap image is mouseover. In the next set of steps, you will change the event to onclick to match the text on the image.

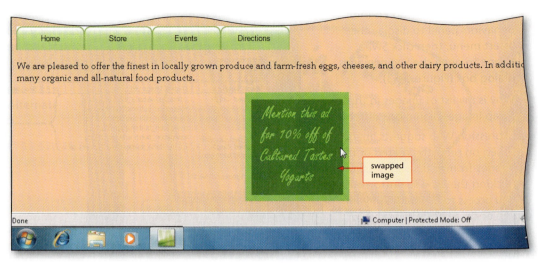

Figure 6–55

To Modify a Swap Image Behavior

The previous set of steps set the image to swap when the user mouses over the image; however, the text on the image specifies that the user should click to see the coupon. The following steps add a restore behavior and change the swap image event so that the user must click the original image to see the second image. The restore behavior event is onmouseout, which means that the original image will reappear when the visitor removes the pointer from the image.

1

• Click the swap_image1.gif file (the "Click here" image you just added) to select it, if necessary.

• Click the Insert button on the Behaviors panel to display the Insert menu, then click Swap Image Restore to open the Swap Image Restore dialog box (Figure 6–56).

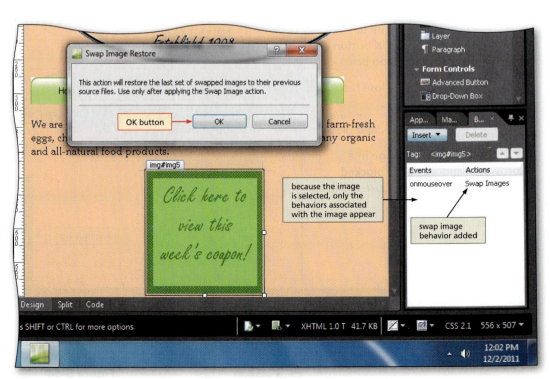

Figure 6–56

2

- Click the OK button to close the Swap Image Restore dialog box and add the swap image restore behavior to the image (Figure 6–57).

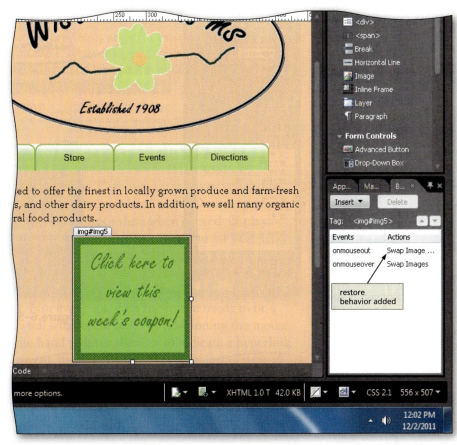

Figure 6–57

3

- Position the mouse pointer over the onmouseover event to display the box arrow, then click the onmouseover event box arrow to open the menu (Figure 6–58).

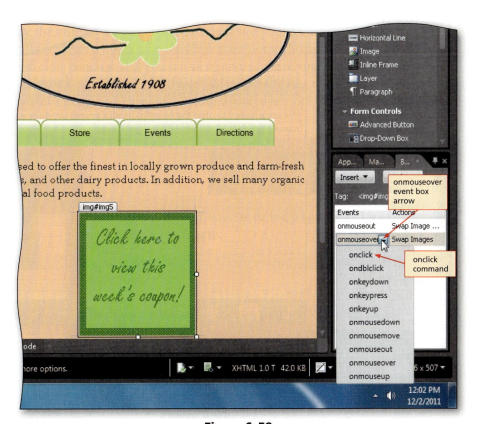

Figure 6–58

6

- Drag the pencil to select the green Dairy rectangle and open the Insert Hyperlink dialog box (Figure 6–66).

- Click the Existing File or Web Page button, if necessary, click dairy in the store_pages folder to select it as the link target, then click the OK button to close the Insert Hyperlink dialog box.

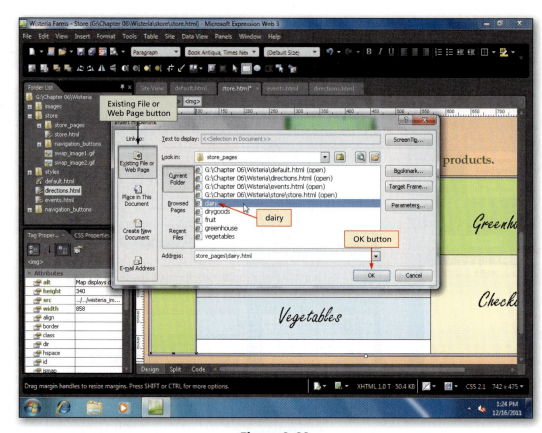

Figure 6–66

7

- Repeat Steps 5 and 6 to create hotspots for the Cereals, grains, and dry goods, Fruits, Vegetables, and Greenhouse sections of the site map with the appropriate links.

- Press CTRL+S to save the store.html page, then click OK to save the embedded image.

- Press F12 to open the page in a browser window, then scroll down to view the image map, if necessary. Allow blocked content, if necessary (Figure 6–67).

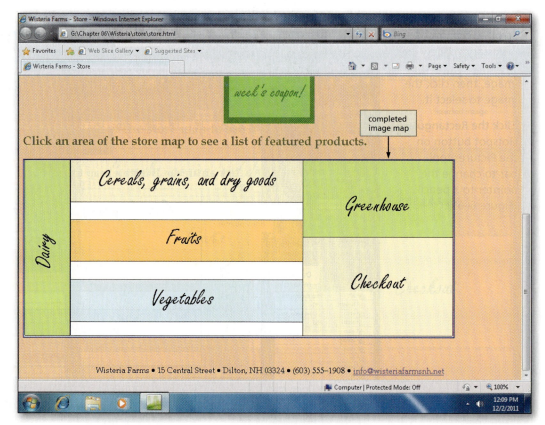

Figure 6–67

8

- Position the pointer over the image map and verify that the hotspots are correct by viewing the path that shows in the status bar (Figure 6–68).

- Click the Close button on the browser title bar to close the browser window.

Status bar shows path to linked file

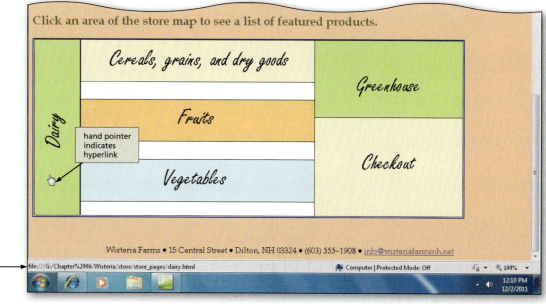

Figure 6–68

To Close a Site and Quit Expression Web

1 On the Site menu, click Close.

2 On the File menu, click Exit.

Chapter Summary

In this chapter, you have learned to create, edit, and test interactive buttons to create a navigation bar that you could paste onto every page. You organized your site by creating folders and moving the button images into them. You learned about behaviors, and created behaviors for a jump menu, a status bar message, and a swap image. You modified the swap image behavior, and also created an image map.

The items listed below include all the new Expression Web skills you have learned in this chapter.

1. Open a Web Site and Web Page (EW 371)
2. Create an Interactive Button (EW 373)
3. Duplicate an Interactive Button (EW 379)
4. Edit an Interactive Button (EW 380)
5. Test Interactive Buttons (EW 382)
6. Copy and Paste the Navigation Bar (EW 385)
7. Organize the Button Images into Folders (EW 387)
8. Add a Jump Menu Behavior (EW 391)
9. Add a Status Bar Behavior (EW 397)
10. Add a Swap Image Behavior (EW 399)
11. Modify a Swap Image Behavior (EW 402)
12. Add an Image Map (EW 405)

For current SAM information, including versions and content details, visit SAM Central (http://samcentral.course.com). If you have a SAM user profile, you may have access to hands-on instruction, practice, and assessment of the skills covered in this chapter. Since various versions of SAM are supported throughout the life of this text, check with your instructor for the correct instructions and URL/Web site for accessing assignments.

Learn It Online

Test your knowledge of chapter content and key terms.

Instructions: To complete the Learn It Online exercises, start your browser, click the Address bar, and then enter the Web address `scsite.com/ew3/learn`. When the Expression Web Learn It Online page is displayed, click the link for the exercise you want to complete and then read the instructions.

Chapter Reinforcement TF, MC, and SA
A series of true/false, multiple choice, and short answer questions that test your knowledge of the chapter content.

Flash Cards
An interactive learning environment where you identify chapter key terms associated with displayed definitions.

Practice Test
A series of multiple choice questions that test your knowledge of chapter content and key terms.

Who Wants To Be a Computer Genius?
An interactive game that challenges your knowledge of chapter content in the style of a television quiz show.

Wheel of Terms
An interactive game that challenges your knowledge of chapter key terms in the style of the television show *Wheel of Fortune*.

Crossword Puzzle Challenge
A crossword puzzle that challenges your knowledge of key terms presented in the chapter.

Apply Your Knowledge

Reinforce the skills and apply the concepts you learned in this chapter.

Creating an Interactive Navigation Bar and Adding a Behavior
Instructions: Start Expression Web. Create a new one-page Web site, create and attach a new style sheet, then copy the default page to create the other site pages as shown in Figure 6–69. You will create a navigation bar using interactive buttons. You will also create a swap image behavior. You will leave most of the site content blank at this point, but you will add folders and move the pages and interactive buttons into them.

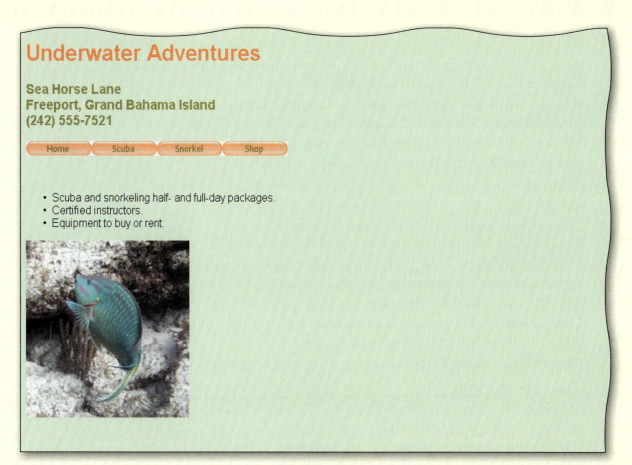

Figure 6–69

Perform the following tasks:

1. Click New Site on the Site menu, then click One Page Site.

2. Click the Browse button, navigate to the drive and folder where you save your data files, open the folder, type `Apply 6-1 Underwater` at the end of the file path in the Location text box, then click the OK button.

3. Point to New on the File menu, then click Page. Click Style Sheets, click the Capsules style sheet type, then click the OK button.

4. Save the new style sheet as `underwater_styles.css`.

5. Open the default.html page, then attach the underwater_styles.css style sheet.

6. Select the Heading 1 <h1> style, then type `Underwater Adventures` as the page heading.

7. Select the Heading 3 <h3> style, then type the following, pressing SHIFT+ENTER at the end of each line:

`Sea Horse Lane`

`Freeport, Grand Bahama Island`

`(242) 555-7521`

8. Press ENTER after the last line to create a new paragraph tag, then save the page.

9. Click the default.html file name in the Folder List to select it, then press CTRL+C to copy the file to the Clipboard.

10. Press CTRL+V to paste a copy of the default.html page in the site folder. Right-click the file name of the copied page, click Rename, type `scuba.html`, then press ENTER.

Continued >

Apply Your Knowledge *continued*

11. Press CTRL+V to paste another copy of the default.html page in the site folder. Click the file name of the copied page to select it, click it again, type `snorkel.html`, then press ENTER.

12. Press CTRL+V to paste a third copy of the default.html page in the site folder. Click the file name of the copied page to select it, click it again, type `shop.html`, then press ENTER.

13. Right-click in the Folder List, point to New, click Folder, type `scuba` as the folder name, then press ENTER. Drag the scuba.html page into the scuba folder.

14. Create folders named `snorkel and shop`, then drag the snorkel.html and shop.html files into their folders.

15. On the default.html page, click in the paragraph tag below the contact information, then click Interactive Button on the Insert menu to open the Interactive Buttons dialog box.

16. Click the Embossed Capsule 3 option from the Buttons list, type `Home` in the Text box, then click the Browse button to open the Edit Hyperlink dialog box. Click default, then click the OK button to close the Edit Hyperlink dialog box.

17. Click the Font tab. Click the Original Font Color box arrow, then click Olive. Click the OK button to close the Interactive Buttons dialog box.

18. Click the Home interactive button to select it, then press CTRL+C to copy it to the Clipboard.

19. Click to the right of the button, then press CTRL+V three times to paste three copies of the button.

20. Right-click the second button from the left, then click Button Properties on the shortcut menu to open the Interactive Buttons dialog box.

21. Change the text of the button to `Scuba`, then change the hyperlink to the scuba page and close all dialog boxes. (*Hint:* The scuba page is in the scuba folder.)

22. Rename the third and fourth buttons `Snorkel` and `Shop`, and link the buttons to the appropriate pages.

23. Save the page and all of the image files.

24. In the Folder List, create a new folder called `navigation_images`, then drag all of the button images into the folder.

25. Click below the navigation bar on the default.html page, press ENTER, click the Bullets button on the Common toolbar, then type:
    * `Scuba and snorkeling half- and full-day packages.`
    * `Certified instructors.`
    * `Equipment to buy or rent.`

26. Press ENTER twice after the last list item, then show the Pictures toolbar if necessary, click the Insert Picture from File button on the Pictures toolbar to open the Picture dialog box. Navigate to the underwater_images folder, select the parrot_fish image, then click the Insert button. Type `Rainbow Parrot Fish` and `Trumpet Fish` in the Accessibility Properties dialog box, then click the OK button.

27. Click the image to select it, then click Behaviors on the Panels menu to open the Behaviors panel if necessary.

28. Click the Insert button on the Behaviors panel, then click Swap Image from the menu to open the Swap Images dialog box.

29. Click the Browse button, navigate to the underwater_images folder, click the trumpet_fish image, click OK, click the 'Restore on mouseout event' check box, then click the OK button.

30. Save the file and embedded files, then preview the site in a browser and test the swap images behavior and the buttons.

31. Change the site properties, as specified by your instructor, then save and close the site.

32. Submit the revised site in the format specified by your instructor.

Extend Your Knowledge

Extend the skills you learned in this chapter and experiment with new skills. You may need to use Help to complete the assignment.

Converting Text to a Table

Instructions: Start Expression Web. Open the site, Extend 6-1 Preschool, from the Data Files for Students. See the inside back cover of this book for instructions for downloading the Data Files for Students, or see your instructor for information about accessing the required files.

You will create a navigation bar using a column of interactive buttons to make the default.html page match the one shown in Figure 6–70.

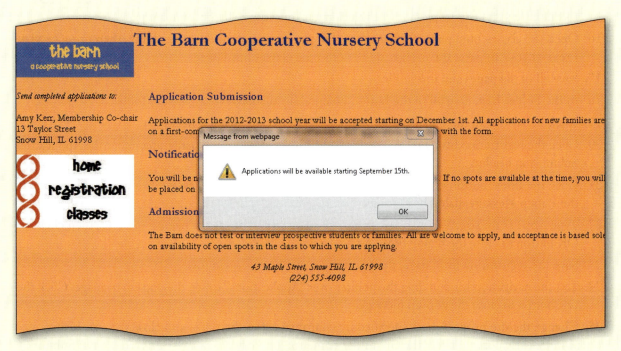

Figure 6–70

Perform the following tasks:

1. Open the default.html page, position the insertion point at the end of the paragraph in the left column, press ENTER, then double-click Paragraph in the Toolbox to insert a new paragraph tag.

2. Click Interactive Button on the Insert menu to open the Interactive Buttons dialog box.

3. Click the Braided Column 3 option in the Buttons list, type home in the Text text box, then click the Browse button to open the Edit Hyperlink dialog box.

4. Click the default file name, then click the OK button to close the Edit Hyperlink dialog box.

5. Click the Font tab, then type Poornut in the Font box to select the font. If the font doesn't appear in the list, then choose another font (such as Matura MT Script Capitals) that resembles the font on the navigation bar in Figure 6–70. Click Bold in the Font Style box, then click 20 in the Size box. Click the Hovered Font Color box arrow, then click Navy from the color palette.

6. Click the Image tab, then type 200 in the Width box. Click the OK button to close the Interactive Buttons dialog box.

7. Click the Home interactive button to select it, then press CTRL+C to copy it to the Clipboard.

8. Press RIGHT ARROW, then press CTRL+V twice to paste two copies of the button.

Continued >

Extend Your Knowledge *continued*

9. Right-click the second button from the top, then click Button Properties on the shortcut menu to open the Interactive Buttons dialog box.

10. Change the text of the button to `registration`, then change the hyperlink to the registration page and close all dialog boxes. If the text doesn't fit on the button, then choose a smaller font size.

11. Rename the third button as `classes` and link the button to the appropriate page.

12. Save the page and all of the image files.

13. In the Folder List, create a new folder called `navigation_images`, then drag all of the button images into the folder.

14. Select the paragraph tag that contains the navigation bar, then press CTRL+C to copy it to the Clipboard.

15. Open the registration.html page, click at the end of the paragraph in the left column, then press ENTER. Press CTRL+V to paste the navigation bar onto the registration.html page.

16. Open the classes.html page, click at the end of the paragraph in the left column, then press ENTER. Press CTRL+V to paste the navigation bar onto the classes.html page.

17. Save all of the pages and image files.

18. In the Folder List, drag all of the button images into the navigation_images folder.

19. Click Behaviors on the Panels menu to open the Behaviors panel if necessary.

20. Click the registration.html tab. Select the word, Applications, in the paragraph under the Application Submission heading.

21. Click the Insert button on the Behaviors panel, then click Popup Message from the menu to open the Popup Message dialog box.

22. Type `Applications will be available starting September 15th.`, then click the OK button to close the dialog box.

23. Save the registration.html page, then preview it in a browser window.

24. Test the navigation bar and drag the pointer over "Applications" to see the pop-up message. Click the OK button to close the pop-up message.

25. Change the site properties, as specified by your instructor, then save and close the site. Using Windows Explorer, change the site folder name to `Extend 6-1 Preschool Site`. Submit the revised site in the format specified by your instructor.

Make It Right

Analyze a site and correct all errors and/or improve the design.

Replacing a Text-Based Navigation Bar with Interactive Buttons

Instructions: Start Expression Web. Open the Web site, Make It Right 6-1 Drama, from the Data Files for Students. See the inside back cover of this book for instructions for downloading the Data Files for Students, or see your instructor for information about accessing the required files.

Create a new navigation bar on the default.html page by replacing the text-based hyperlinks with interactive buttons. Copy and paste the navigation bar to the main site pages, and create folders to store the button images to create the home page shown in Figure 6–71.

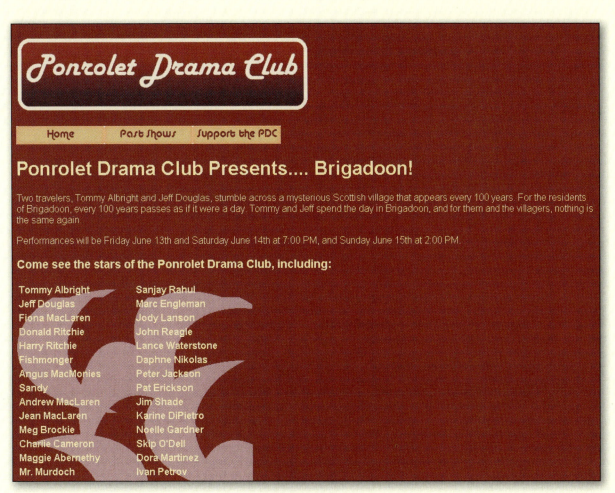

Figure 6–71

In the default.html page delete the content, in the h3 tags, which contains the hyperlinks. Open the Interactive Buttons dialog box. Create a button using the Soft Rectangle 3 button, with Home as the text, that links to the default.html page, with Alba as the font (or a similar font such as Viner Hand ITC), 14-point font size, Maroon as the original font color, and 150 pixels wide. Create two copies of the button in the navigation bar. Edit the second button so that its label is Past Shows and that it links to the past_shows.html page. (*Hint:* the past_shows.html page is in the past_shows folder.) Edit the third button so that its label is Support the PDC and that it links to the support.html page. (*Hint:* the support.html page is in the support folder.) Copy the <h3> tag, with the navigation bar containing the interactive buttons, and paste it over the text-based navigation bars on the support.html and past_shows.html pages. Create folders for the navigation images in the main site folder, the support folder, and the past_shows folder, and move the button image files into them. Change the site properties, as specified by your instructor. Save and close the site. In Windows Explorer change the site folder name to Make It Right 6-1 Drama Site. Submit the revised site in the format specified by your instructor.

In the Lab

Design and/or format a Web site using the guidelines, concepts, and skills presented in this chapter. Labs are listed in order of increasing difficulty.

Lab 1: Adding Interactive Buttons

Problem: Your client, the manager of a senior center, has asked you to create a new multi-page Web site and add an interactive navigation bar. You will create a new one-page site, add a preformatted style sheet, then copy the page twice. You will add interactive buttons to create a navigation bar that includes links to the three site pages, copy it to each page, then create a folder for the buttons to create the page shown in Figure 6–72.

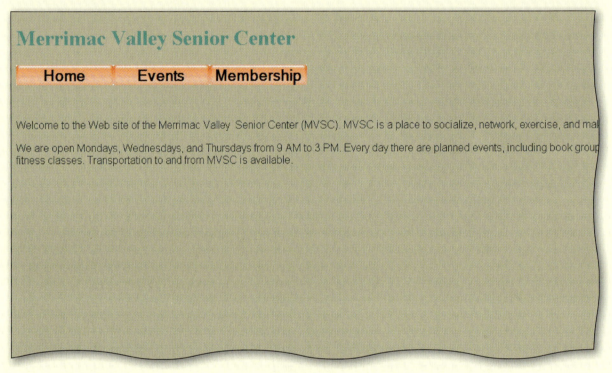

Figure 6–72

Instructions:

1. Start Expression Web.

2. Create a one-page Web site called `Lab 6-1 Senior Site`, then open the default.html page.

3. Create a new style sheet based on the Bars style sheet, save it as `senior_styles.css`, then attach it to the default.html page.

4. Select the Heading 1 <h1> style, then type `Merrimac Valley Senior Center`. Save the page.

5. In the Folder List, click the default.html page, press CTRL+C, then press CTRL+V twice.

6. Rename the two copies of the default.html page so that you have two new pages: events.html and membership.html.

7. Create a paragraph tag on the default.html page under the heading. Type `Welcome to the Web site of the Merrimac Valley Senior Center (MVSC). MVSC is a place to socialize, network, exercise, and make new friends.` Press ENTER, then type `We are open Mondays, Wednesdays, and Thursdays from 9 AM to 3 PM. Every day there are planned events, including book groups, games, and fitness classes. Transportation to and from MVSC is available.`

8. Save the default.html page.

9. Add a new paragraph tag to the default.html page, then click Interactive Button on the Insert menu.

10. Create a button using the Embossed Rectangle 3 button with the text Home that links to the default page. Make the button font bold, use the Tahoma font, set the font size as 14-point, and make the button 150 pixels wide.

11. Copy the button and paste it twice. Edit the two pasted buttons to refer and link to the two other site pages (events and membership), then select the paragraph containing the buttons and copy it to the Clipboard.

12. Copy the navigation bar, then open the events.html and membership.html pages and paste the navigation bar onto each page. Attach the senior_styles.css style sheet to both pages.

13. Save all pages at once and click OK three times to save the embedded images.

14. Create a new folder in the Folder List called navigation_images. Using the Site View pane, move all button images into the folder.

15. Preview the default.html page in a browser.

16. Close the site, then submit the site in the format specified by your instructor.

In the Lab

Lab 2: Adding a Jump Menu

Problem: You want to create a menu of sample worksheets for your math tutoring business. You will add a jump menu and reorder the menu items to create the default.html page, as shown in Figure 6–73.

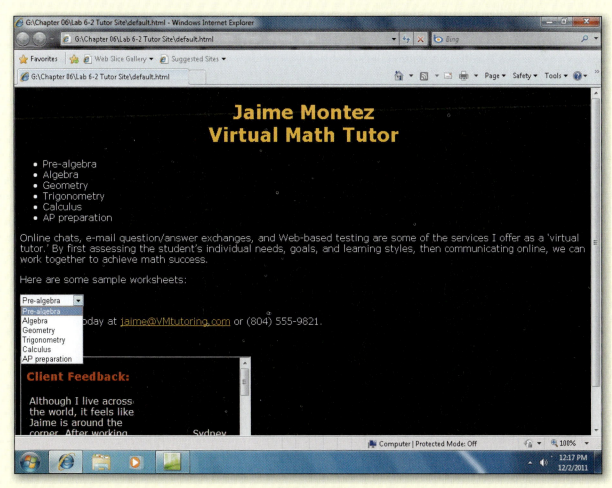

Figure 6–73

Continued >

In the Lab *continued*

Instructions: Start Expression Web. Open the Web site, Lab 6-2 Tutor Site, from the Data Files for Students. See the inside back cover of this book for instructions for downloading the Data Files for Students, or see your instructor for information about accessing the required files.

Perform the following tasks:

1. Open the default.html page.
2. Create a new paragraph tag above the tag that starts, Contact me. Type Here are some sample worksheets:, then press ENTER.
3. Open the Behaviors panel, if necessary, then open the Jump Menu dialog box.
4. Use the table below to create the menu items. The pages shown in the Value column are in the sample_worksheets folder within the main site folder.

Choice	Value
Algebra	algebra_sample.html
AP preparation	AP_preparation_sample.html
Calculus	calculus_sample.html
Geometry	geometry_sample.html
Pre-algebra	prealgebra_sample.html
Trigonometry	trigonometry_sample.html

5. Use the Move Up and Move Down buttons to change the order to: Pre-algebra, Algebra, Geometry, Trigonometry, Calculus, AP preparation.
6. Save the page, preview the site, and test the jump menu.
7. Change the site properties, as specified by your instructor, then save and close the site.
8. In Windows Explorer, rename the site folder as Lab 6-2 Tutor Site, then submit the site in the format specified by your instructor.

In the Lab

Lab 3: Creating an Image Map

Problem: You are on your school's fundraising committee and need to show supporters the funds raised this school year. You create a one-page Web site folder and a new style sheet using a preformatted style sheet, and add content and pages. You then insert an image and create an image map to link to the pages to create the page shown in Figure 6–74.

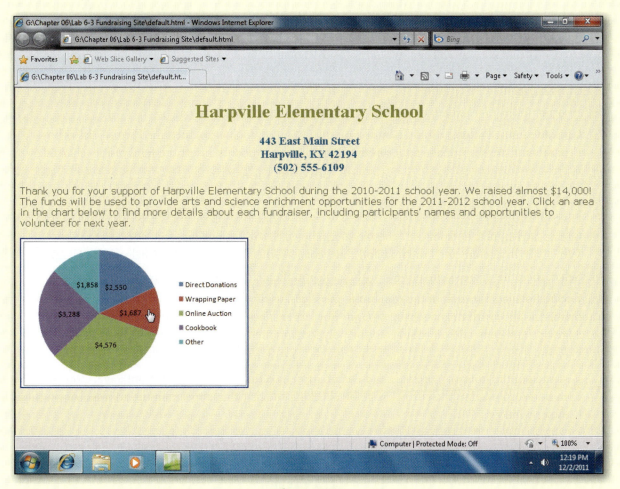

Figure 6–74

Instructions:

1. Start Expression Web.

2. Create a one-page Web site called Lab 6-3 Fundraising Site, then open the default.html page.

3. Create a new style sheet based on the Arcs style sheet, save it as fundraising_styles.css, then attach it to the default.html page.

4. Select the Heading 1 <h1> style, type Harpville Elementary School, then press ENTER.

5. Select the Heading 3 <h3> style, then type the following, pressing SHIFT+ENTER after each line:

   443 East Main Street

   Harpville, KY 42194

   (502) 555-6109

6. Center the address.

7. Click below the address, then insert a new paragraph tag. Type the following:

   Thank you for your support of Harpville Elementary School during the 2010-2011 school year. We raised almost $14,000! The funds will be used to provide arts and science enrichment opportunities for the 2011-2012 school year. Click an area in the chart below to find more details about each fundraiser, including participants' names and opportunities to volunteer for next year.

Continued >

In the Lab *continued*

8. Save the default.html page. Copy and paste the default.html page in the Folder List five times. Rename the copied pages as `direct.html`, `wrapping.html`, `auction.html`, `cookbook.html`, and `other.html`.

9. Insert a new paragraph tag below the paragraph on the default.html page.

10. Click the Insert Picture from File button on the Common toolbar to open the Picture dialog box. From the fundraising_image folder in the Data Files for Students, insert the fundraising_chart file.

11. Type `Pie chart showing donation percentages for 2010-2011 school year` as the alternate text.

12. Select the image, display the Pictures toolbar if necessary, then click the Polygonal Hotspot button.

13. Create a triangular hotspot over the pie slice labeled $1858 by clicking each corner of the slice. When you have connected the first and third corners, the Insert Hyperlink dialog box will open.

14. Select the other page as the target for this hotspot, then close the dialog box.

15. Create hotspots for each of the remaining pie slices, using the legend to the right of the chart to match the slice with the page name. (*Hint:* For larger slices, click multiple times along the rounded edge of the slice to add more sides to the polygon and include more of the slice in the hotspot.)

16. Save the default.html page and the embedded image, then preview the site in a browser.

17. Test each of the hotspots, pressing the Back button to return to the default.html page. Confirm that each hotspot linked to the correct page by checking the text that appears in the address bar on the browser window.

18. Change the site properties, as specified by your instructor, then save and close the site.

19. Submit the site in the format specified by your instructor.

Cases and Places

Apply your creative thinking and problem-solving skills to design and implement a solution.

• EASIER   ••MORE DIFFICULT

• 1: Creating a Navigation Bar Using Interactive Buttons

Create a new one-page Web site for a car wash. Create a new style sheet based on a preformatted style sheet and attach it to the page. Add a header and div into which you will add a navigation bar. Copy the page using the Folder List to create three other pages, and rename them. Create and test a navigation bar on the default.html page for the home page using the interactive button of your choice. Specify different font colors for original, hovered, and pressed states, then change the vertical or horizontal alignment. Specify the height and width of the button. Copy and paste the button, then modify the text and hyperlink to create navigation for all pages in your site. Save the page and embedded images, then create a folder to store the images. Test the navigation bar in the browser, then copy it to all site pages. Create folders as necessary to store the button images for the navigation bars. Save and close all pages, then quit Expression Web.

• 2: Creating and Modifying a Swap Image

Create a new one-page Web site for a florist. Insert an image using a file from this chapter, a previous chapter, or an image file of your own. Add a swap image behavior using another image of similar size. Accept the defaults in the Swap Images dialog box, then save the page and preview the image in the browser. Return to the default page, then modify the swap image behavior to add a restore behavior and change the event to onclick. Save the page, and refresh the browser window. Test the modified behavior. Return to the default page, then modify the restore image behavior to an event of your choice. Save the page, and refresh the browser window. Test the modified behavior, then save and close the site and the browser window.

•• 3: Adding Behaviors to a Dynamic Web Template

Create a new site for a computer repair shop using a dynamic Web template. Open the default page and preview it in a browser window to see the interactive buttons for the navigation bar. Open the master. dwt page, and set a status bar message. Add a jump menu to the default page that links to at least two site pages. Save all open pages, then refresh your browser to view the status bar message on the default page. Test the jump menu to go to another page and view the status bar message on that page. Close the browser window and the site.

•• 4: Creating a Travel Site

Make It Personal

You want to create a Web site that includes information about a travel spot you have visited or would like to visit. Create a site with at least three pages, using blank pages or a CSS layout and a preformatted style sheet. Enter information on the pages, and create a navigation bar for the site pages using interactive buttons. Create an image swap using two photos from your trip or that you find for public use on the Internet or from the projects in this book. Save the pages and style sheets, then close the site.

•• 5: Planning Navigation for Other Site Pages

Working Together

A department store wants to create a site that has four main site pages: a home page, directions, contact information, and products. Working as a team with several of your classmates, you plan and create the four site pages, and at least four other site pages for store departments. You will focus on creating the pages and navigation, not on creating elaborate content for each page. Each team member should contribute to planning the layout, formatting, and navigation for the site. As a group, decide on the departments for which you will include pages, and decide the best way to include that information on your site. Start by creating a site folder, and add a page using a CSS layout. Create and attach a style sheet using a preformatted style sheet. Copy that page to create additional site pages, and name each of them appropriately. Create a navigation bar using either a column or row format, and add it to each of the main site pages. Create an interactive behavior such as an image map or jump menu to link to the other site pages. Create folders as necessary to keep your site organized. Preview the site, and test the navigation bar and behavior. Save and close the pages and style sheet, then close the site.

In the Lab *continued*

2. Include in your report a list of the steps necessary to integrate Chris's existing Web site with the chosen third-party processor. You will find this information at the processor's Web site.

3. Save your report as `Lab SF 2-2 Third-party Payment Processor`. At the direction of your instructor, print the report.

In the Lab

Lab 3: Selecting an All-in-One E-Commerce Solution

Problem: Refer to the Web site you created in Chapter 5 for The Upper Cut. Owners Marcus and Elisa have developed their own brand of custom hair care products. Customers are buying the shampoos, conditioners, and specialty treatments as fast as the salon can stock the shelves. To exploit the popularity of their new products to increase sales, Marcus and Elisa want you to add a product sales component to their existing Web site. You know that you need a way to add a product catalog and shopping cart software to the Web site. You also know that most online payments are made using credit cards; therefore, you need a way to handle online credit card payment and processing. To save time and get the Web site's e-commerce capability up and running, you decide that an all-in-one e-commerce solution would work best for The Upper Cut.

Instructions: Search the Web to identify and then review at least three all-in-one e-commerce solution vendors. Take advantage of any vendor tutorials or demos. Then select the solution that you think offers the best combination of cost and services for the salon's online store.

1. Write a report that summarizes the services provided and costs for those services for each reviewed all-in-one e-commerce solution. Choose the all-in-one e-commerce solution that best meets the needs of The Upper Cut Web site's online store and discuss the reasons for your choice.

2. Include in your report a list of the steps necessary to integrate the salon's existing Web site with the chosen all-in-one e-commerce solution. You will find this information at the vendor's Web site.

3. Save your report as `Lab SF 2-3 All-in-One E-Commerce Solution`. At the direction of your instructor, print the report.

Appendix A

Using the Microsoft Expression Web User Guide

Introduction

You might have a question about how to use a specific Expression Web feature, or perhaps you want to learn more about the different features offered by Expression Web for creating, editing, and publishing Web pages. You can search for information on specific topics, look up a topic in an index, or browse available topics by category in the **Microsoft Expression Web User Guide window**.

To open the Expression Web User Guide window, click the User Guide command on the Help menu. The User Guide window (Figure A–1) contains standard Windows 7 operating system window features, including a title bar and the Minimize, Maximize or Restore Down, and Close buttons. Additionally, the User Guide window contains a **toolbar** with the Hide or Show, Back, Print, and Options buttons; a **tabs pane** containing the Contents, Index, and Search tabs; and a **viewing pane** in which selected Help topics appear. In Figure A–1, the Getting started folder in the Contents tab is selected and the Getting started Help topic page is visible in the viewing pane.

Appendix D

Microsoft Expression Studio 3

Introduction

Microsoft Expression Studio 3 is a family of related software products — Expression Web 3, Expression Design 3, Expression Blend 3 plus SketchFlow, and Expression Encoder 3 — used by Web developers to create standards-compliant Web pages. In addition to creating Web pages, the Expression Studio products help developers import, create, and edit vector and bitmap graphics; create interactive Web-based applications; create user interface prototypes; and produce audio and video content for Web-based applications.

Expression Web

A **WYSIWYG (What You See Is What You Get) editor** is software that automatically inserts markup language tags as you work with the software's graphical interface, including menu commands, toolbar buttons, and task panes, to create and edit a Web page. **Expression Web**, which you learn about in the chapters of this text, is a WYSIWYG editor used by both novice and professional Web developers to create standards-compliant Web pages. Expression Web is the replacement software for Microsoft FrontPage, which is no longer supported by Microsoft.

Expression Web provides easy-to-use Web site and page templates for the beginner while also delivering more sophisticated tools required by Web development professionals, such as Cascading Style Sheets for layout and formatting, the SuperPreview feature that allows you to see how a page will look in different browsers and browser versions, and a feature for Web standards compliance testing.

Expression Design

Vector graphics are images created by drawing shapes and lines, while **raster graphics**, also called **bitmaps**, are images created one pixel at a time. An example of a vector graphic is a company logo created by combining different drawing shapes and lines. Examples of bitmaps include animated images and photographs.

Expression Design (Figure D–1) is software you can use to import, create, and edit vector graphics and bitmaps. Expression Design includes features that let you apply special effects to graphics, combine vector graphics with bitmaps, and convert bitmaps into vector graphics and vice versa. Expression Design also offers tools for exporting graphics into Expression Web and Expression Blend.

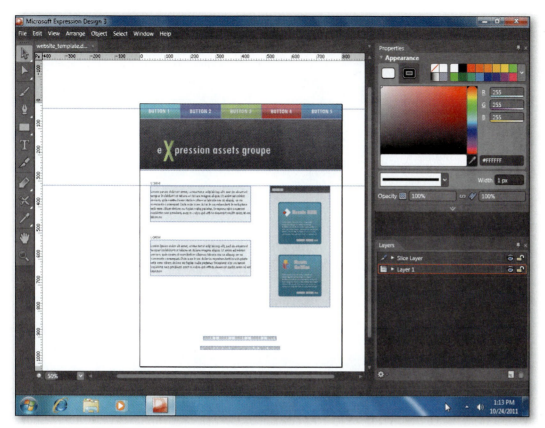

Figure D–1

Expression Blend

Expression Blend is software designed for professional developers who need to create graphical user interfaces (GUIs) for Windows desktop applications using the Microsoft .NET Framework platform.

Expression Blend can also be used to create GUIs for rich interactive applications using XAML (Extensible Application Markup Language) and the Microsoft Silverlight plug-in technologies. A **rich interactive application**, or **RIA**, is a Web-based application with multimedia content. Silverlight is a browser plug-in that works with different browsers and different operating systems to display the multimedia content included in RIAs. For more information on Silverlight, check out the Silverlight appendix.

Blend (Figure D–2) provides tools for professional developers to combine images, animation, video, audio, text, and controls, such as buttons, list boxes, and scroll bars, in creating rich content for desktop or Web-based applications. **SketchFlow** (Figure D–3), a feature of Expression Blend, is a set of tools a developer can use to mock-up a prototype for the user interface for an application or Web project in development, such as a series of interactive Web pages.

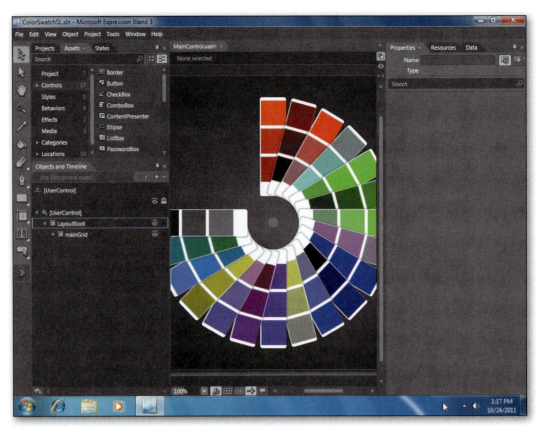

Figure D–2

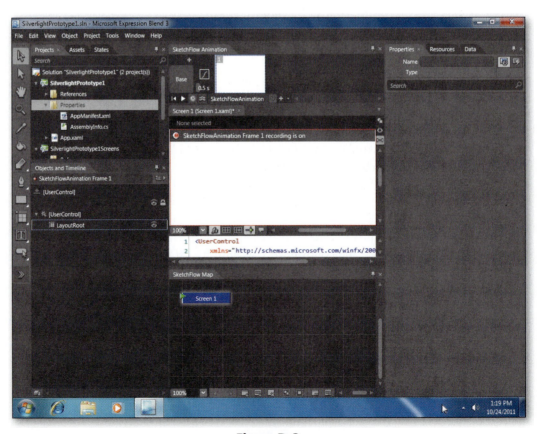

Figure D–3

For more information about the Microsoft .NET Framework, XAML, Microsoft Silverlight, or SketchFlow, visit **scsite.com/ew3/websources** and click a link under Appendix D, Microsoft Platforms.

Expression Encoder

Encoding software is used to compress audio and video files and output the files in a specific audio or video format. **Expression Encoder** (Figure D–4) is encoding software designed specifically to work with Silverlight technologies.

A variety of audio and video file formats can be imported into Expression Encoder, including AVI, WMV, WMA, MPEG, and QuickTime files. The encoded files can be output as WMV or WMA files or encoded using a Silverlight output template. Expression Encoder also contains the Screen Capture feature that allows you to capture on-screen actions, Webcam video, and sound.

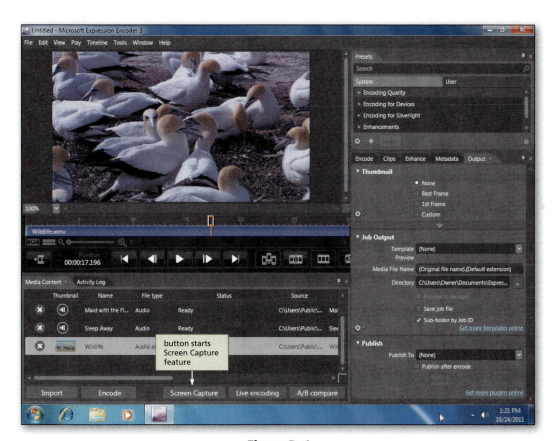

Figure D–4

For more information about the individual software products that make up Expression Studio, visit **scsite.com/ew3/websources** and click a link under Appendix D, Expression Studio 3.

Appendix E
Using Expression Web in Windows XP

The step-by-step instructions and illustrations in this text are based on Expression Web running on the Windows 7 operating system. If you are running Expression Web on the Windows XP operating system, your instructor might modify certain step-by-step instructions as necessary to perform tasks.

You also will see some variances between the desktop, the Windows taskbar and Start menu, the Expression Web window, and Expression Web dialog boxes on your screen with the illustrations in this text, including the:

- Default Windows color scheme and desktop background
- Size and color of the Minimize, Maximize, Restore Down, and Close buttons on the Expression Web title bar
- Program's title text color on the title bar
- Taskbar color and the Start button size and shape
- Start menu colors, arrangement, contents, and style
- Dialog box colors, boundary style, and, in some instances, dialog box content

This appendix illustrates examples of these differences by showing how to start Expression Web and then open and close an existing Web site.

To Start Expression Web

The following steps, which assume Windows XP is running, start Expression Web based on a typical installation. Your instructor might provide alternate instructions for starting Expression Web on your computer.

- Click the Start button on the Windows XP taskbar to display the Start menu.

- Point to All Programs on the Start menu to display the All Programs submenu.

- Point to Microsoft Expression on the All Programs submenu to display the Microsoft Expression Web 3 command (Figure E–1).

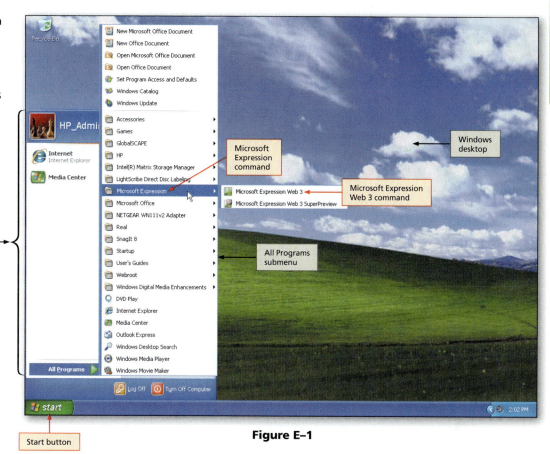

Figure E–1

- Click Microsoft Expression Web 3 to start Expression Web.

- If the Expression Web window is not maximized, click the Maximize button to the left of the Close button on the Expression Web title bar to maximize the window (Figure E–2).

Figure E–2

Other Ways

1. Double-click the Microsoft Expression Web 3 icon on the desktop, if one is present

2. Click Microsoft Expression Web 3 on the Start menu, if present

To Open an Existing Web Site

The following steps close the Untitled_1.html page, if necessary, and open the Boon Mountain Resort Web site data file from the USB flash drive where you save your data files. When you open a Web site, you will see two Open Site dialog boxes. The first Open Site dialog box allows you to select a site from a list of recently opened sites or key the path to a site. You can click the Browse button in this Open Site dialog box to open the second Open Site dialog box and use your computer's drive and folder structure to browse for a site. Your drive and folder information will likely differ from what is shown in the Open Site dialog box figures.

1

• Click File on the menu bar.

• Click Close to close the Untitled_1. html page (Figure E–3).

Figure E–3

2

• With your USB flash drive connected to one of the computer's USB ports, click Site on the menu bar.

• Point to Open Site on the Site menu (Figure E–4).

Figure E–4

3

- Click Open Site to display the first Open Site dialog box (Figure E–5).

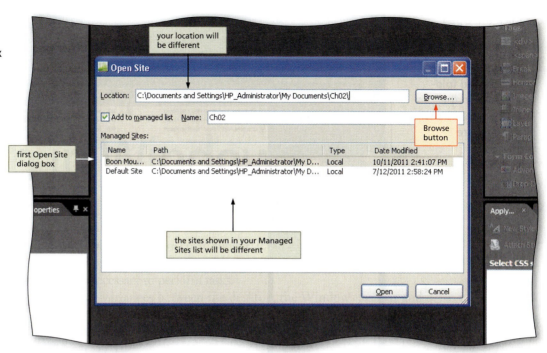

your location will be different

first Open Site dialog box

Browse button

the sites shown in your Managed Sites list will be different

Figure E–5

4

- Click the Browse button to open the second Open Site dialog box and browse for the location of your data files.

- Click the Look in box arrow to view the list of available drives.

- Click the USB flash drive to select it and view its contents.

Q&A

How do I locate the site to open if I am not using a USB flash drive?

Use the same process, but select your device or network folder from the Look in list.

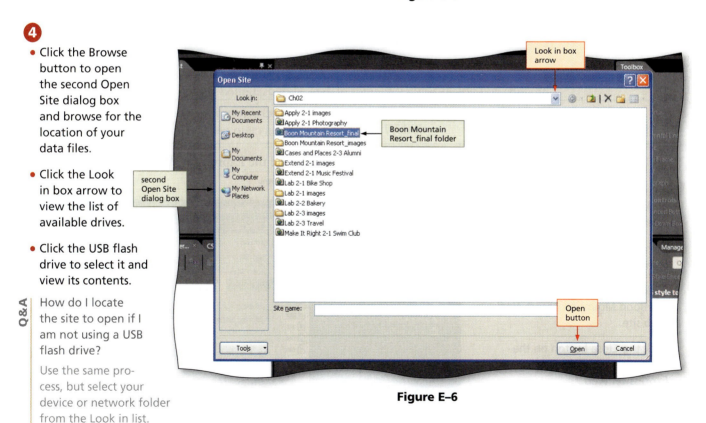

Look in box arrow

second Open Site dialog box

Boon Mountain Resort_final folder

Open button

Figure E–6

- Double-click the data file folder, if necessary, to open it.

- Click Boon Mountain Resort_final to select the site name (Figure E–6).

To Start Expression Web

The following steps, which assume Windows Vista is running, start Expression Web based on a typical installation. Your instructor might provide alternate instructions for starting Expression Web on your computer.

- Click the Start button on the Windows Vista taskbar to display the Start menu.

- Click All Programs on the Start menu to display the All Programs list.

- Click Microsoft Expression on the All Programs list to display the Microsoft Expression Web 3 command (Figure F–1).

Figure F–1

- Click Microsoft Expression Web 3 to start Expression Web.

- If the Expression Web window is not maximized, click the Maximize button to the left of the Close button on the Expression Web title bar to maximize the window (Figure F–2).

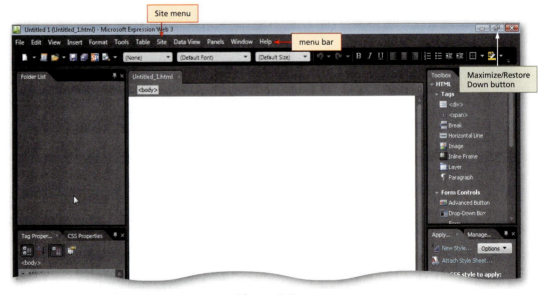

Figure F–2

Other Ways
1. Double-click Expression Web icon on desktop, if present   2. Click Microsoft Expression Web 3 on Start menu, if present

To Open an Existing Web Site

The following steps close the Untitled_1.html page, if necessary, and open the Boon Mountain Resort Web site data file from the USB flash drive where you save your data files. Your drive and folder information will likely differ from what is shown in the figure.

 1

• Click File on the menu bar (Figure F–3).

• Click Close to close the Untitled_1.html page.

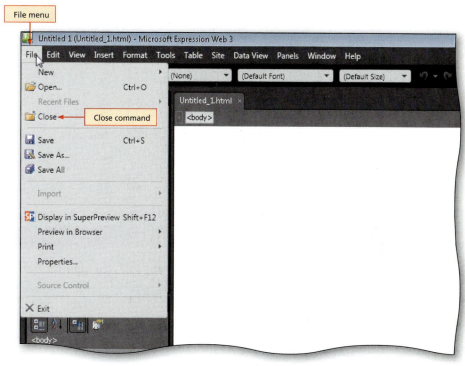

Figure F–3

2

• With your USB flash drive connected to one of the computer's USB ports, click Site on the menu bar (Figure F–4).

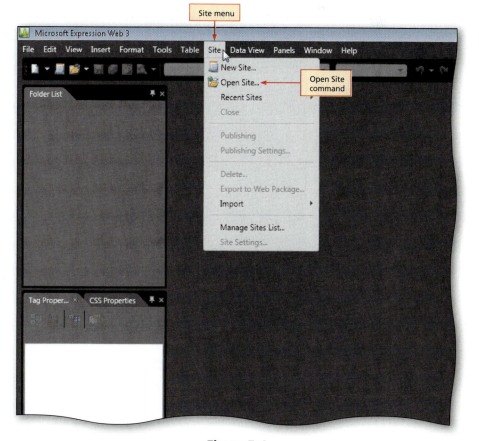

Figure F–4

3

- Click Open Site to display the Open Site dialog box.

- Click the Browse button to view the list of available drives.

- Click the Computer link in the Open Site dialog box to display the contents of the computer.

- Double-click the USB flash drive to select it and view its contents.

Q&A

How do I locate the site to open if I am not using a USB flash drive?

Use the same process, but navigate to your desired location from the Computer folder window.

- Double-click the data file folder, if necessary, to open it.

- Click Boon Mountain Resort_final to select the site name (Figure F–5).

Figure F–5

4

- Click the Open button to display another Open Site dialog box.

- Click the Open button to open the site and all of its files and folders in the Microsoft Expression Web 3 window (Figure F–6).

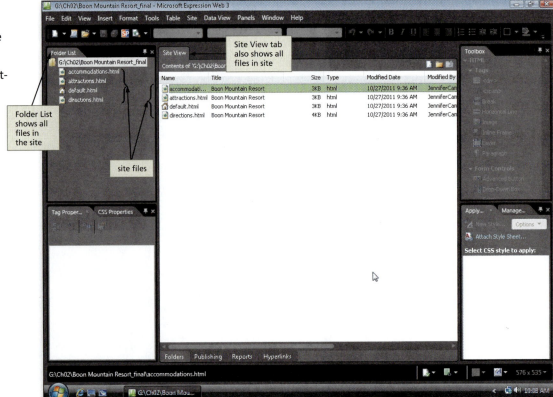

Figure F–6

To Close a Web Site

The following steps close the Boon Mountain Resort Web site and the Expression Web program.

- Click Site on the menu bar to open the Site menu (Figure F–7).

- Click Close to close the Boon Mountain Resort_final Web site.

- Click the Close button on the Expression Web 3 title bar.

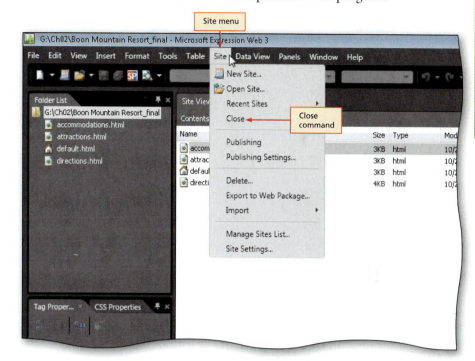

Figure F–7

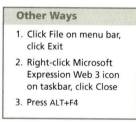

Other Ways

1. Click File on menu bar, click Exit

2. Right-click Microsoft Expression Web 3 icon on taskbar, click Close

3. Press ALT+F4

Appendix G
Changing Screen Resolution

A **pixel** (short for picture element) is a single point of light on a computer screen. **Screen resolution** is a setting that determines the number of pixels necessary to display the program windows, pictures, text, and icons you see on your screen. Screen resolution usually is stated as the two numbers that represent the width and height of the pixels. For example, a screen with a 1024×768 screen resolution, the most common resolution used today, displays 1,024 pixels in width and 768 pixels in height; the screen illustrations in this book were created using the 1024×768 screen resolution. Other less common screen resolutions include the 800×600, 1152×720, 1280×768, and 1440×900 screen resolutions.

When you increase the screen resolution, you see more information on the screen, but the size of the information (text characters, toolbar buttons, dialog boxes, icons, pictures, and so forth) decreases; this might make the information more difficult to see for certain users. Alternatively, if you decrease the screen resolution, the size of the information increases, resulting in less visible area in which to view the information. Decreasing the screen resolution might, therefore, cause desktop icons to overlap or program toolbar buttons to be hidden.

Toolbars, buttons, and other elements can look different or appear in various locations in the program window when viewed at different screen resolutions. Variations in monitor shapes and sizes can also cause two screens set at the same resolution to look slightly different.

To Change the Screen Resolution

The following steps change your screen resolution to 1024 × 768 to match the illustrations in this text.

● Minimize all open windows so that the Windows 7 desktop appears.

● Right-click the Windows 7 desktop to display the Windows 7 desktop shortcut menu (Figure G–1). Your shortcut menu might have additional commands.

Figure G–1

● Click the Screen resolution command on the shortcut menu to open the Screen Resolution window (Figure G–2).

Figure G–2

3
- Click the Resolution button and drag the slider in the Resolution pane to the 1024 × 768 position (Figure G–3).

- Press the ESC key to close the Resolution pane.

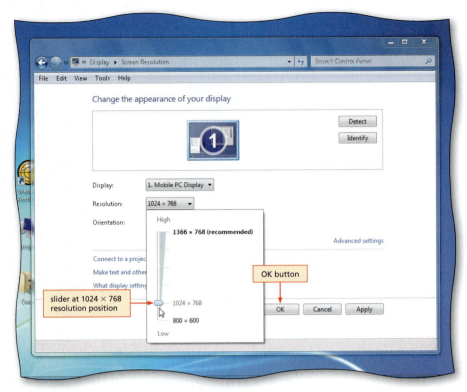

Figure G–3

4
- Click OK to open the Display Settings dialog box (Figure G–4).

- Click Keep changes to change the resolution to 1024 × 768.

- Click the Close button on the title bar to close the Screen Resolution window.

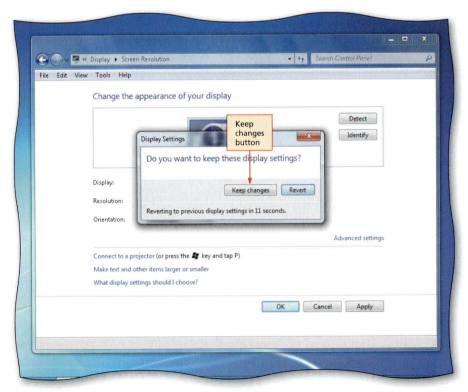

Figure G–4

Index

Note: **Boldface** entries include definitions.

2Checkout.com, EW 436

A

about_artist file, EW 277
accessibility, EW 320, EW 398
Accessibility Checker, APP 14
accessibility properties, EW 75–76
Accessibility Properties dialog box, EW 306, EW 327, EW 332, EW 400, EW 406
accredited registrar, **APP 15**
Add Choice dialog box, EW 393, EW 394
advertising business model, EW 424
aligning images, EW 94
alignment, **EW 233**
all-in-one e-commerce solution, **EW 437–438**
alternate text, **EW 75–76**, EW 236
alternative fonts, EW 262
Amazon.com Web site, EW 425
animated GIFs or images, EW 236
Apple Safari, EW 54
Apply Styles panel, EW 31, EW 84, EW 195, EW 249, EW 252, EW 254, EW 256
artist.html page
  adding content and link to, EW 276–280
  attaching multiple style sheets, EW 280–282
  attaching style sheets, EW 274–276
  links, EW 283–284
artist_image style, EW 254, EW 256
artist_styles.css file, EW 273
aspect ratio, **EW 89**
ASP.NET Framework for Web pages, APP 17
assistive technology, EW 320
asymmetric arrangement, EW 232
Attach Style Sheet dialog box, EW 280–281, EW 313–315
attached, **EW 242**
audio, EW 236
audio files, compressing, APP 27
AutoFormat, EW 340, EW 346–348
AutoFormat dialog box, EW 347–348
avatars, EW 236
AVI file format, APP 27

B

B2B (business-to-business) e-commerce business models, **EW 425–426**
B2C (business-to-consumer) e-commerce business models, **EW 425**
B2C e-commerce sites, EW 425
B2E (business-to-employee) e-commerce, **EW 428**
B2G (business-to-government) e-commerce business models, **EW 427**
B2GMARKET Web site, EW 427
Back button, **APP 4**
back office operations, **EW 429**
background colors, EW 228, EW 230
background images and tables, EW 316
backing up Web site files, APP 18
BACKSPACE key, editing text with, EW 183
balance, **EW 232**
behaviors, **EW 368**
  defining, EW 390
  improving site visitors' experiences, EW 370
Behaviors panel, EW 392
Bidmain Web site, EW 427
bills of lading, EW 426
bitmaps, **APP 24**, EW 236
BlueHost, APP 16
bookmarks, **EW 120**, EW 134–136
borders, **EW 95–96**
box-like divs, EW 154
breadcrumb trail, **EW 224**, EW 226
Browse dialog box, EW 401
browsers, **EW 48**
  ActiveX content restricted, EW 378
  automatically blocking interactive sites, EW 372–373
  bookmarks, EW 120
  CSS (Cascading Style Sheets), EW 194
  interactivity, EW 372–373
  previewing in, EW 54–55, EW 203
  security, EW 372–373
  unable to *see* status bar, EW 398
bulleted list, **EW 25–27**
business documents, exchange of, EW 426
business models, **EW 424**

business-to-business. *See* B2B (business to business) e-commerce business models
business-to-consumer. *See* B2C (business-to-consumer) e-commerce business models
business-to-employee e-commerce. *See* B2E (business-to-employee) e-commerce
business-to-government. *See* B2G (business-to-government) e-commerce business models
button file names, EW 379
buttons
  image files for each state, EW 372
  organizing images into folders, EW 387–390

C

C2B (consumer-to-business) e-commerce business models, **EW 427**
C2C (consumer-to-consumer) e-commerce business models, **EW 426**
Call Script behavior, EW 390
captions, **EW 316**, EW 317–319, EW 336
card not present/card holder not present risk, **EW 434**
cascading, **EW 193**
Cascading Style Sheets. *See* CSS (Cascading Style Sheets)
CCNow, EW 436
cells, **EW 302**, EW 316, EW 337
  combining, EW 304
  content on two lines, EW 323
  entering text, EW 323–326
  images, EW 326–329
  line breaks, EW 323
  margins, EW 320
  merging, **EW 336–337**
  properties, EW 319–322
  splitting, **EW 336**, EW 338–339
centering text, EW 36
Change Property/Restore behavior, EW 390
chargebacks, **EW 433–434**, EW 436
Check Browser behavior, EW 390
Check Plug-in behavior, EW 390
checkout process, **EW 430**
Cisco Web site, EW 426

Quick Reference Summary

In the Microsoft Expression Web 3 program, you can accomplish a task in a number of ways. The following table provides a quick reference to each task presented in this textbook. The first column identifies the task. The second column indicates the page number on which the task is discussed in the book. The subsequent four columns list the different ways the task in column one can be carried out.

Microsoft Expression Web Quick Reference Summary

Task	Page Number	Mouse	Menu Bar	Shortcut Menu	Keyboard Shortcut
Add Folder	EW 167		File	New	Folder	New	Folder	
Behavior, Insert	EW 391	Click the Insert button in the Behaviors panel, then click the behavior to add			
Behavior, Modify	EW 402	Double-click behavior in Behaviors panel to open *behavior* dialog box			
Bold	EW 30	Bold button on Common toolbar or Formatting toolbar	Format	Font	Font	CTRL+B
Bookmark, Insert	EW 134		Insert	Bookmark		CTRL+G
Bullets	EW 25	Bullets button on Common toolbar or Formatting toolbar	Format	Bullets and Numbering		
Caption, Add to Table	EW 317		Table	Insert	Caption	Insert	Caption	
Cell Properties, Change	EW 320		Table	Table Properties	Cell	Cell Properties	
Cell, Split	EW 338	Split Cells button on Tables toolbar	Table	Modify	Split Cells	Modify	Split Cells	
Cells, Merge	EW 337	Merge Cells button on Tables toolbar or Formatting toolbar	Table	Modify	Merge Cells	Modify	Merge Cells	
Center Text	EW 36	Center button on Common toolbar or Formatting toolbar	Format	Paragraph		CTRL+E
Close Page	EW 57	Close button on editing window	File	Close	Close	CTRL+W
Close Site	EW 57		Site	Close		
Copy	EW 103		Edit	Copy	Copy	CTRL+C
Crop an Image	EW 106	Crop button on Pictures toolbar	drag cropping handles	Crop button on Pictures toolbar again			
CSS Layout Page, New	EW 271		File	New	Page	CSS Layouts		
CSS Report, Run	EW 286		Tools	CSS Reports		

Task	Page Number	Mouse	Menu Bar	Shortcut Menu	Keyboard Shortcut
Delete File or Folder	EW 166		Edit | Delete	Delete	DELETE
Delete Text (Left of Insertion Point)	EW 183				BACKSPACE
Delete Text (Right of Insertion Point)	EW 183				DELETE
E-mail Link, Add	EW 137	Insert Hyperlink button on Common toolbar	Insert | Hyperlink	Hyperlink	CTRL+K
Find Text	EW 186		Edit | Find		CTRL+F
Font	EW 44	Font box arrow on Common toolbar or Formatting toolbar	Format | Font	Font	
Font Color	EW 37	Font Color arrow on Common toolbar or Formatting toolbar	Format | Font	Font	
Font Family, Create	EW 262		Tools | Page Editor Options | Font Families tab		
Font Size	EW 39	Font Size box arrow on Common toolbar or Formatting toolbar	Format | Font	Font	
Heading Style, Add	EW 33	Style box arrow on Common toolbar or Formatting toolbar			
Hotspot, Add	EW 405	*Shape* Hotspot button on the Pictures toolbar | draw hotspot shape			
Hyperlink, Insert	EW 122	Insert Hyperlink button on Common or Standard toolbar	Insert | Hyperlink	Hyperlink	CTRL+K
Image, Align	EW 94	Double-click image to open Picture Properties dialog box	Format | Properties | Appearance tab	Picture Properties | Appearance tab	
Image, Insert	EW 80	Insert Picture from File button on Common toolbar, Formatting toolbar, or Pictures toolbar	Insert | Picture | From File		
Image Margins, Modify	EW 97	Drag margin border Or Double-click image to open the Picture Properties dialog box	Format | Properties | Appearance tab	Picture Properties | Appearance tab	
Image, Resize	EW 89	Drag corner resize Or Double-click image to open Picture Properties dialog box	Format | Properties | Appearance tab	Picture Properties | Appearance tab	
Images, Borders and Padding	EW 95	Borders button arrow on Common or Formatting toolbar	Format | Borders and Shading		Hold SHIFT | drag blue lines around graphic
Indent Text	EW 41	Increase Indent Position button on Common or Formatting toolbar	Format | Paragraph		CTRL+M
Inline Frame, Add Link	EW 352	Set Initial Page button in I-frame			
Inline Frame, Insert	EW 349	Double-click Inline Frame button in Toolbox	Insert | HTML | Inline Frame		
Interactive Button, Create	EW 373		Insert | Interactive Button		
Interactive Button, Edit	EW 380	Double-click to open Interactive Buttons dialog box		Button Properties	

Microsoft Expression Web Quick Reference Summary *(continued)*

Task	Page Number	Mouse	Menu Bar	Shortcut Menu	Keyboard Shortcut
Italicize	EW 42	Italic button on Common or Formatting toolbar	Format | Font	Font	CTRL+I
New Folder, Create	EW 116		File | New | Folder	New | Folder	
New Web Page	EW 169	New Document arrow on the Common toolbar | Page	File | New | Page	New | HTML Or New | ASPX Or New | ASP Or New | PHP Or New | CSS	CTRL+N
Page Properties, Set	EW 15		File | Properties	Page Properties	
Panel, Close	EW 85	Close button on panel title bar	Panels | panel name		
Panel, Dock	EW 84	Drag panel title bar to edge of window			
Panel, Maximize	EW 84	Turn off AutoHide button on panel title bar			
Panel, Minimize	EW 84	Turn on AutoHide button on panel title bar			
Panel, Open	EW 84		Panels | panel name		ALT+F1
Panel, Undock	EW 84	Drag title bar to blank area			
Paste	EW 103		Edit | Paste	Paste	CTRL+V
Paste Formatted Text	EW 177		Edit | Paste		CTRL+V
Paste Unformatted Text	EW 177		Edit | Paste Text		
Preview Site	EW 54	Preview in *browser* button arrow on Common toolbar | *browser*	File | Preview in Browser | *browser*		F12
Print	EW 56		File | Print | Print Or File | Print | Print Preview | Print		CTRL+P
Quick Tag Selector, Use	EW 31	Tag on Quick Tag Selector			
Quit Expression Web	EW 58	Close button on program window title bar	File | Exit		ALT+F4
Remove Formatting	EW 177	Paste Options button below pasted text | Remove Formatting	Format | Remove Formatting		CTRL+SHIFT+Z
Rename File or Folder	EW 161	Click file or folder name | click file or folder name again | type new name		Rename	
Replace Template Text	EW 172	Select tag on Quick Tag Selector | type replacement text Or Select tag tab | type replacement text			
Replace Text	EW 186		Edit | Replace		CTRL+H
Reset Workspace Layout	EW 9		Panels | Reset Workspace Layout		

Microsoft Expression Web Quick Reference Summary *(continued)*

Task	Page Number	Mouse	Menu Bar	Shortcut Menu	Keyboard Shortcut
Rulers, Show or Hide	EW 87		View | Ruler and Grid | Show Ruler	Show Ruler	
Save Web Page	EW 30	Save button on Common toolbar	File | Save	Save	CTRL+S
ScreenTip, Add to Hyperlink	EW 138		Insert | Hyperlink Or Format | Properties	Hyperlink Properties	CTRL+K
Select Paragraph	EW 183	Triple-click paragraph			
Select Text (One Character at a Time)	EW 183				SHIFT | left or right arrow
Select Text (One Word at a Time)	EW 183				CTRL+SHIFT | left or right arrow
Select Word	EW 183	Double-click word			
Snapshot View	EW 49		Panels | Snapshot		
Spell Check	EW 46		Tools | Spelling | Spelling		F7
Style, Apply	EW 201	*Style* button in Apply Styles panel			
Style, Create Code	EW 266	Type first letter(s) of selector name or value, then double-click selector from shortcut menu		Type first letter(s) of selector name or value, then press down arrow and ENTER	
Style, Create New	EW 198	New Style link in Apply Styles panel	Format | New Style	New Style	
Style, Modify	EW 195	*Style* button arrow in Apply Styles panel | Modify Style		Modify Style	
Style, New	EW 254	New Style link in Apply Styles panel	Format | New Style		
Style Sheet, Attach	EW 268	Attach Style Sheet link in Apply Styles panel	Format | CSS Styles | Attach Style Sheet		
Style Sheet, New	EW 260		File | New | CSS	New | CSS	
Style Sheet, New from Preformatted	EW 310		File | New | Page | Style Sheets		
Switch Views	EW 49	Show *view type* View button at bottom of editing window	View | Page | *view*		CTRL+PAGE DOWN Or CTRL+PAGE UP
Table AutoFormat	EW 347	Table AutoFormat button on Tables toolbar	Table | Modify | Table AutoFormat	Modify | Table AutoFormat	
Table Column, Add	EW 330	Column to the Left button on Tables toolbar Or Column to the Right button on Tables toolbar	Table | Insert | Column to the Left Or Table | Insert | Column to the Right	Insert | Column to the Left Or Insert | Column to the Right	
Table Column, Delete	EW 330	Delete Cells button on Tables toolbar	Table | Delete | Delete Columns	Delete | Delete Columns	CTRL+X
Table, Convert to Text	EW 342		Table | Convert | Table to Text		
Table, Fill	EW 334		Table | Fill | Down Or Table | Fill | Right		

Microsoft Expression Web Quick Reference Summary *(continued)*

Task	Page Number	Mouse	Menu Bar	Shortcut Menu	Keyboard Shortcut
Table, New	EW 316	Insert Table button on Common toolbar	Table | Insert Table		
Table, New from Text	EW 342		Table | Convert | Text to Table		
Table Properties, Change	EW 320		Table | Table Properties	Table Properties	
Table Row, Add	EW 330	Row Above button on Tables toolbar Or Row Below button on Tables toolbar	Table | Insert | Row Above Or Table | Insert | Row Below	Insert | Row Above Or Insert | Row Below	
Table Row, Delete	EW 330	Delete Cells button on Tables toolbar	Table | Delete | Delete Rows	Delete | Delete Rows	CTRL+X
Tag, Add	EW 20	Double-click tag in Toolbox Or Drag tag from Toolbox to desired location Or *tag* button on Common toolbar	Insert | HTML | *tag*		
Thumbnail, Create	EW 113	Auto Thumbnail button on Pictures toolbar		Auto Thumbnail	CTRL+T
Transparency, Set Around an Image	EW 99	Set Transparent Color button on Pictures toolbar			
Undo Action	EW 21	Undo button on Common toolbar	Edit | Undo		CTRL+Z
Visual Aids, Show or Hide	EW 52	Visual Aids button on status bar | Show	View | Visual Aids | Show		CTRL+/
Web Page, Delete	EW 164		Edit | Delete	Delete	DELETE
Web Page, Open	EW 14	Open button arrow on Common toolbar | Open Or Double-click page in Folder List or Site View tab	File | Open		CTRL+O
Web Page, Rename (Folder List)	EW 162	Click file name in Folder List | click file name in Folder List again | type new name		Rename	F2
Web Site, Create from Template	EW 157		Site | New Site		
Web Site, Open	EW 77	Open button arrow on Common toolbar | Open Site	Site | Open Site		